JUDGING WORSHIP MUSIC

EIGHT STANDARDS OF EXCELLENCE

Dwight Riggs

INFINITY
PUBLISHING.COM

ISBN 0-7414-5759-8

Published by:

INFINITY
PUBLISHING.COM
1094 New DeHaven Street, Suite 100
West Conshohocken, PA 19428-2713
Info@buybooksontheweb.com
www.buybooksontheweb.com
Toll-free (877) BUY-BOOK
Local Phone (610) 941-9999
Fax (610) 941-9959

Printed in the United States of America
Published September 2010

TABLE OF CONTENTS

PREFACE

Worship music is the new battleground turf among evangelical churches----uniting or dividing congregations. Should we sing only hymns or the new Contemporary Christian Music (CCM) of "praise and worship choruses?" Passions run deep on both sides of the fence, and both traditional and CCM camps muster their respective supporting arguments. Tragically congregations divide and good Christians leave the church in search for another place of worship-----leaving in their wake ruptured feelings, broken friendships, fractured fellowship, and disunity in the Body of Christ.

For over fifty years I have personally witnessed the influence of the church growth movement and its matching cousin, Contemporary Christian Music. I well recall the early days of CCM in the 1960s when converted hippies gave fresh expression to their new faith through the use of rock and roll music with added Christian words. Since then the music industry, especially CCM, has blossomed into a myriad of music publishers promoting the expanded range of CCM-----rock and roll, soft rock, jazz, pop artists, hip hop----all incorporating into our worship services. Is this proliferation of CCM with its divergent tentacles and musical variety contributing to Biblical worship? Leaders in the CCM movement agree with a resounding "YES!" On the other hand many pastors and mature Christians wave red flags of caution.

Numerous books are available on this issue of CCM-----books supporting and rejecting the music and/or its philosophy. Some of the books are popular and easy to read; other books are musically technical; other books are historical relying on Martin Luther and John Wesley as support for using CCM; other books use proof texts of Scripture in defending CCM. This book is not a cursory use of proof texts of Scripture, but a detailed, in depth exposition of key passages from the Bible relating either directly or indirectly to the issue of music in worship, and pagan influence encroaching on Biblical worship. Scripture can be interpreted correctly or incorrectly, and the reader must decide if I am misinterpreting, abusing, mishandling God's Word, violating the established rules of hermeneutics (rules of Biblical interpretation). I hope this book will add Biblical insights to the clamorous confusion among sincere Christians over what is appropriate and inappropriate in Christ-centered worship.

1

INTRODUCTION

PURPOSE OF THIS STUDY:

(1) Explore the Biblical/theological history of ancient Hebrew music.

The Bible has over 500 references to music-----vocal, instrumental, choral, types, and usage. This study will not examine all 500-----only three early occurrences of music in the early life of Israel: **(a) the song heard around the golden calf at Mt. Sinai-----Ex. 32:17-18; (b) the song of Moses at the Red Sea---Ex. 15:1-18; (c) the second song of Moses at the entrance to the Promised Land---Deut. 32:1-44.** In addition, the passage of **"strange fire" offered by Nadab and Abihu----Leviticus 10:1-8** will be explained even though it does not directly address the issue of music, but it relates in principle to music. Knowledge of this history forms a solid foundation for **<u>DUAL</u>** evaluation of other references to Israel's music, and to our present-day music confusion rampant in the evangelical church.

(2) Evaluate the logic of Gamaliel.

Acts 5:33-42 is a watershed passage in determining Biblical and humanistic philosophy of success in Christian service, and Christian leaders resort to the counsel of Gamaliel as validation of divine methodology in proving growth and results in Biblical endeavors. His words are considered as the sunum bonum of wise counsel from a knowledgeable, seasoned sage of rabbinic lore. This study will examine the person of Gamaliel, his reputation, and the logic of his argument---specifically as it applies to the area of music and the wide-spread acceptance and popularity of contemporary Christian music and its methods of worship style. He does not address the issue of music in his counsel, but his philosophy and logic definitely applies to music, as well as other areas of Christian ministry.

(3) Correlate New Testament teaching regarding standards in music discernment.

Unity pervades the Bible in all subjects----including the sphere of music-----and the task of wise Biblical interpretation is to form discernment in evaluating appropriate and inappropriate music for worship. Paul prayed a pointed, powerful prayer for the Philippian Christians in Philippians 1:9-10: **<u>"My prayer: that your love may abound more and more in knowledge and depth of insight, so that you may be able to discern what is best........."</u>** Note that vital word---**_"discern"_**-----and that measurement word----**"best"**. Discern means to form judgments, assess value to something, weigh the presence/absence of certain qualities. It is a good word, though much maligned by many Christians who believe in standard-less opinions. Paul wanted the Philippian Christians to discern between evil and purity, then advance to deciding between what is good, better, and best. That's the goal of discernment----of evaluating worship music.

Paul does not leave his prayer unanswered, but under the inspiration of the Holy Spirit, gives a pregnant verse in Philippians 4:8 providing eight bench marks or standards of judgment------how to discern what is best in worship music. Chapter 6 will probe the depth of these eight words of discernment, relate them to the surrounding context, measure their applicability to the music of Moses, and project their relevance to our own time in the issue of worship music.

(4) Examine the subtlety of humanistic philosophy in musical acceptance.

Paul addresses in Colossians 2:4,8 the entrance of human-centered philosophy into the Colossian church and its damaging, theological influence on the person of Christ and the gospel message of salvation. The Colossian Christians are naïve, lack spiritual discernment, and embrace worldly philosophies without realizing their gullibility corrupts the Christian message of Christ. Music is not addressed in the context of Colossians 2:4,8, but Paul's principles directly relate to music, and this study will examine in depth the commands Paul gives in warning the Colossian Christians about the fine-sounding arguments of man-centered thinking.

(5) Contribute overall support for non fleshly worship music.

I know of no other issue more controversial in today's churches than the issue of music, and the category in question is called Contemporary Christian Music (CCM). This kind of music developed in the 1960s out of the Jesus movement from young people who were involved in the "hippie" lifestyle, but became converted to Christ and added Christian words to their existing music style of rock n roll. Their enthusiasm for Christ was refreshing as they attempted to share their faith through a new musical expression which evolved into the term we know today as CCM.

Since the 1960s this new type of music has entered the church and brought heated division, often resulting in church splits between Christians who supported or opposed traditional hymns of worship. This study will not criticize **ALL** CCM-----only CCM which does not measure up to Biblical standards of worship music. I maintain in this study **ALL** Christian worship music (both traditional hymns and CCM) must meet Biblical and Christian philosophical standards----not human-centered, contrived logic of worldly wisdom. There is an ongoing need for trained, gifted musicians to write both contemporary lyrics and musical melodies for freshness in worship-----but it must be judged by Biblical standards, and one key word summarizes the issue: **DISCERNMENT.** Unfortunately this prized Biblical word is lost or clouded by the politically correct term of **PLURALISTIC EXPRESSION** rampant in Christian thinking.

LIMIT OF THE STUDY:

I will not examine the numerous technical aspects of music theory, or components: cultural diversities in music is beyond the Biblical/theological scope of this treatment. Other books are available in evaluating these technical parts of Contemporary Christian Music and how it compares to traditional hymns, vocals, choral arrangements, and instrumental music Christians have used for generations in their worship services. In Chapter 8 I will list several books centering on why much of Contemporary Christian Music fails to meet accepted music standards of good music.

SCOPE OF THE STUDY:

This exposition encompass three areas: **(1) Background information** to Exodus 32:17-18; Ex. 15:1-18; Leviticus 10:1-8; Deut. 32:1-44; Acts 5:33-42; Philippians 4:8; and Colossians 2:4,8. **(2) A detailed explanation** of these seven passages, and **(3) Twenty-four points of application** emanating from the principles contained in these six passages. Several charts and diagrams will also be displayed to make the exposition and application more understandable and memorable. A useful chart for evaluating worship music appears in Chapter 6 targeted around the eight words of Philippians 4:8-----true, noble, right, pure, lovely, admirable, excellent, praiseworthy.

ORGANIZATION OF THE STUDY:

Chapters 1-6 consists of examining the passages of Scripture as a **FOUNDATION**. Apart from the Bible, we have no other certain foundation to form doctrine and philosophy of music ministry. Several popular books advocating Contemporary Christian Music (called CCM) will use the Bible for proof texts, but many times the texts are ripped from the context---- resulting in wrong interpretations with resulting wrong applications.

Chapter 7 consists of extracting twenty-four points of **APPLICATION** from the **FOUNDATION**. If you are like me (and I'm sure many are), you will be tempted to read Chapter 7 first, because that section is the practical outworking, the methodology of developing a Biblically based music ministry in the church. Reading Chapter 7 first may give you a popular, superficial understanding of pagan music/methods, but you will not fully understand the strong, foundational, necessary evidence in Chapters 1-6. Resist this strong temptation. Force yourself to read and think through the exposition of these six chapters; then the application section of Chapter 7 will be more understandable.

CHAPTER 1:

Golden Calf Music

**"When Joshua heard the noise of the people shouting,
He said to Moses, 'There is the <u>sound</u> of war in the camp.'
Moses replied: 'It is not the <u>sound</u> of victory,
It is not the <u>sound</u> of defeat;
It is the <u>sound</u> of singing that I hear.'"**

I. BACKGROUND OF EXODUS 32:17,18

The Hebrew people had been in Egyptian bondage for 400 years, but God miraculously delivered them from the clutches of Pharoah and his army by drowning them in the Red Sea following the tenth plague sent on the nation of Egypt. These Israelites under the leadership of Moses travel to Mt. Sinai where they will remain for eleven months before beginning their 40 year wilderness wandering. After only a few weeks at Mt. Sinai, God gives the 10 commandments to Moses and the Israelites vow to obey them, but they become impatient with Moses because he ascends Mt. Sinai a second time and remains there 40 days while God gives further revelation of the Law.

In his absence the people plead with Aaron to make a golden calf; Aaron, being a weak leader, consents, and the golden calf is formed from the gold jewelry brought out of Egypt by the Israelites. They sing and dance around the calf, but Moses is unaware of this breach of conduct until God reveals this evil to him (Ex. 32:7-8). Moses descends Mt. Sinai, hears at a distance the **"sound"** of their worship, and hears the words of Joshua: **"There is the sound of war in the camp."**

II. EXPLANATION OF EXODUS 32:17,18

Two elements are pertinent in this brief passage: **(1) word meaning for "singing," and (2) associated behavior to this "singing."**

(1) Word meaning

The Hebrew word for **"SOUND"** (NIV Translation) **(KOLE, or QOWL)** occurs four times in Exodus 32:17,18. This Hebrew word is used in other references in the Old Testament for the **bleating sound of sheep, the crackling sound of thunder, or the yelling sound of someone who calls out loud.** The first time Joshua thinks the sound is a sound of war in the camp, but he misunderstood the sound, for Moses replied, **"It is not the sound of victory; it is**

not the sound of defeat." John Durham says, "it was neither the exultant victory cry of triumph or the keening lamentation of defeat," **1** Joshua failed to properly interpret the singing or sound; his spiritual senses were dulled, preventing him from accurately interpreting the music

But Moses correctly interpreted this sound; he said it was the sound of **"singing."** The Hebrew word for **"singing"** is **AW-NAW**, but what kind of singing is inferred in the context, since there are obviously different kinds of singing? The context provides the answer: it is *CHAOTIC SINGING or CONFUSED NOISE*---as evidenced by the chaotic behavior of the worshipping Israelites. This same Hebrew word can also mean to depress literally or figuratively; to beat down, to afflict; to answer back. Chaotic singing or confused noise will produce these emotions of depression and affliction. Moses knew the distinction between triumphant and lamenting music, and neither is chaotic, but this **"singing"** of the Israelites was totally different. Rabbi Ramban makes a wise observation about Moses' ability to discern different kinds of music: **"Moses however with his mastery of the sciences knew how to differentiate between the various kinds of noise. He said that it was the noise of song that was audible to him." 2** Aaron nor Joshua could not properly discern the kind of music, but Moses, because of his training in Egypt, could discern the true nature of music and what conduct it produced in the Israelites.

(2) Associated behavior

All music, whether jazz, rock and roll, blues, classical, country western, hip hop, or Christian, produces a **DISTINCT** sound, and thus produces **DISTINCT** effects in the listener. What were the effects produced in the children of Israel as they worshipped the golden calf they carved with their hands? Exodus 32:6,25 provides the answer: revelry and running wild. Revelry is associated with sexual orgies in pagan worship; running wild means casting off restraint---letting emotions override clear thinking. How did other people react to this **"new kind of music"** being played and sung by the Israelites? Exodus 32:25 says these Israelites became a **"laughingstock"** or a shame to their enemies. The Hebrew word for "laughingstock" literally means according to S.R. Driver, **"a whispering among those who rose up against them." 3** These surrounding pagans whispered among themselves in a mocking manner. At what were these pagans mocking and laughing? The context of verse 25 provides the answer: (1) **IMMORAL BEHAVIOR:** the Israelites were running wild and out of control in sexual frenzy, and (2) **ABANDONMENT OF GOD:** these pagans knew the Hebrews were non-idolatrous worshippers of Jehovah God, and now they have abandoned this worship by adopting pagan methods of music and idolatry. The Israelites worshipped God in music, danced around the golden calf, and the surrounding pagans laughed and laughed.

What kind of music was used by these recently-liberated Israelites? According to the Hebrew word for singing (**AW-NAW**) in this context it was a chaotic, depressing, afflicting, beating down type of music. No, it was not a funeral dirge kind of music which is slow in tempo and eliciting a feeling of normal grief and sadness, but an **UPBEAT, FAST TEMPO, REPETITIVE, MONOTONOUS, DISCORDANT, DRIVING** kind of music designed to evoke positive happiness and excitement. How do we know the music was characterized this way? Because of its effects on the Israelites: revelry, dancing, running wild, casting off all normal moral restraints. *Quiet, slow, harmonious, melodic, reflective, relaxing music does not*

produce this effect. The word for "dancing" in verse 19 is the same word describing the dancing of Miriam and the women in Exodus 15:20, but in that passage the dancing does not appear to be out of control. That music was more conducive to a dance of joy measured by restraint, but here in Exodus 32:19 the dancing is definitely out of control and casting off all moral restraint.

Why would this kind of music be classified in the Hebrew word **(AW-NAW)** and labeled as **chaotic, depressive, afflicting, beating down?** How could such upbeat music be depressive, afflicting? ***Because of its effect on true worship of God.*** Normally a fast-tempo music with a positive upbeat produces excitement and happiness, and it certainly did with these Israelites, but it also produced a depressive affliction on the true emotions of worship. It majors on human, self-centered feelings of giddiness, rather than the character and attributes of God. Their worship was an **ILLUSION OF TRUE WORSHIP!** They worshipped the true God in a false way, with false music! ***Unwholesome music depresses, beats down, afflicts true worship.***

Exodus 32:6 tells us the Israelites **"sat down to eat and drink and got up to indulge in revelry."** It was a raucous, indecent celebration, bordering on the obscene. The Israelite camp had become a place of drunken carousing, pagan revelry, and bawdy singing. What Moses and Aaron heard was the sound of people partying. Durham further interprets this word "singing" as **"disorganized, conflicting answering of random singing; racket,"**------an antiphonal singing of Israelites answering back to each other seemingly in conflicting words, off-beat rhythm, or discordant tones. **4** Alfred Syndrey calls this singing and behavior **"savage skipping." 5** God's Word Translation (GWT) gives this translation of the "singing" as **"wild celebration."** Moses hears this so-called "worshipful singing," this discordant, disorganized, fast-tempo, driving, bawdy music, sees the Israelites dancing around the calf, and in anger throws down the tablets----breaking them into pieces.

(3) Source of this music

Where did these Israelites learn this kind of bawdy music? Seemingly from the Egyptians whom they observed for 400 years under Egyptian captivity. During these long years of exile they watched the Egyptians in their worship of a pantheon of gods-----witnessed their behavior, the kind of music, the emotional atmosphere. Sendry comes to this same conclusion by stating the Israelites experienced a "relapse......into the Egyptian pagan practices with worshipping an idol and with ritual customs, which were familiar to the Hebrews from their recent place of slavery." **6**

(4) Nature of Egyptian Music: monophonic and chanting

History records Egyptian, Arabic, and even early Hebrew worship music was not harmonious (given to rich harmony), but "monophonic" (melody alone) played or sung on a minor pentatonic scale of five tones and without half tones, as verified by the position of holes in the flute found in archaeological digs. The music was highly developed, served an integral part of religious worship in ancient Egypt, and played a central role in the religious rituals, hymns, and prayers. Ritual temple music was largely a matter of the rattling of the sistrum, and party scenes showing naked female acrobatic dancers performing the same movement in unison. This music was accompanied by a dominant, driving beat of drums, lutes, flutes, cymbals, clappers, tambourines, percussion instruments, and wind flutes. Such a dominant, driving beat will definitely capture and control the emotions of worshippers leading to sensual urges and minimal reflective thought. The emphasis in this type of music targets the physical pleasure of the beat, not the flowing melody accompanied by blended harmony and wedded to meditative thought of the words. **The music is the major component; the words (when they exist) are of minor importance.** These Israelites thus became the first group of God's people to **"borrow"** a worldly music style and incorporate it into their own worship of Jehovah God.

The actual singing was more of a chant than a true melody such as we know today in our Western culture. Melody was present on the five note scale, but the singer would sing several words on one note before progressing to a different pitch level. Both the monophonic melody and repetitious changing of the words accompanied by the driving, dominant beat of the drums and instruments explains why the **"chaotic singing"** of the Israelites impacted on their immoral behavior as they savagely danced around the golden calf. Three elements characterize this early Egyptian music: **(1) Driving beat, (2) Repetition, and (3) Loud volume.** The first two elements are evident from previous discussion, and the third (loud volume) element is clearly seen in Moses and Joshua hearing the noise from a considerable distance. According to Exodus 24:13 Joshua accompanied Moses to the top of Mt. Sinai, and perhaps Joshua only went half way up the mountain, allowing Moses alone to ascend the remaining distance to the summit where he received the Law from God during a forty-day time span. Following reception of the Law, Moses descended the mountain: joining Joshua at the half way point. From this distance Moses and Joshua heard the loud "noise" coming from the Israelites. These identical three elements are seen today in rock music and much CCM in our churches: **(1) Driving beat, (2) Repetition, and (3) Loud volume.** Combined they form a trilogy of manipulation and control----hypnotically controlling the emotions and conduct of the innocent worshipper. At Mt. Sinai three thousand Israelites were controlled by Egyptian pagan worship music, and today thousands and thousands of Christians are also being manipulated with this same style of **"worship music."**

REPETITION IN MUSIC. The technical term in music for repetition is **OSTINATO**---rhythmic or melodic phrase repeated constantly in music. How does this repetition **(OSTINATO)** in music affect the brain? The brain receives musical information, arranges it into an orderly pattern, and decides whether subsequent repetition of the music is different or identical. If the musical repetition is identical in lyrics, melody, rhythm, volume, or chord structure, the music becomes displeasing, creating mental **"fatigue,"** 7 and prompting either a state of sub-conscious thinking of numbness and susceptibility to suggestion, or a state of anger and rejection toward the music. Under these conditions, the human mind becomes bored, **"fatigued,"** and shuts down after three or four repetitions of a rhythm, melody, or a harmonic progression. This explains why people become bored today in repeating "praise and worship" choruses in monotonous repetition. Excessive repetition causes people to release control of their thoughts, and this rhythmic repetition is often employed by people pushing certain ethics in music. Initial usage of identical repetition may not be a deliberate, conscious motivation of the musical performer or leaders in worship, but he soon discovers its power of influence and continues using it for further mind and conduct control in the listener or worshipper.

Repetition is wholesome---provided it varies the chord structure, melody, rhythm, lyrics, volume, and emotional tension/relaxation. Our brain welcomes this refreshing repetition, as is evident in many classical pieces of music employing a simple melody repeated numerous times in diverse arrangements and rhythms as in Beethoven's fifth symphony, first movement. This musical masterpiece with its various settings is definitely not boring or monotonous, but stimulating, energizing, tense yet relaxing, and triumphantly resolving in its concluding chords.

Singing a hymn usually consists of four or five stanzas with a chorus or refrain repeated at the end of each stanza. The chorus is often shorter and does not create "fatigue" because it occurs after each stanza. But if the chorus was sung eight or ten times in succession detached from the stanzas, then mental "fatigue" would certainly develop. This is how many current "praise and worship" choruses are repeatedly sung with their short fragments of vapid lyrics---- resulting in mental "fatigue."

Repetition in Egyptian worship music served one element in prompting the wild, lewd, raucous behavior of the Israelites worshipping at the golden calf. Some Israelites may have become bored by constant repetition of the same lyrics, or driving beat and walked away in disgust, but three thousand remained----mesmerized, controlled by the hypnotic sound. This same hypnosis is evident in much CCM today by using a short, lyrical fragment repeated numerous times to the same melody, beat, and rhythm of the music----resulting in a form of hypnotic mind control. The evangelical worshipper may not give full vent to the sensual practices of the Israelites, but the sensual foundation remains under the veneer of a diluted, deceptive **"worshipping experience."**

Their immoral behavior at Mt. Sinai contrasts sharply with the Song of Moses in Exodus 15:1-18 at the edge of the Red Sea. In Moses' song of deliverance there is no hint of immoral behavior, chaotic singing, revelry, or sensual movements. Around the golden calf the music was objectionable, but not at the Red Sea. Moses knew the difference between **APPROPRIATE** and **INAPPROPRIATE** worship music, and our obligation as Christians is to follow his discerning example, not the pagan worship music Aaron allowed.

(5) Results of the music

Seven events occurred from using pagan, worldly music (Exodus 32:19-35) (the idolatry can not be separated from the music: both intertwined): (1) Moses burned with anger; (2) he threw down the tablets of stone, breaking them into pieces; (3) he destroyed the golden calf by grinding it into a powder which he forced the guilty to drink; (4) he ordered the Levites to kill with a sword 3,000 people who participated in golden calf worship that same day; (5) he interceded to God again for these corrupt Israelites; (6) God forgave the sin; (7) God sent a plague on the people. We learn from this incident the absolute importance of using the right kind of music in Biblical worship.

(6) Influence of the mixed multitudes

The exodus of the Israelites from Egypt included also a **"mixed multitude"** (Ex. 12:38--- KJV) of disenchanted pagan Egyptians, perhaps slaves or descendants of the Hyksos (foreign kings of Egypt from the fifteenth and sixteenth dynasties) and a few God-fearers (Ex. 9:20) who desired to leave their native land (Ex. 12:38) and were called "rabble" (disorderly mob) in Numbers 14. How many composed this group? We don't know, but the Hebrew word for

"mixed multitude" can also be translated a **"great swarm."** This group became a source of trouble in Israel and led the Israelites in complaining and opposing Moses (Numbers 14). These pagan Egyptians brought with them their pagan idolatry, music, values, and no doubt exercised a corrupting influence on many Israelites there at Mt. Sinai in the absence of Moses ------ convincing them of the "rightness" of Egyptian idols and accompanying "worship music."

(7) Motives of the mixed multitude

What were the motives of this **"mixed multitude"** who joined the Israelites in the Exodus from Egypt? Scripture does not indicate, but we can project possibly four motives: **(a) genuine belief, (b) personal betterment, (c) fearful reprisals, and (d) attractive success.**

(a) FIRST---genuine belief. A few Egyptians were God-fearers (Ex. 9:20); they apparently, sincerely converted to the worship of Jehovah as a result of seeing the work of God through Moses in the ten plagues. **(b) SECOND---personal betterment.** Some Egyptians perhaps felt defeated working as slaves and desired to improve their conditions in life by joining the Israelites. **(c) THIRD----fearful reprisals.** Some Egyptians may have emotionally and personally supported the Israelites during their 400 year captivity, and feared Governmental reprisal on them if they remained in Egypt. **(d) FOURTH-----attractive success.** Many Egyptians no doubt were amazed at the miracles Jehovah performed in the ten plagues, and thus became attracted to the "glitzy, showy" benefits of Israel's God, and hoped they too would become successful by identifying with Israel.

Whatever the motives, this **"mixed multitude"** did have a corrupting influence on the Israelites by cunningly convincing Israel to adopt their pagan values, ideas, music, and idolatry. How did this **"riffraff,"** this **"great swarm"** of pagan Egyptians incorporate themselves into the estimated two million Israelites? Scripture does not indicate; we can only guess. They either isolated themselves apart from the main body of Israelites or dispersed individually into the throng of two million followers of Jehovah. The diagram on the left illustrates their isolation or separation as an entity by themselves-----part of the Israelites, yet distinct from them; the diagram on the right illustrates their dispersion or infiltration into the mass of Israelites. The circles represent Israelites; the stars represent pagan Egyptians.

ISOLATION OF EGYPTIANS   INFILTRATION OF EGYPTIANS

```
O O O O O O O O O O        O * O * O * O * O * O * O * O
O O O O O O O O O O        O * O * O * O * O * O * O * O
O O O O O O O O O O        O * O * O * O * O * O * O * O
         * * * * * * *
         * * * * * * *
```

Infiltration or blending into the mass of Israelites would seem best to explain the corrupting influence of these Egyptians with their pagan music and values on the Israelites, giving the Egyptians a more ready, natural access to all the Israelites.

(8) Sin of Syncretism

The Israelites knew to worship Jehovah God exclusively and erect no idols of God, but seemingly they adopted the Egyptian **"style of worship"** by making a golden calf and then singing music in the style of the Egyptians. Their sin was **SYNCRETISM: combining different or opposing beliefs in religion.** It is highly unlikely they developed this **"new style of worship music"** on their own; rather they observed how the Egyptians worshipped using a variety of musical instruments and incorporated this musical style to accompany veneration of the golden calf. In Ezekiel 20:7 God is rehearsing with Ezekiel the words He spoke to the Israelites when they departed Egypt: **"get rid of the vile images you have set your eyes on, and do not defile yourselves with the idols of Egypt."** Some of these Israelites had worshipped false gods while in Egypt for 400 years (Joshua 24:14), and even now are continuing to combine the worship of Jehovah with Egyptian idolatry and its pagan music.

Scripture teaches Satan appears as a roaring lion and a sly serpent. Arthur Pink in his commentary on Exodus wisely observes the Jews for 400 years were under the galling control of the Pharaoah and harassed like the **fearful lion;** now in the desert at the base of the mountain they are deceived by the **serpent** to incorporate pagan Egyptian music as the **"new way to worship God." 8** Today, the sly, cunning, crafty, seemingly logical serpent has "conned" many Christians into accepting the style of contemporary Christian music as the most relevant medium to reach people. The golden calf with its attendant "worship music" is alive today.

(9) Impatience leads to sin

Moses went up to the mountain for 40 days and there received further instruction from God. Why 40 days? Could not God have given revelation to Moses in four days, two days, even one hour? Yes, definitely, for nothing is impossible with God. Why 40 days? Because the number 40 is the number of testing, as Jesus was tested 40 days and nights in the desert by Satan. Was Moses being tested? No, the Israelites were being tested to determine their stated loyalty to God and His Word, and they failed the test, for Exodus 32:1 states, **"When the people saw that Moses was so long in coming down from the mountain, they gathered around Aaron and said, 'Come, make us gods who will go before us. As for this fellow Moses who brought us up out of Egypt, we don't know what has happened to him.'"** They were impatient and wanted some visual, aesthetic, physical assurance of the presence of gods. They were not content to wait patiently for Moses' return; unwilling to trust God in the absence of Moses. They desired immediate results, immediate assurance of their senses, quick response to worship the invisible God in a visible, sensual manner. They wanted to "sense" God now, not later; they desired to see results now, not later; therefore they resorted to idolatry and sensuality. Yes, they were tested----and failed the test!

The evangelical church today, like these Israelites, is impatient to see God working; unwilling to trust God in His sovereignty to bring about fruit in evangelism, a greater sense of worship, so the church resorts to **"pagan Egyptian music"** to satisfy fleshly desires, secure quick results, see fast growth in churches. Evidence for this thinking is seen in the words of Christians who remark, **"I like this modern music; I like the beat and jazzed up tempo; it makes me feel motivated! It is relevant to the music I hear it in school, on the radio, and in rock and roll concerts."** Note the clues of idolatry: **"makes me feel good, motivated, jazzed up, relevant, the beat."** Will such "pagan" music get immediate results in pleasing our sinful flesh? Yes, definitely-----but at what price to Biblical worship? It gained immediate results for these Israelites------but 3,000 worshippers were killed that day! (Ex. 32:27)

Spirituality and its blood brother, maturity, cannot be rushed by such "pagan" music and idolatry. Maturity in Christ takes time----much time spent learning of Christ, patience in worship services in quietly listening to His still small voice, (not loud, syncopated, heavy-beat, jazzed-up music), and many "closet" experiences with Christ in prayer. Maturity can not be rushed! And neither can fruitfulness in evangelism----by **"get-happy-get-modern worship music."**

(10) The Training of Moses

Luke tells of the training of Moses in Acts 7:22: **"Moses was educated in all the wisdom of the Egyptians and was powerful in speech."** He was being groomed for leadership by the Egyptian priestly caste, and thus received training in all areas: agriculture, science, math, languages, religion, and music. Sendry concludes: Moses was "thoroughly conversant with the musical art of the Egyptians." **9** Philo of Alexandria comments on the theoretical and practical effects of music Moses gained from training: "Arithmetic, geometry, the lore of metre, rhythm and harmony (i.e. poetry), and the whole subject of music as shown by the use of instruments or in textbooks and treatises of a more special character, were imparted to him by learned Egyptians."

Music received major emphasis among the priests and senior clergy of the state, headed by the Pharoah who gave special attention to music training. As a result of this prominent emphasis by the Pharoah, there was a special school in Memphis, Egypt at that time called **"Academies for Sacred Music,"10** and since Moses was trained by the Egyptian priestly caste, he may have attended and graduated from this prominent school of music. Justin Martyr **11** in his Apologia Prima pro Christianmis, comments of Moses training and influence in music by noting prominent people who excelled in music and poetry-----among them Orpheus, Pythagoras and Homer-----**"had taken advantage of the history of Moses, when they had been in Egypt, and profited by his godliness and his ancestry."**

What is the importance of Moses' training in music? It qualifies him in two areas: (1) compose lyrics and melodies which are appropriate, and (2) discard music inappropriate to the occasion. Hearing the "sound" of singing emanating from the giddy, twirling Hebrews around the golden calf immediately connected with his discernment, and he knew this **"new style of worship music"** was not appropriate in worshipping Jehovah God. Moses was not only a godly man, but also courageous, musically informed, and discerning.

Moses had spent 40 days alone with God on the Mountain before descending to the ribald "worship music" of the Israelites. He alone had the formal training in music and the spiritual discernment to detect inappropriate "sounds" of music. Neither Joshua nor Aaron possessed this rare virtue; he alone had the "hearing ear." Yes, he knew from his formal training what music was acceptable in worship, but even greater was his spiritual discernment gained from 40 days alone in the presence of God.

(11) Application to Contemporary Christian Music

Many evangelical church leaders (pastors, church musicians, seminary professors), like Aaron, adopt the musical styles of contemporary rock and roll, soft rock, jazz, heavy metal, hip hop, rhythm and blues, sprinkle a few Christian words in the music, and use this new musical style in worship services under the banner "praise and worship" choruses. This prevalent practice is nothing more than borrowing pagan music for Christian worship, a practice further amplified in the application section of the book.

CHAPTER 2:

Red Sea Music

I. Background of Exodus 15:1-18

God performed a miracle when He opened the Red Sea to allow the Israelites to escape 400 years of Egyptian captivity. Safely on the other side, they look behind them and see a second miracle: drowning of Pharoah's soldiers, horses, and war chariots as the high wall of water covered them. Upon seeing these two great miracles, the people rejoiced, feared the Lord and placed their trust in Him and in Moses (Exodus 14:20-31).

II. Explanation of Exodus 15:1-18

At this high emotional event, Moses composes a masterpiece of music-----both in lyrics and melody just a few weeks before the golden calf incident in Ex. 32:17-18. We have the lyrics (Ex. 15:1-18), not the melody or tune, but this song represents the first song composed by Moses and serves as an example of contemporary music------contemporary to the time of Moses, and illustrates how words are to be written for grand, worship music. This song is also classified as a hymn of joy for God's deliverance of the Israelites through the Red Sea and the drowning of the Egyptian army. Some people call this hymn "Victory at Sea" because it truly was a victory over the Red Sea. A second song from Moses (Deut. 32:1-44) occurs 40 years later as the Israelites are ending the wilderness wanderings, and getting prepared to enter the promised land.

1. Talmudic rules

The importance of both songs is displayed in Talmudic rules requiring the songs be written in the Pentateuch in a distinctive manner----=-separate in their style and arrangement on the page of Hebrew Scripture----and are written in different column formations and extra space between the words to highlight the importance of the song. Furthermore, these two songs are included in the Jewish lectionary for home and synagogue readings. Why are the songs written in different format style from the remaining parts of the Pentateuch, and why include them in the Jewish lectionary? Because of the **TEACHING VALUE.** God inspired Moses to compose these songs so succeeding Jewish generations would sing them to imprint the lessons on the majesty, power, and greatness of God. They form a **THEOLOGICAL BASTION** of worship lyrics and truth----unlike much of the Contemporary Christian Music today with its anemic, vapid, weakly sentimental lyrics and often ear-grating ditty tunes.

2. Content of the song

Sendry identifies this song as "the first religious national song found in the Bible." **1** and describes it as ***"artistically the most relevant, song of the Old Testament,"*** The first verse of this chapter tells us **"Then Moses and the Israelites sang this song to the Lord."** The Hebrew word for singing is **YASHIR**---the most common word referring to illustrious singing, unlike the "singing" around the golden calf which was chaotic, confused noise. Verses 2-18 describe the mighty acts of God, and His miraculous power in delivering His people. Examine the words and they reveal a total God-centered focus on His majesty, wisdom, sovereignty, and power over all the pagan gods of Egypt and the Egyptian army. There is not the slightest hint in this hymn of any emphasis on Moses' feelings of giddiness, hilarity, or desire to **"feel good"** by the heavy beat and rhythm of the song.

3. Structure of the song

The lyrics are masterfully composed in Hebrew poetical format, not like our rhyming concept of poetry. The words are formed into three strophes (stanzas): 1-6, 7-11, 12-18 with each stanza ending on a hinge or refrain-----similar to our "chorus" sung at the end of each stanza of a hymn. Note this trilogy hinge**: "RIGHT HAND"** (v. 6); **"RIGHT HAND"** (v. 12); **"POWER OF YOUR ARM."** (v.16) This flowing style of writing and excellent use of technique in the trilogy hinge reveals again the musical knowledge and skill of Moses: he was fully qualified to discern appropriate from inappropriate music; worship from "feel good" music; ennobling lyrics from anemic lyrics.

4. Antiphonal singing

We do not know the melody or tune Moses used to accompany the lyrics, but we do know how it was sung: antiphonally. The term "antiphonal" means "answering back"----one choral group sings a phrase followed by another group of singers repeating back the same words. As children most of us learned the French tune to "Row, row, row your boat gently down the stream. Merrily, merrily, merrily, merrily life is but a dream." I recall singing this antiphonally or "in rounds." Sendry **2** believes the singing of Moses was antiphonal, not because the text of 15:2-18 indicate such, but rabbinical sources in the Mishna (the teachings of the Rabbis regarding oral traditions of the law) confirm explicitly this kind of rendition. The seraphim in Isaiah 6:3 cried out antiphonally, "Holy, Holy, Holy, is the Lord of Hosts; the whole earth is filled with his glory." One group of seraphs uttered these words, followed by other seraphs all in praise to God.

Furthermore, the response of Miriam indicates antiphonal singing in Ex. 15:20-21 where Miriam took a timbrel in her hand, and all the women went out after her with timbrels and with dances. Miriam sang to the women, "Sing to the Lord, for he is highly exalted; the horse and its rider he has hurled into the sea." We can assume Moses led the men in antiphonal singing of this miracle of God's deliverance.

Miriam is called a "**prophetess**," (Ex. 15:20), a term Sendry defines as **"her mastery in music and singing"** **3** (Alfred Syndrey, Music in Ancient Israel, London: Vision Press Limited,

1969, p 480) along with eloquent speaking abilities. In early Jewish history, therefore, the term "seer" or "prophet" would be synonymous with "musician" or "singer." How did she acquire this musical knowledge and insight into music? Sendry believes "there is a great probability that she owes her mastery to none else than her brother Moses." **4**

The following simple chart reveals 400 years under Egyptian slavery----with no record of any worship while they were in bondage; if the Hebrews did worship (and I'm confident many did) there is no record of any worship or singing among them. But immediately after crossing the Red Sea we have the first song from Moses: Hymn----- "Victory at Sea." (Ex. 15:1-18) accompanied by the Israelites. Another 40 years passes in the wilderness and again no singing. At the end of the wilderness journeys, God inspires Moses to record a second song (Deut. 32:1-44). Was Moses opposed to "contemporary" music? Hardly! He himself composed two contemporary songs by using his training in Egypt and spiritual discernment. His example is for our imitation.

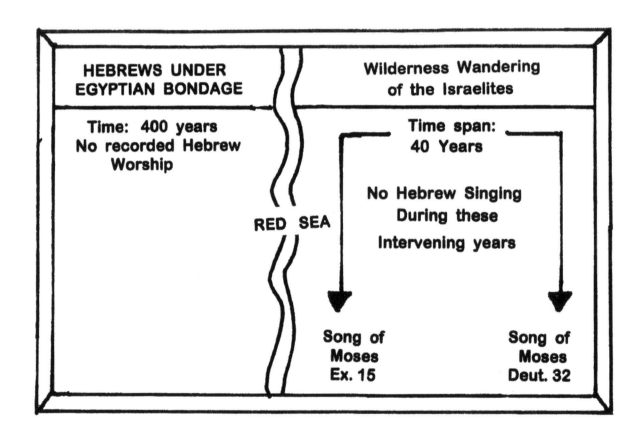

CHAPTER 3:

Promise Land Music

I. BACKGROUND OF DEUTERONOMY 32:1-44

The second "contemporary" song composed by Moses (contemporary to his time) is recorded in Deut. 32:1-44 near his death (Deut. 31:16). Joshua had already been chosen (Deut. 31:1-8) to lead the Israelites into the promised land of Canaan because God would not allow Moses to lead any further. The Lord summoned both Moses and Joshua at the Tent of Meeting, and there revealed the song (lyrics) to teach the people. Moses may have composed the tune or melody, but the words (lyrics) are direct revelation from God to Moses. Historically we attribute this song to Moses as though he composed the words, but the words came straight from God.

The purpose of the song is not to entertain the people, but **TEACH** them: **"Now write down for yourselves this song and teach it to the Israelites and have them sing it, so that it may be a witness for me against them."** The song was not to entertain the worshipping Israelites, but teach them. **"Then Moses recited the words of this song from beginning to end in the hearing of the whole assembly."** (Deut. 31:30) I will call this song: Moses' Farewell Song.

II. EXPLANATION OF DEUTERONOMY 32:1-44

1. Length of the song

The first obvious feature is its length: 44 verses long and occupying about 90% of the chapter, in comparison to the Song of Moses at the Red Sea with its 18 verses occupying about 70% of the chapter. Why so long? There are two reasons: **CONTENT** and **TIMING.** In content this farewell song of Moses covers much more material in Israel's history than does the Song at the Red Sea. In timing this farewell song was planned; the Song at the Red Sea was spontaneous. God knew in advance of Moses' death and thus summoned him to receive God's revelation of the lyrics. Moses at the Red Sea did not plan to compose "Victory at Sea," but was caught up in the euphoria of the parting of the Red Sea. His inspiration was **SPONTANEOUS.**

2. Meaning of the song

The Hebrew word for "**sing**" or "**song**" used in Exodus 15:l and Deut. 32:1-43 is totally different from the "**singing**" of Exodus 32:18. At the Song of the Red Sea in Exodus 15:1 and the farewell song of Moses in Deuteronomy 32:1 the Hebrew word is **YASHUR,** _meaning a song of joy,_ but around the golden calf in Exodus 32:18 the Hebrew word is **AW-NAW,** _meaning a song of depression._ Both the Song of the Red Sea and the farewell song of Moses emphasize joy, even though heavy thoughts on judgment are instilled in the song.

3. Theme of the song

The theme of the Song of the Red Sea is the _**MAJESTY OF GOD;**_ Moses' farewell song is the _**JUDGMENT OF GOD!**_ In the Song of the Red Sea, Moses extols the might of God in performing miracles in Egypt and anticipates the entrance of Israel into the promised land; so the view is **PROSPECTIVE** for Israel's bright future in their new homeland. In Moses' farewell song God extols His power in performing miracles during Israel's 40 years of grumbling, complaining, and on-going rebelling; the farewell song thus results in God's future judgment on His people. So the view is **RETROSPECTIVE** and **PROSPECTIVE.** In its retrospective view, Moses' farewell song looks back on the amazing, faithful miracles of God meeting the needs of 2 million people for 40 years living in desert conditions. Each time the song would be sung by an Israelite they would be reminded of God's loving faithfulness, despite their persistent sinning. In its prospective view, Moses' farewell song warns the Israelites of future judgment they will face because of their determined will to disobey God.

4. Balance of the song

Israel (and us also) needed both songs: songs lifting up the majesty of God in worship, and songs of rebuke for sinfulness. Reading through the farewell song of Moses here in Deut.32:1-44 is ponderous but profitable; tedious but timely; rebuking but rewarding; reminiscent but revealing. I don't read this important song in a joyful, but saddened spirit because verse after verse recounts the miraculous power of God with the ungrateful Israelites, but they kept on sinning, and as a result He must judge them.

5. Category of the song

The length of this song would be classified in musicology today as an **ORATORIO: a long, dramatic musical composition consisting of arias, duets, trios, and choruses sung to orchestral accompaniment.** Usually this major music production is conducted in music halls and music conservatories where large crowds attend. Moses' farewell song would clearly not fit into our **"ditty praise and worship choruses"** used profusely today. What congregation wants to sing forty-three verses or stanzas of Deut. 32:1-44? And yet God gave this song as a **TEACHING INSTRUMENT** (Deut. 32:19) for families in homes, synagogues, and local churches. Deep theology is communicated in the forty-three verses of this song-----a need, I believe, is dire among professing Christians. This lengthy song of God's determination to judge Israel and us also is reinforced by II Timothy 3:16: **"All scripture is useful for teaching, rebuking, correcting and training in righteousness."** And yes, that includes a lengthy song from the Old Testament.

This song is definitely not trite, infantile, syrupy, nor boringly repetitious-----as are so many modern Christian songs and choruses of today, which in reality **"dumb-down"** the intelligence level of Christians----retaining them in effect to on-going "babyhood" and spiritual immaturity----sucking on milk bottles! **TRITE WORDS PRODUCE TRITE CHRISTIANS. SYRUPY TUNES PRODUCE SENTIMENTAL CHRISTIANS!** God through Moses composed this music to **TEACH THEOLOGY!** Paul in Colossians 3:16 repeats that same purpose: **"teach and admonish one another with all wisdom and as you sing psalms, hymns, and spiritual songs."** Note Paul did not command: *"entertain, amuse, cajole one another with.......psalms, hymns, and spiritual songs."* Nor did Paul command: *"Evangelize one another with psalms, hymns, and spiritual songs."* This pithy verse gives an incisive clue: **Christian music is aimed at Christians----not unbelievers!** Sadly, much Contemporary Christian Music today is pathetically weak in sound theology-----articulating only inane, insipid, simplistic truth.

The importance of teaching is the major point at the beginning of the song: **"Let my teaching fall like rain, and my words descend like dew...."** Deut. 32:2 Note the two figures of speech (similes): **"fall like rain"** and **"descend like dew."** What is the significance of these two similes? The first simile emphasizes constant repetition of truth as rain falls in repetition to the earth; the second simile emphasizes quiet nourishment of truth as dew forms quiet condensation of the air from the cold ground. Both rain and dew were essential for the continued flourishing vegetation. November through March were the months for rain, and April through October were the months for the dew. The rain and dew were vital for vegetation, and the constant repetition of the words of the song, and the quiet reflection on these words would produce growth and blessing.

Moses, as the trained musician, taught the Israelites not only the words, but the melody and rhythm: he was the choral director. Did Moses consider this song as authoritative? Definitely, for Moses told the people in Deut. 32:46, **"Take to heart all the words I have solemnly declared to you this day, so that you may command your children to obey carefully all the words of this law."** *NOTE: this song is on the same level as the actual law of God!* Is Moses overstating his case? No, because the words of the song recount the complete history of Israel, God's majesty, His holiness, moral demands, and judgment on sin.

6. Influence of the song

What kind of influence did this song have on the Israelites? According to the words of Moses, **"They (these words, accompanying qualitative melody, and structured rhythm) are not just idle words for you-----they are your life. By them you will live long in the land you are crossing the Jordan to possess."** Note Moses' connection to rich words in theology wedded to the right kind of appropriate music: **"they are your life."**

The Hebrew word for **"life"** used here means more than physical existence; **it refers to holistic life---body, mind, and spirit or emotions**. Rich words of poetry wedded to right musical forms will produce nourishment or healing to your physical body, clearness and depth to your thinking, and balanced emotions regulated by healthy discipline. All three conditions were absent in the Israelites with their chaotic singing around the golden calf, but are here present in the words and music of Moses in Deut. 32. Note Moses' connection to the words of the song to longevity: ***"By them you will live long in the land you are crossing the Jordan to possess."*** (Deut. 32:47) Obedience to the right music and theological words will mean living a long time.

I often hear Christians say about rich hymns with their theologically based words: **"I don't like hymns: they are boring; they don't reach me; they don't rouse my emotions; they are not 'fun;' they are not entertaining."** Moses would respond to these entertainment-oriented Christians today: **"Sing them again and again; they are true life, and you will live a long time."**

But did succeeding Israelites follow Moses' command regarding singing the song? Yes, they did. When Solomon built the beautiful, grand Temple in Jerusalem where animals were sacrificed for sins, the Levites would lead out in singing this very song on the Sabbath to commemorate the drink-offering. Sendry records: "They divided the song into six portions, verses 1-6, 7-13, 14-18, 19-28, 29-39, and 40-43, each one of these being still further broken up into three parts. After each of these subdivisions the priests gave three blasts of trumpets, and the people prostrated themselves." **1** In the Sabbath-eve service they sang, in addition, the "Song of the Red Sea" (Ex. 15)

Note what happened when the rich theological words of Deut. 32 were sung to the right kind of worship music: the worshippers fell on their faces. There was no hand clapping, swaying, stiffened torso, hip thrusting, sexy voice, screams of delight, or rowdy behavior----only quiet prostration before God Almighty: a holy hush in the presence of holiness.

7. Application to music today

Much music today in our churches is short, simplistic choruses, repeating a few words over and over and over, but Moses' song here in Deut. 32 is long and rich in profound theology: long and profound because it recapitulates God's 40 year dealings with the temperamental Israelites. I don't believe we should sing 20 stanzas of a hymn, but I do believe Moses is setting an example to write songs reflective of deep theology, and we can ask God in prayer to raise up gifted musicians like Moses to write new tunes and lyrics measuring up to the eight standards of Philippians 4:8, and words of deep doctrine.

CHAPTER 4:

"Strange fire"

Leviticus 10:1-8

1. ABSENCE OF MUSIC:

This passage in Leviticus 10 does not directly address **MUSIC,** but **METHODS** of worship. In Nadab and Abihu we see how their well-intentioned, sincere efforts to gain coals of fire from pagan sources for Tabernacle worship resulted in their deaths, and by extraction of the Biblical principle of worship we can indirectly relate false methods to false music.

2. REGULATIVE AND NORMATIVE WORSHIP:

The regulative principle of worship, from the Westminster Confession of Faith in 1646 and the Baptist Confession of Faith in 1644, teaches public worship should be regulated by elements instituted, commanded, or appointed by command or example in the Bible. God clearly indicates in His Word how He is to be worshipped and thus limits or restricts our worship. He never gave permission and freedom to worship Him **"any old way we choose,"** with any new method, with a novel technique, to the sound of hot jazz, soft rock, heavy metal, twanging guitars, or bodily gyrations of praise team members with their sensual pulsations. We do not have this option! The normative principle agrees worship must consist of direct commands of God, but **_also may include_** methods not specifically prohibited by Scripture. The normative philosophy believes **"if it isn't expressly forbidden in scripture, then we are free to innovate and create 'NEW FORMS OF WORSHIP.'"** Regulative worship is practiced by Reformed Baptists and Presbyterians. Normative worship is practiced by Lutheran, Anglican, Methodist, Nazarene, Church of God, Assembly of God, many independent Baptist and Bible churches, as well as in the Roman Catholic church.

3. BACKGROUND INFORMATION:

The normative principle of worship and its chilling consequences is illustrated in Leviticus 10:1-11 with the sudden deaths of Nadab and Abihu----sons of Aaron. They were anointed as priests (Leviticus 8-9) and thus began their first day of functioning as priests for the people in Leviticus 10, but they were killed on this momentous day for offering to God **"strange fire"** or **"unauthorized fire:"** _"So fire came out from the presence of the Lord and consumed them, and they died before the Lord." (Leviticus 10:2)._

The procedure for the priests was to (1) take hot coals of fire from off the great bronze altar in the Tabernacle where a fire burned constantly, (2) place these coals in their censer pans; (3)

sprinkle finely ground fragrant incense (Lev. 16:12) over the hot coals; and (4) place the censer and incense before the Lord, allowing smoke from the incense to rise, filling the Tabernacle with its sweet aroma, and conceal the atonement above the Testimony on the Ark of the Covenant. This sweet smelling incense was offered by the priests twice a day (morning and evening) on the inner altar (Exodus 30), and once a year by the high priest as part of the Day of Atonement (Leviticus 16). What precisely was this **"strange fire"** or **"unauthorized fire"** warranting God's judgment on Nadab and Abihu? Biblical scholars for years have debated this issue and have proposed various interpretations: (1) the fire was inappropriate incense placed over hot coals, (2) drunkenness of Nadab and Abihu, (3) coals of fire taken from a pagan source outside the Tabernacle rather than from the brazen altar inside the Tabernacle. This last interpretation appears the most valid and is presented by Richard S. Hess,[1] professor at Denver Seminary.

4. **PRACTICE OF A CONTINUAL FIRE:**

Three times in Leviticus 6:9,12,13 God specified the fire on the brazen altar must never be extinguished or go out whenever the Israelites were encamped, but the fire must burn continuously day and night. God Himself started the first fire (Leviticus 9:24). Why was this fire commanded to burn continuously? Because the fire represented God's presence, and perpetual sacrifice for sins was always ready and available, even as Christ always lives to intercede for Christians when we sin (Heb. 7:25). Furthermore the priest each morning was instructed to add firewood to the existing embers which burned the previous night (Leviticus 6:12). Did they fail to keep the fire burning during the night? If they failed this inattention would have been a direct sin against God's commandment, but Scripture does not tell us! Did they fail to add new firewood to the extinguished fire? Again Scripture is silent! We can only assume the initial fire started on the brazen altar by God in Leviticus 9:24 was still burning the next morning when Nadab and Abihu commenced their new ministry as priests in Leviticus 10:1. Thus Nadab and Abihu seemingly had access to coals of fire from the brazen altar, but they chose to acquire coals from a pagan source.

What caused these priests to commit such a serious sin resulting in their immediate deaths? Bryan D. Bibb offers three possible explanations: ignorance, carelessness, or maliciousness.[2] He observes there is no evidence in the context of Leviticus 10:1-8 they were careless or malicious, but rather they were ignorant because God had not given a specific command **PROHIBITING** acquiring coals of fire from pagan sources. They were functioning as priests within a "gap" or absence of God's commandment.

Richard S. Hess **3** bases his view of coals from a pagan source on two elements: (1) the Hebrew word ('es zaru) meaning "strange fire," and (2) archaeological evidence of sacred rituals of fire associated with anointing pagan priests in the West Semitic world of Emar, a prominent, ancient city on the Euphrates River---now in Syria. It has been the source of many cuneiform tablets revealing historical evidence of both secular and sacred practices, and ranks with Ugarit, Mari and Ebla among the most important archaeological sites of Syria. This archaeological evidence from Emar occurred in north Palestine------far from south Palestine where Nadab and Abihu were commissioned at the base of Mt. Sinai, but it does provide a connecting link to fire rituals. Leviticus 10 occurs during the year they encamped around Mt. Sinai where pagan temples and practices were prevalent, and Nadab and Abihu may have acquired hot coals of fire from these pagan altars in their censers on their way to the Tabernacle to inaugurate their official priesthood. The Hebrew root word for "strange fire" is **ZWR** (pronounced ZOR) and is often used with reference to a person outside the nation of Israel or as a description of deities other than Jehovah. The fire, according to Phillip J. Budd, may have been brought from an outside pagan source into the Tabernacle, thus making the fire "unauthorized fire," or fire not commanded by God. **4**

These instructions (Leviticus 8-9) on the ordination of Nadab and Abihu occur during the eleven months the Hebrews are encamped around Mt. Sinai in southern Palestline prior to commencing their 40 year wilderness wanderings. Also located in this dry land were the Midianites with their false gods Baal-Peor, and Ashera, meaning **"lord of the opening."** Baal-Peor was considered the male consort of Ashera, the female goddess. The Ashera pole was an erect wood pole (symbol of the male phallus) depicting Ashera, the female goddess of fertility with her visible breasts and associated sexuality of her vaginal opening------hence **"lord of the opening."** God gave explicit commands in Deut. 16:21 *"**Do not set up any wooden Ashera pole beside the altar you build to the Lord your God.**"* Around this Ashera pole numerous, deviant sexual practices occurred in the belief these practices would give fertility to crops, animals, and people, but God despised mixing His worship with any pagan symbol or practice. Such mixing is called the sins of **SYNCRETISM** or **ACCOMODATION.**

Their pagan tribes lived as Bedouins (nomadic desert people) in this hot, difficult terrain and often travelled through this desolate area with their sacred tent called a **QUBBAH** (pronounced KUBAH)---a small temple shrine, and precursor to the modern, permanent Islamic mosque. This leather tent was portable, like the Tabernacle, vaulted, domed, and displayed a miniature red leather top. Some **QUBBAHS** were suitable for mounting on camel back, and contained the tribal idols or betyls. Due to its religious nature it conveyed in some way "holiness". "It was both a palladium and a place of worship," **5** observes Frank M. Cross, an archaeologist. Blood sacrifices were made in this tent, and the blood would be sprinkled on it. **6** Seemingly fire may also have been used in this sacrificial manner by the Midianites. We do not know for certain but the Hebrews (Israelites) may have seen these pagan tribal people traverse through the land near Mt. Sinai, and Nadab and Abihu may have "borrowed," or acquired hot coals of fire from the altar in a nearby **QUBBAH,** and placed them in their censers prior to entering the Tabernacle.

Prominent in this passage of Leviticus 10 is an obvious **ABSENCE** of a direct command from God: nowhere in Leviticus or any other book in the Pentateuch does God give a definite command telling Nadab and Abihu what **NOT TO DO;** He only gives positive commands of **WHAT TO DO.** He never stated to Aaron or his sons, Nadab and Abihu, *"Don't acquire coals of fire from pagan deities or their altars."* Nadab and Abihu perhaps thus assumed they had freedom to secure coals of fire from any source, and thought **"fire is fire----regardless of the source. We can use any fire in the Tabernacle acquired from any external source as long as we are sincere and properly execute the mechanics of worship to Jehovah."** Their sin was **SYNCRETISM:** fusing together two opposing belief systems----the worship of Jehovah with the worship practices of the false gods of the Midianites, borrowing practices from false gods and meshing them with worship of God. This same sin is committed today by Christians fusing together the worship of God, and adding worldly methods and philosophies from pagan systems of thinking in an attempt to be **RELEVANT** in this secular society.

5. <u>RULE FOR INTERPRETING GOD'S COMMANDS.</u>

God gave to Aaron, Nadab, and Abihu in Leviticus detailed commands concerning sacrificial offerings, the brazen altar, how the fire on the altar must be maintained, and what sacrificial offerings could be eaten by the priests. But nowhere in these chapters does God give a negative command prohibiting coals of fire from pagan altars. If this prohibition is so important, why did God fail to expressly give a negative command, and thus spare the lives of Nadab and Abihu? He expected them to ponder, reflect, and discern how this positive command can best be fulfilled to revere the glory of God. The Biblical reason is the rule of interpretation: *INTERPRET A POSITIVE COMMAND AS AUTOMATICALLY INCLUDING THE UNSTATED NEGATIVE PROHIBITION OF ANY SIN DETRIMENTAL TO ITS FULFILLMENT.* When God gives a positive command or example, He expects obedience and compliance------without any added human inventions, innovations, or creativity from worldly sources. For example, the fourth commandment in the ten commandments is expressed positively: **"Honor the Sabbath day to keep it holy,"** (Exodus 20:8). Therefore, any activity which detracts from making holy the Sabbath day is sinful, prohibited, and God specifically prohibited working on this day. The fifth commandment (Exodus 20:12) is also framed in a positive manner: **"Honor your father and your mother......"** Therefore, by logical implication this positive command prohibits disobedience, disrespect, or emotional injury to them in any form. Nadab and Abihu ignored this important rule: they failed to fully grasp the significance and import of God's positive command and positive example, choosing to misinterpret this vital rule to their own destruction.

Another example of a positive command revolves around repainting the exterior of a house. I could give a positive command to painters to begin painting at the top of the house and paint downward and ignore speaking any negative prohibitions about procedure. The painters might say to themselves, **"Painting is painting, and there is no difference whether we start at the top or bottom, so we will begin first at the bottom and work our way upward."** The skill of repainting involves scraping old peeling paint and sanding prior to actual painting, but if the painters begin at the bottom with scraping, sanding, and painting, then the old peeling paint and dust from higher elevations will fall downward onto the newly painted surfaces-----resulting in reworking the lower paint surfaces. Even though I gave a positive command, the painters should have reasoned and projected the negative results of starting at the bottom.

God does not always give a prohibition for everything; rather He gives us positive commands about living an obedient, holy life; if we fully obey these positive commands we will reason many activities and attitudes must be rejected because they will hamper our Christian life. Jesus in Matthew 22:37-40 answers the Pharisees regarding which commandment was the greatest: "Love the Lord your God with all your heart and with all your soul and with all your mind. This is the first and greatest commandment. And the second is like it: 'Love your neighbor as yourself. All the law and the prophets hang on these two commandments."

Loving God with all my heart, soul, and mind and loving my neighbor as myself implies also obedience to any unstated negative prohibition of sin which would prevent my full love to God and my neighbor. Note the conspicuous **ABSENCE** of any negative prohibition in Jesus' answer, demonstrating the above rule: **A POSITIVE COMMAND AUTOMATICALLY INCLUDES ANY UNSTATED NEGATIVE PROHIBITION.**

6. **IMMATURITY AND MATURITY IN DISCERNMENT.**

Both Nadab and Abihu displayed spiritual immaturity by their actions of securing coals of fire from pagan sources: they failed to reason from God's positive command of exclusive worship and concluded no negative command therefore gave them freedom to borrow pagan coals of fire. Their approach was **LEGALISTIC:** they wanted a specific command for every circumstance. They reasoned: *"If there is no specific negative command forbidding certain actions, then we are free to select any method."* This legalistic approach was common, not only to Nadab and Abihu, but also to the Israelites, as described by Paul in Galatians 3 and 4 where he compares the law with the full revelation of faith in Christ. Prior to Christ's coming, the Old Testament believer was under the law which served as a schoolmaster, or a child conductor----instructing the immature child in what he should and should not do. This immature child did not possess the spiritual ability to properly discern truth from error, ethical from unethical, right from wrong, wise from wise. He was bound by a legalistic system preventing spiritual discernment and judgment in many areas of life.

But Christ's coming freed men from **"childhood"** to **"manhood"** or **"mature sons"** (Galatians 4:4-5), and now God deals with the believer as a mature son who can make mature judgments----no longer as a child who must be instructed in every detail of life. Nadab and Abihu, even though they were priests in the Tabernacle, did not possess spiritual maturity to properly reason, judge, and discern God's positive command; they misinterpreted, misapplied God's positive command as permission to borrow coals of fire from pagan deities, their evil associations, and practices. They knew the expressed law of God, but were ignorant of implied principle. By definition the word "law" means a collection of specific rules and regulations applicable to conduct. *Principle is the collection of morals, values undergirding specific rules. Law is specific---requiring little reasoning, just strict compliance; principle is broad----requiring much reasoning of values and morals to discern proper application to detailed situations.*

Moses was one exception of an Old Testament believer, because he did possess spiritual maturity: he not only saw the error of a golden calf violating the second commandment, but he also realized the pagan Egyptian music played and sung by the Hebrews was inconsistent with the true worship of God. Aaron, the High Priest, also displayed lack of spiritual discernment which was manifested in his sons, Nadab and Abihu.

7. **ILLUSTRATION OF LAW AND PRINCIPLE:**

God does not expressly command in His Word: "You shall not smoke Camel cigarettes." The legalistic Christian would thus infer, "God does approve of smoking Lucky Strike cigarettes, or else He would have forbidden this brand." God's expressed command regarding Camel cigarettes **INCLUDES** all cigarettes. That is a principle! Here is another example of law: "Don't drink Budweiser beer." The legalist would claim: "I am free to drink Miller high life beer, or else He would have forbidden this brand also." Legalism is always looking for small details, and fails to grasp the broad principle of morals, values, judgment, discernment.

Nadab and Abihu were obeying the **POSITIVE** commands of worship and believed they were exercising personal **FREEDOM** to borrow fire from pagan sacrificial altars in adding to worship in the Tabernacle. They were wrong------and instantly killed by God's fire consuming them. This is the **NORMATIVE** principle of worship: obeying the direct commands of worship, but adding corruptive, innovative, self-generated new methods of worship.

8. APPLICATION TO MUSIC.

How does this incident of Nadab and Abihu apply to the issue of music or any other innovative method? It teaches we must remain loyal to the **REGULATIVE** principle of worship: ***use only methods commanded by God***. And what are these direct commands of worship? There are seven: **(1) preaching from the Bible**---Matt. 26:13; Mark 16:15; Acts 9:20; II Tim. 4:2; **(2) public reading the Word of God**---Mark 4:16-20; Acts 13:15; I Tim. 4:13; Rev. 1:13; **(3) meeting on the Lord's day**---Acts 20:7; I Cor. 16:2; Rev 1:10; I Cor. 11:18; **(4) observing the sacraments of baptism and the Lord's Supper**---Matt. 28:19; Matt. 26:-29; I Cor. 11:24-25; **(5) hearing the Word of God**---Luke 2:46; Acts 8:31; Rom. 10:41 James 1:22; Luke 4:20; **(6) prayer to God**----Matt. 6:9; I Thess. 5:17; Heb. 13:18; Phil. 4:6; James 1:5; I Cor. 11:13-15; **(7) singing praise to God with psalms, hymns, and spiritual songs**---I Chron. 16:9; Psalm 95:1-2; Psalm 105:2; I Cor. 14:26; Eph. 5:19; Col. 3:16. But how should we sing? Can we use pagan music with its evil associations in worship? No---the incident of the golden calf in Exodus 32:17-18 clearly shows the folly of adding "New worship styles" tainted with sinful living. Adding worldly, pagan music styles revives the "strange fire," "unauthorized fire" of Nadab and Abihu. It corrupts, not completes, Biblical worship.

Distinction must be made between these seven **REGULATIVE ELEMENTS** of worship, and the **CIRCUMSTANCES** of worship. The elements of worship are both **TRANSCULTURAL**----applicable to all cultures of people in all areas of the world, and **CULTURAL**----specific application to present cultural circumstances. We use electricity in our worship services----the Tabernacle had no electricity. We use air conditioning in our services;-----the Tabernacle had no air conditioning. We use padded pews in our churches----the Tabernacle had no pews. We use amplification to enable all people to hear----the Tabernacle had no such aid.

These are circumstances of worship----applicable to our modern Western culture, but they do not abrogate worship. Yes, our circumstances of worship may vary, but the seven regulative elements of worship will not vary. At first, John Calvin prohibited the use of the organ in worship, but later rescinded his view to allow organ music to accompany congregational singing, realizing organ music facilitated singing in tune, time, and support.

What are we to say about other innovative "methods" such as a clown ministry leading the music in the worship service, or casual dress of tennis shoes, foot thongs, and shorts to make visitors feel comfortable, or offering free gifts to visitors, or distributing condoms in the offering plate to prevent the spread of disease, or a mime show prior to the sermon, or the current fad among evangelicals of preaching "lite" sermons of superficial scriptural truth with heavy emphasis on personal illustrations, humorous ante dotes, pop psychology, and personal self-esteem? Are such methods pleasing to God? The mind of man is creative in devising many other modern methods to make Biblical worship "popular" and enticing to sinners, but these methods compromise God's regulative principle of worship

9. <u>VIOLATION OF SECOND COMMANDMENT.</u>

The second commandment in Exodus 20:4-5 states: ***"You shall not make for yourself an idol in the form of anything in heaven above......or bow down to them or worship them."*** Idolatry is not limited to carving an actual idol from stone, metal, or wood, but also involves **MENTAL IMAGES** formed in the mind to enhance worship. Nadab and Abihu needed coals of fire to worship God and mentally imagined pagan fire would facilitate worship since all fire burns the same. Thus, they violated the second commandment through their mental image of equal fire.

The first commandment teaches **WHOM** to worship------God exclusively. The second commandment teaches **HOW** (or the manner) to worship------exclusively spiritual------not emotionally, sensuously, entertainingly, selfishly, relevantly, popularly, easily, craftily, creatively, nor equally with methods from false deities. The third commandment teaches **WHY** of worship------respect God's holy name. The fourth commandment teaches **WHEN** to worship----- the Sabbath day. We can worship the correct God incorrectly, or as one person observed------worshipping God with poison! Nadab and Abihu worshipped the true God, but worshipped Him incorrectly by acquiring coals of fire from pagan altars, and thus violated the second commandment----like their father, Aaron.

He violated the second commandment by idolatry of the golden calf and by borrowing pagan Egyptian worship music to "enhance" a contemporary musical style. His sons Nadab and Abihu violated the second commandment by obtaining coals of fire from pagan altars----- poisoning the worship of God with pagan methods. Both pagan music and pagan methods corrupt divine worship.

10. <u>THREE MAJOR PRINCIPLES IN WORSHIP.</u>

Three major principles are involved in worship: ***(1) Adhere to Biblical worship. (2) Search for a command. (3) Use freedom----cautiously, fearfully.*** The first principle of regulative worship as discussed above is both Biblical and preventative from the enticements of modern methodology. ***"But,"*** say many evangelicals, ***"this worship approach doesn't***

work! ***It does not attract the crowds; it is tied to the past and does not relate to the present."*** This common criticism is a smoke screen for the three words discussed in Chapter 7, Application #9: **CASUISTRY, PRAGMATISM, UTILITARIANISM.** We as Christians are asking the wrong question; instead we should ask what is truth, what does the Bible teach----not what works, is easy, produces results, gives gigantic growth, is popular, entertaining, satisfies our self-centered desires. Spiritual growth of individuals and churches comes from God-----in His own timing and sovereignty. Our task is to be faithful and wait on Him.

The second principle in worship is *(2) Search for a direct command.* Pastors and elders must search the Scriptures for a direct command or example of how to plan a worship service------what methods may or may not be used. God considers worship as the highest priority for Christians, and He does not leave us to our own man-centered creativity and inventiveness: that was the problem of Nadab and Abihu----they invented a new resource: fire from pagan deities. ***Where there is no direct command or example, we must rely on human reason and spiritual discernment in thoughtfully reflecting on the total revelation of Scripture and its holistic picture of worship.*** Nadab and Abihu had no direct command from God forbidding the use of pagan coals of fire obtained from pagan deities, but they should have used their spiritual reasoning process to consider the total picture of worshipping Jehovah in His holiness, beauty, grandeur, and majesty as revealed in the Law---- the Pentateuch. In these five books of Moses God had clearly stated all other pagan gods are false and an illusion. Had they used their reasoning process they would have concluded the utter inconsistency of using pagan goals of fire to worship the One and only True God.

An artistic painting illustrates this reasoning process. You and I may view a famous painting on display in an art gallery and concentrate on the tiny brush strokes of the artist in painting the masterpiece. But this microscopic procedure prevents us from standing back and viewing the painting as a whole------basking in its majestic scene of beauty and grandeur. Nadab and Abihu looked for the specific, (tiny brush strokes) forbidding commands of God, and since these specific commands were absent, they used their freedom and chose the wrong pagan resource, and were consumed by the fire of God. Had they viewed the whole picture of worship in the Pentateuch and grasped the grandeur of worshipping God, they would know the sinfulness of a pagan source for fire.

"What is so 'wrong' about acquiring coals of fire from the pagan altars?" many Christians ask? **"What is the big deal over such a small issue? After all, fire is fire: it all burns the same."** Three reasons are offered by God: (1) God's command, (2) Demonic influence, and (3) Worshipper evolvement. **(1) FIRST**, He commands a complete break from all false gods and their pagan practices: that is precisely the nature of the first commandment-----**"You shall have no other gods before me."** (Exodus 20:3) This commandment can be paraphrased: "Don't possess, practice, participate, or pilfer from any other false gods. Worship Me alone." **(2) SECOND**, demons influence false deities and their practices. False gods do not exist, except in the mind of men, nor do they possess any power, but according to I Corinthians 10:19-21 **REAL DEMONS** operate within illusory false, pagan deities, and silently motivate evil practices of the misguided worshiper. Paul in Romans 1:21-25 records the downward spiral of men who reject the knowledge of God, replace Him with false gods, exchange the truth of God for a lie, and thus open themselves to a long list of sins (Romans 1:29-32). Demonic influence therefore accompanies pagan coals of fire acquired from pagan altars, and when Nadab and Abihu brought these coals of fire into the Tabernacle they were introducing the real power of demons into the worship of God----corrupting, polluting God's holiness and majesty.

(3) THIRD, worshipper evolvement. Psalm 115:1-8 describes the falsity and futility of idols carved from gold or silver incapable of speaking, hearing, smelling, feeling, walking, or seeing. Then in verse 8 the Psalmist concludes: **"Those who make them will be like them, and so will all who trust in them."** What precisely does he mean regarding the worshipper becoming like the idol? One word summarizes both the idol and the worshipper: **POWERLESS**----unable to respond, understand, or escape a crisis of need. The worshipper by honoring the idol evolves and becomes senseless, irrational, hollow, equally stupid-----like his idol! The idol can not assist the worshipper and neither can the worshipper affect situations in his life. The idol is unreal, false, and so is the worshipper----not genuine in his personhood. This evolvement of the worshipper describes the individual who worships an idol.

11. <u>EVOLUTION OF IDOLATRY.</u> The following diagram reveals the three stages of idolatry.

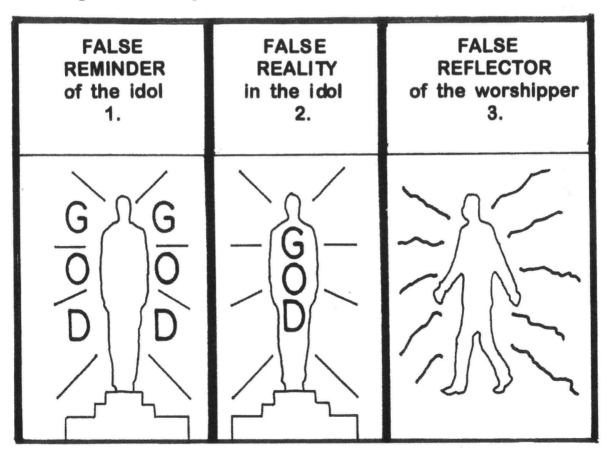

In **stage one** the idol is used as an **AID,** a reminder of worship, and is never conceived as possessing power, authority. Aaron and the Israelites at the golden calf did not believe the idol was actually God, but only reminded them of God. The golden calf was selected because it represented virility, youth, energy, power: that is how the Israelites perceived God. Viewing the calf helped them better focus their thoughts on God. It was not a **REPLACEMENT,** but a **REMINDER** or symbol of God. Superstition over time takes control converting the idol into **stage two** where the idol is perceived as God. Moses, on the instructions of God made a bronze serpent and set it on a pole. Israelites who had been bitten by a snake and who looked at the bronze serpent were healed (Numbers 21:6-9). Centuries later Hezekiah breaks the serpent in pieces, because the people had been burning incense to it (II Kings 18:4). The symbol of the serpent (deliverance in the wilderness) ceased to be a **REMINDER** and became in **REALITY** the God of worship. Nadab and Abihu also considered the fire coals taken from pagan sources was merely an **AID**, a **REMINDER** of worship.

Stage three occurs in the worshipper: he becomes like the material or mental idol. Psalm 115:1-8 graphically describe this third stage: **"Those who make them will be like them, and so will all who trust in them."** The idol is false-----and so is the worshipper: he becomes a false, superficial, plastic reflector of God. Every man is like his idol, and if he acquires a false notion of God through his idol or image, then he becomes as false and spiritually superficial or dead as his idol. What occurs to the Christian who worships the true God with worldly, pagan methods? In what ways does he evolve?

He evolves into (1) superficiality of interpersonal relationships; (2) shallowness in worship; (3) lacking in spiritual discernment; (4) dominated by a need of selfish entertainment in worship; (5) difficulty in distinguishing truth from error; (6) driven by sensuality in music selection; (7) minimal appreciation of deep knowledge in God's Word; (8) dominated by self-centered emotions as a gauge of spirituality; (9) reluctance and resistance to think on things true, noble, right, pure, lovely, admirable, excellent, praiseworthy (Philippians 4:8). These nine factors of evolvement are summarized by one Biblical word: the **"milk"** Christian (Hebrews 5:13). Real demonic influence from worldly, pagan sources not only contaminates God's holiness, but also infects and stifles spiritual maturity in the Christian-----preventing him from becoming a **"meat"** or solid food Christian (Hebrews 5:14).

Over these past several years I have observed this "evolvement" of worshippers caught up in the Contemporary Christian Music movement; I do not question their sincerity, but I discern these above nine traits characteristic in them. ***"You are judgmental and caustic,"*** claim my critics swept up in this "new sound movement." Yes, I honestly admit I attempt to be discerning: that is the task of every mature Christian (I Cor. 2:14,15)---to make judgments about all things. But I am not caustic----meaning harsh, cutting, stinging, burning, sarcastic. God commands me and every other Christian to examine all things in light of God's Word, and make loving observations or discernment about them.

Years ago in my research I discovered two valuable diagrams depicting religious imagery which gives me new insight into the idolatry of the second commandment, but I have been unable to locate its precise source or author, and give due credit. The following diagram shows

human religious imagery appealing externally to our five physical senses of smelling, tasting, touching, seeing, and hearing-----causing mere conformity to the object. This human imagery appeals to the natural heart, whose inclination is toward control by these physical and mental senses. Material or mental imagery molds our emotions, intellect, and will, but leaves our spirit (represented by the "I" in the center) qualitatively the same though somewhat altered into conformity with the controlling image.

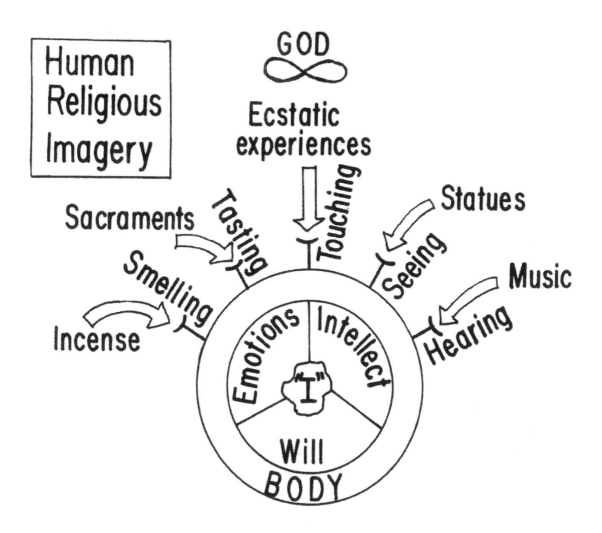

Consequently our spirit which communicates with God is ultimately left in a state of dissatisfaction and lack of fulfillment. Image control temporarily satisfies only part of the whole man, but restricts the potential expression of the spirit to the limitations of the influential image. The final result is the person is not free to be in totality what he was created to be------a lover and worshipper of God. This lack of communication with God results in the worshipper remaining superficial, shallow, false-----like the material or mental idol he worships. Note in the diagram the sense of hearing----the auditory ability to hear music. Unwholesome music in worship can affect the emotions, but it is weak to influence and change our true spirit (the "I" in the center).

In contrast, **divine re-incarnate imagery** by means of the Word of God transforms our spirit by replacing it with the unlimited Spirit of Christ as revealed in this diagram where God (represented by the horizontal figure eight at the top), through the Word of God, transforms our spirit and heart (at the center of the circle; the visual heart with God's presence replaces the "I" of the previous diagram.) Spiritual growth and maturity develops internally to externally (note the direction of the arrows), not externally to internally as shown in the diagram of human religious imagery. God's Word, especially Philippians 4:8, and the discernment gained from this one verse, thus affects the kind of music which changes our spirit. Wholesome music, filled with theological teaching and wedded to majestic, excellent music measuring up to Philippians 4:8, radiates outward from our spirit in honor and worship to God.

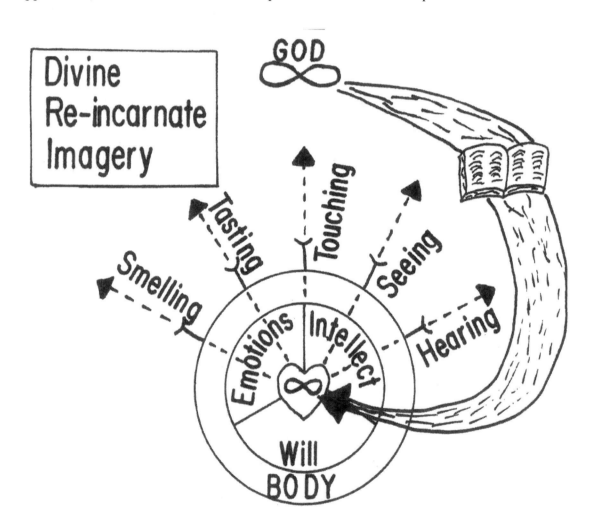

Our spirit is distinct from our emotions-----by a fine line-----and even good, wholesome, secular music, such as a classical overture, may stir our emotions, but leave our spirit untouched. Likewise, some CCM or a "praise and worship chorus" may stimulate our emotions of happiness and self-pleasing, yet fail to reach our true spirit of humble, reverent worship toward God. Biblical discernment alerts us to know when music is moving our emotions--------or prompting our spirit in worship.

Ephesians 4:27 records this command: **"Do not give the devil a foothold."** Paul here describes how Satan can use our sins, such as anger against other people, to bring about greater evil. If we harbor anger in our emotions, the devil can establish a foothold, a beachhead in our lives to incite greater sin. He gains entrance through our personal sins, and in the experience of Nadab and Abihu he gains entrance through association with pagan deities and their practices. We must avoid any contact or borrowing new methods or practices from pagan, evil deities so Satan will not establish a foothold and influence in the worship of God.

Today sincere, but misguided, Christians, like Nadab and Abihu, introduce new methods, appealing innovations, and musical **"coals of fire"** from pagan sources of worldly music and pagan philosophy into worship services in an effort to be **"relevant, modern, entertaining, contemporary, trendy, cool, meeting the needs of the consumer"** to gain bigger crowds and increased numerical success in evangelism. Yes, this new **"strange fire"** may initially appear to "work" for a time-----***but the power of demons is slowly corrupting true worship, degrading the holiness of God, imprisoning Christians into 'milk' immaturity, and artfully preparing for the thirty-two sins of Romans 1:29-32.*** This catalogue listing of sins does not imply every person will commit every sin, but the gamut of sins will be seen in the population. These sins are not immediately apparent with "strange fire," but like the Trojan Horse in Greek times, they lie dormant under the delusion of true worship-----waiting to reveal their true nature at the right time.

God's Word does not give a direct command forbidding clowns with their garish, outlandish clothing styles from leading in worship. Nor does His Word directly forbid using pornographic videos in the worship service as an illustration of evil. Nor does the Word of God expressly forbid the use of pagan music in worship as a **"new aid"** to reach young people (though its negative example of the golden calf in Exodus 32:17-18 illustrates its sinfulness). But using godly human reason, we conclude these methods are inconsistent with the total picture of holy worship in the Bible.

The third principle in worship is *(3) Use freedom------cautiously, fearfully.* Nadab and Abihu used their freedom as priests-------but suffered immediate death because they chose and acquired pagan coals of fire, **"strange fire,"** from pagan altars. In the absence of a direct command from God prohibiting obtaining fire from pagan deities, they used their freedom to their own destruction. Galatians 5 teaches we have freedom from legalism, but our freedom must not be used to serve our sinful, sensual, selfish natures, but by the law of love we are to serve each other (Gal. 5:13). This passage is addressing personal freedom, not worship freedom of the corporate assembly, yet the principle still applies to pastors and elders in planning the public worship service. We are not free from the seven Biblical commands of corporate worship, but these seven commands must be fleshed out in practical methods and this requires cautious, careful, reflective thinking on Biblical principles rightly interpreted and applied. What ever methods are employed in public worship, the methods must reflect dignity, majesty, holiness, reverence, severance from evil pagan practices, and full harmony with Biblical teaching. Pastors and elders may use their freedom in planning corporate worship-----but they must tremor, quake, and quiver in fear lest they, like Nadab and Abihu, select worldly, self-centered, sensuous, infantile, repugnant methods of entertainment and casualness in worship.

12. <u>CLOTHING STYLES IN TODAY'S CULTURE.</u>

A current trend or "fad" among pastors today is dressing down in their leadership role in worship services: wearing blue jeans, tennis shoes, sport shirt, or a sport coat clashing in color with the shirt or blue jeans------all for the purpose of presenting a casual, **"come-as-you-are"** appearance to the congregation. This casual appearance is also seen in worship services among many Christians who also dress in casual clothes. Does God give a direct, unequivocal command requiring pastors to wear dark, pin stripe suits, dress shirts with a matching tie, and set off with polished shoes? No, He does not! But He gives a pertinent principle in Exodus 28:2 regarding the garments of Aaron the High Priest: ***"Make sacred garments ('garments of holiness') for your brother Aaron, to give him dignity and honor."*** In subsequent verses in Exodus God gives commands to skilled tailors to sew garments of gold, blue, purple and scarlet yarn and fine linen. (Exodus 28:4-5) Note the purpose of the High Priest's garments: to show ***dignity and honor.***

The Hebrew word for "dignity" means glorious reverence, and the Hebrew word for "honor" means beauty, finery of garments. Aaron's priestly clothes were designed to set him apart to sanctuary service and ministry and are called garments of holiness----distinct from ordinary clothes. His garments were to exalt the office of the high priest as well as beautify the worship of God. In the book of Exodus this word "dignity" or glorious reverence is used for the brilliance of God's presence, and so the magnificence of these garments would strike the worshipper with the sense of exaltation in the service of worship. The Israelite entering the Tabernacle would immediately see the High Priest in his beautifully designed robes of gold, blue, royal purple, and sense these garments pointed to the majestic holiness and grandeur of Jehovah's presence.

"But we no longer live under the law and its regulations," claim modern day "cool" pastors. I agree fully, but we are not set free from the principles and morality of the law; rather the moral principle imbedded in Exodus 28:5 remains reverence and dignity in dress among pastors who lead worship. The worship service is not just another **"casual event"** in the week's calendar, or **"relevant motivational"** meeting to arouse emotional fervor, nor **"orchestrated musical entertainment"** to gain a bigger audience, but congregating of God's people in the awesome, dignified, beauty of God's presence to worship Him. Pastors and other staff leaders in church can set the example to people by dressing in clothing signifying dignity, honor, beauty, and reverence.

Does this mean a pastor must wear long colorful robes like Aaron with a mitered, turban hat? No-----but he is to dress with dignity and honor. In our Western culture dignity and honor is not perceived as blue jeans and a sport shirt, but by tasteful suits, pressed pants, dress shirts, matching tie, and polished dress shoes. In other cultures different garments symbolize dignity and honor, and in these circumstances the pastor and staff leaders must ascertain from society what is appropriate clothing to represent this divine principle of dignity, honor, and beauty. Even in other cultures Philippians 4:8 applies: think on things (such as clothes) true, noble, right, pure, lovely, admirable, excellent, praiseworthy. (A thorough exposition of these eight words appears in Chapter 6.) Does the pastor have freedom in how he dresses to lead a worship service? Of course he does-------as long as his garments portray dignity, beauty, and honor of leadership.

Let me further illustrate liberty in worship with three illustrations: (1) an overhead projector, (2) printed outline, and (3) free meal. As a teacher of God's Word I preach/teach by using the overhead projector to display visual charts, diagrams, and pictures to illuminate the passage of Scripture. Furthermore, I make available a printed outline in the bulletin of the sermon for people to follow and add written notes. Did the Israelites have an overhead projector in the Tabernacle, and were they given a printed outline of the sermon delivered that day by the priest? Of course not! My use of these two modern methods, in my opinion, do not conflict with Scripture; they facilitate worship, not impede worship. They are the **CIRCUMSTANCES** of worship----not the **ELEMENTS** of worship.

A local church has an effective outreach to college students here in this city of Columbia, S.C.------a free meal following the evening service. Presently the pastor is delivering a series of excellent, expository sermons on Romans in the evening service, the numerous college students take copious notes of the sermon, and then they gather in the fellowship hall for a free meal provided by the church. This meal is, in my opinion, an excellent method of arousing interest in the evening service, and provides rich fellowship for Christian students in the midst of a secular, humanistic university. I personally don't see any contradiction with the scriptural principles of worship.

13. <u>COMPARE AARON AND HIS SONS.</u>

Why did God kill Nadab and Abihu here in Leviticus 10, yet spare Aaron in Exodus 32? We don't know why Aaron did not suddenly die, but we do know why his two sons instantly perished by God's consuming fire: God's pronouncement of judgment in the second commandment----Exodus 20:4-6: *__"I am a jealous God, punishing the children for the sins of the fathers to the third and fourth generation of those who hate me".__* God pronounced He would judge Aaron's genealogy family down to the third and fourth generations, meaning his sons, grandsons, and great grandsons would suffer judgment because of Aaron's sin of syncretism.

Did such judgment occur? Yes----exactly as God promised. **FIRST GENERATION:** Aaron was the first high priest appointed by God to serve in the priestly duties of the Tabernacle, but he sinned through idolatry of the golden calf and allowing Egyptian pagan music in worship; he, however, was not judged instantly by God. **SECOND GENERATION:** Nadab and Aibhu were the second generation sons from Aaron and God killed them because their sin of syncretism passed from Aaron to his sons resulting in their death. **THIRD GENERATION:** Eli the priest was the third generation through the son of Ithamar---another son of Aaron. He failed to restrain his two sons who violated Tabernacle worship by sacrilege and immortality of sacred prostitution, and he died a sudden, tragic death at the age of 98 when he fell backwards at the city gate and died of a broken neck upon hearing of the deaths of his two sons. **FOURTH GENERATION:** Hophni and Phinehas, were also priests, sons of Eli, but they died also because of their sins of sacrilege and immorality (I Samuel 2:17). The following diagram reveals this four generation judgment of God.

FIRST GENER-ATION	SECOND GENER-ATION	THIRD GENER-ATION	FOURTH GENER-ATION
Aaron ↓ Father	Nadab & Abihu ↓ Sons of of Aaron	Eli ↓ Grandson of Aaron	Hophni & Phineas ↓ Great Grandsons of Aaron

Both Aaron and his sons were guilty of using pagan methods and resources in worship; both were priests; both led others in worship----but God spared Aaron. In one sense Aaron incurred greater guilt of syncretism by allowing idolatry and pagan Egyptian music in worship, but Nadab and Abihu only borrowed pagan coals of fire. Their sin appears less in magnitude than the sin of Aaron, yet God judged them for perpetuating the sins of their father, and because His holiness was corrupted with pagan practices of worship.

Often the charge is lodged against God for being **"unfair"** in passing judgment to the third and fourth generations, but this accusation overlooks God's limit of judgment: the judgment extends only to four generations. He could have pronounced judgment to the tenth, fortieth, or the ninetieth generation, but He limited Himself---thus showing His gracious mercy. Many of us can give thanks to God for honoring His Word in allowing us to be born into a godly line extending back several generations. In my own family I see this long line of Riggs generations who have loved God and His Word; I take no personal credit for this act of God's grace, but rejoice in honoring some godly ancestor in our family tree---some unknown man or woman who determined to honor God above all cost, and I am humbled for God's gift to me. (Exodus 20:7)

14. LIBERTY IN WORSHIP.

Liberty is not removal of boundaries, but the power to move easily among established boundaries, as illustrated in driving rules. Would we really be liberated by dismantling all stop signs, yield signs, one-way direction signs, and all speed markers? Of course not, for that would mean pure bedlam and mounting accidents. True liberty in driving means recognition of these traffic markers, and operating safely within these guidelines.

Is regulative worship rigid, binding, inflexible? No-----creativity is welcomed-----as long as it does not conflict with Biblical principles of dignity, reverence, orderliness, holiness, and respect of Christ-centered worship. Should we sing only Psalms or should we sing Psalms, hymns, and spiritual songs? Should we sing two hymns or 30 hymns in a worship service? Should our worship service last one hour or ten hours? Should our singing be all somber, or all joyful? Should public Scripture reading consist of reading an entire chapter or reading the entire book of Genesis? God does not give a specific command in these areas. In these and other related questions there is liberty for pastors and elders in designing a worship service. Can secular music be adapted to Christian lyrics? Yes----provided the music style is free from sinful associations, and measures up to the eight positive benchmarks of Philippians 4:8 (covered later in this book). Many of our present popular hymns were originally adapted to noble, majestic, uplifting secular tunes.

CHAPTER 5:

Gamaliel's Counsel

I. BACKGROUND OF ACTS 5:34-40

NOTE: This famous passage is not directly addressing the issue of music, as did the four previous Old Testament references, but its logic is often used to support questionable methods, techniques, and philosophies advanced by Gamailel-----a chief Rabbi on the Sanhedrin council-----as approval of contemporary methods, techniques, and philosophies. Once the passage is closely examined, I believe, the logic errors of Gamaliel will be revealed and its irrelevancy to music in our churches.

Following the resurrection and ascension of Christ in Jerusalem (Acts 1:1-9), the disciples were filled with the Holy Spirit, spoke in foreign languages, and began an effective, though daunting, task of world evangelism, resulting in thousands of people being converted to Christ. The Sanhedrin (the official ruling party of 70 men legislating on religious issues) became incensed at the explosive growth of this new religious movement, jailed Peter and John, rebuked them for preaching about the resurrection of Christ, and ordered them to cease all teaching and preaching ministries. They continued teaching and preaching, so the Sanhedrin arrested the apostles again and placed them in jail, but during the night an angel of the Lord opened the doors of the jail and brought them out. (5:17-19)

Next morning the furious Sanhedrin realized the apostles were set free, yet the guards remained at their duty position in the jail, and all doors and windows were locked. The Sanhedrin realized counseling the apostles is a futile effort; they therefore, decide to kill the apostles. (5:33) Gamaliel steps forward in 5:34-40 to offer his counsel about the disposition of the apostles.

II. EXPLANATION OF ACTS 5:34-40

1. Identify Gamaliel

Gamaliel was a seasoned, highly respected Jewish Rabbi of the Pharisees party, and the leading member of the Sanhedrin. He was enormously popular, served as Paul's teacher (Acts 22:3), and was moderate in his views. In the Talmud his name bears the title "Rabban," meaning "our teacher, a title higher in honor than rabbi, meaning "my teacher." He was the most respected Pharisee of his day. The Mishnah, a collection of commentaries on the oral laws of Israel published toward the end of the second century A.D. contains the following statement about him: "**Since Rabban Gamaliel died there has been no more affection for the law; and purity and abstinence died out at the same time.**"

He did not embrace this new religion of Christianity, nor could he explain the sudden growth of the movement or its miracles. As a Jewish Rabbi, he was not a Christian; yes, he was moral, decent, knowledgeable in the Old Testament scriptures, and wise in giving counsel to the best of his human insight, but since he was not a Christian and disciple of Christ, the counsel he would offer would be limited and skewed----certainly not reflective of spiritual maturity.

2. Access his dilemma

Gamaliel faces a dilemma regarding what to do with these apostles who are determined to teach about Christ. Two options confronted Gamaliel: (a) death desired by the Sadducees on the Sanhedrin Council, or (b) release. If death is chosen, Gamaliel knows the strict regulations Jewish law required to perform justice and he sensed such a "fair" trial would not be possible with the open hostility of the Council. If release is chosen, the apostles will again be free in their teaching, further growth will occur from this new religious movement, and the Sanhedrin Council itself would diminish in authority and prestige in the eyes of the Jewish nation. He is in a "**tough**" spot, and needs the wisdom of Solomon to revolve this impasse. I'm sure as a Jewish Rabbi he well knew the dilemma of Solomon when confronted by two women both claiming to be the mother of the child

3. Examine Gamaliel's logic

Gamaliel makes **seven major mistakes** or errors in his logical reasoning process which lead to errors of application. I learned years ago a monumental principle in Bible Interpretation that has aided me in studying and interpreting the Bible:

A strong, correct interpretation will lead to a strong, correct application;
A weak, incorrect interpretation will lead to a weak, incorrect application.

These seven logic errors are often overlooked by sincere Christians, leading them to embrace the thinking of Gamaliel-----without realizing their deception. I will fully apply these seven logic errors in the book, but for now will only provide one illustration of how many Christians are deceived in the area of much of Contemporary Christian Music. Often I hear Christians describe in glowing euphoria their attachment to CCM: **"This music must be of God because He is blessing its ministry. Young people are flocking to our churches and concerts, and many people are being saved because the music is relevant to their time and age. It communicates; it excites them; they get turned on by it."**

This thinking by thousands of dear pastors, youth directors, music ministers, parents, and other Christians is pure, unadulterated **PRAGMATISM:** what ever works! Another term for it is **CASUISTRY**----meaning the end justifies the means. Both terms are embedded in the false logic of one of the seven errors.

Because of the seven errors in Gamaliel's reasoning process, Christians today misapply his advice. These seven errors of logic will be discussed: (a) false analogy, (b) poisoning the well, (c) appeal to force, (d) appeal to many, (e) bifurcation, (f) hasty generalization, and (g) appeal to ignorance. I can already hear devoted pastors blurting out, **"But Gamaliel's advice is in the Bible, and therefore inspired by God!"** I agree 100%, but there is a major flaw in understanding inspiration of Scripture. ***Inspiration is an accurate recording of his words, but not approval of his words!*** The Bible records the statements and views of many unbelievers, but does not approve and endorse them: it is merely an accurate recording of their speech.

Psalm 14:1 is a clear and easy proof, for it reads: **"There is no God."** Is this verse advocating atheism? Of course not, for the entire verse reads, **"The fool has said in his heart,"** 'There is no god." This verse is an accurate recording of the beliefs of the atheist, but not endorsement of his views. Another example is in Gen. 3:4 where the serpent spoke to Eve and commanded her **"Eat the fruit. You will not surely die."** Is God approving of the serpent's views? That is an easy question to answer--------and you only get one chance!

Reading and interpreting the Bible involves many skills, but one of the simpler ones is to always identify the speaker: is he/she a believer or unbeliever; is he/she an immature or mature believer. Here in Acts 5 it is clear Gamaliel is not a Christian: he is a devout Rabbi who loves God, but has rejected Jesus as the Messiah; therefore, any counsel he may give must always be suspect, for he does not have the mind of Christ.

a. FALSE ANALOGY

(1) Definition of false analogy

The first technique in false logic is false analogy. An analogy means comparison, such as comparing an orange to an apple, but this comparison is not valid, even though both of them are classed as fruit: there are major differences between apples and oranges; therefore, comparing apples to oranges is a **FALSE ANALOGY.** A **TRUE ANALOGY** would be comparing two apples or two oranges. In the reasoning process, people resort to false analogy in an attempt to prove something by improper comparison, such as the apple and orange. A common French proverb says it well: **"To compare is not to prove."** Metaphors don't prove; they illustrate. Things may be alike in many ways, and yet, be very different.

(2) Gamaliel's analogy

Gamaliel begins his reasoning process (Acts 5:35) to the Sanhedrin by referring to two historical insurrections against the Roman Government: Insurrection of Theudas (the only time he is mentioned in the Bible) who led an insurrection of 400 men against Rome, but he and his followers were all killed. The movement thus failed. Judas the Galilean also led an insurrection against Rome, but he too was killed, but the movement did not permanently die; it lived on in the party of the Zealots who increased in number, but never successfully gained major influence to oppose Rome (See Acts 1:13 and Matt. 10:4).

(3) Gamaliel's application

Gamaliel applied these two insurrections to the apostles: since Theudas and Judas failed in their insurrection attempt; therefore, you apostles and your teaching will also fail. Here he is basing his counsel on two grounds: **PAST FAILED HISTORY** of Theudas and Judas, and **FUTURE POTENTNIAL PROSPERITY**: this new Christianity may grow and prosper. The past failed history is revealed in Gamaliel's words **"If their purpose or activity is of human origin (like Theudas and Judas), it will fail."** (Acts 5:38). His implied counsel is **"Let the movement die a slow death,"** (like Theudas and Judas). The future potential prosperity is revealed in Gamaliel's words: **"But if their purpose or activity is from God, you will not be able to stop these men; you will only find yourselves fighting against God."** (Acts 5:39). Gamaliel's direct counsel is **"The apostles may be from God, so let them go and observe."** His counsel is summed up in three words: **TOLERATE, TIME, TERMINATE.** He counsels in effect, **TOLERATE** these Apostles and defer any evaluation to a later time; allow the movement of **TIME** to transpire and monitor what may happen; judge the movement by **TERMINATION** of its quantitative (numerical) growth and success, because success indicates God's approval; numerical failure indicates God's disapproval.

(4) Reasons for false analogy

Years ago I read an excellent, concise contrast between Theudas, Judas, and the apostles, but have been unable to recall and locate the precise source to give proper credit, so I am here listing from this unknown author the six reasons why Gamaliel's logic and counsel was wrong:

(a) Theudas and Judas both led insurrections; the Apostles are not leading insurrections.

(b) Theudas and Judas advocated political policy; the Apostles advocated a spiritual message.

(c) Theudas and Judas led a human-centered movement; the Apostles led a divine-centered movement.

(d) Theudas and Judas did not display miracle-working powers; the Apostles did display miracle-working powers.

(e) Theudas and Judas were crushed by Roman government officials; the Apostles were opposed and beaten by spiritual authorities: the Sanhedrin.

(f) Theudas and Judas started with a small following and watched it grow to 400 people; the Apostles started by a small following and watched it grow to more than 8,000 in the first early years of the Church (Acts 2:41; 4:4).

This list reveals little comparison between the insurrections of Theudas and Judas and the Apostles; therefore, Gamaliel's use of false analogy cancels out his reasoning and conclusion; this false analogy gives new meaning to the hermeneutical rule: **A strong, correct interpretation will lead to a strong, correct application. A weak, incorrect interpretation will lead to a weak, incorrect application.** If I misinterpret a passage, I will misapply the passage.

(5) Lessons learned

What lessons can we learn from Gamaliel's false analogy counsel? There are four lessons: (a) **REGARD**, (b) **REGULATE**, (c) **RESIST**, (d) **RESPOND.**.

(a)   Regard a new movement. Gamaliel's counsel was to retard or delay action on this new movement of Christianity; the Sanhedrin wanted to kill the apostles for their teaching, but Gamaliel advocated delay, deferment, postpone action. He said in effect: **"Let these men go free, because if this movement is not from God, it will not grow nor succeed. Give this issue time so we can better judge it."**

New trends and philosophies, such as CCM and the church growth movement forge onto the Christian and secular scene. In medicine the issue of cloning is a present hot potato in discussion: whether or not to create life in chemical laboratories with perfect DNA. What should be our response to this medical advance of creating life apart from God's eternal plan through normal human reproduction? How should churches respond to modern philosophies of building a church congregation? Can jazzy music be used in worship services? Can drama be used in worship services?

Learn from Gamaliel: don't ignore these trends and movements; don't delay and defer your thinking, but regard them: analyze them for their beliefs and practices. If a new cult develops, don't ignore it and hope it will go away by itself; it may not recede, but increase in power and influence. Paul teaches in I Cor. 2:15: **"The spiritual man makes judgment about all things."** Stay informed so you can be an effective judge. Paul commands us to **"TEST ALL THINGS."** (I Thess. 5:2) In the context of this passage Paul includes prophetic utterances to determine validity, and by extension also test any questionable philosophy, movement, or method for ministry. Does this include the whole area of music? Definitely.!

(b)   Regulate a new movement. Regulate and measure a new movement according to established rules and regulations of morality, ethics, qualitative standards of excellence taught in the Bible. This book you now hold and read is about modern music infiltrating our churches, and our response should not merely be **"I like it"** or **"I don't like it."** Rather, use objective, measureable standards for judging music which will be explored in Chapter 6 on Philippians 4:8 listing eight benchmarks as a useful tool in judging. If you are musically trained and desire more technical knowledge on judging, evaluating music, then consult books written by professional teachers and professors of music listed in Chapter 8. Study the Bible, because there are over 500 references to music in Scripture: it will illuminate your mind on different kinds of music, how music must be performed, and for whom it is performed.

(c) Resist the movement. Resist the movement (in music, teacher education, issues such as abortion, cloning, homosexual marriages) if the movement does not comply with guidelines given in God's Word. Resistance, if necessary, may involve you speaking out to proper officials in the areas of concern (music, teacher education, etc), or writing letters to these people, or as I am now doing-------writing a book.

(d) Respond to the movement. Respond with positive affirmation if the movement or methods conform to Biblical guidelines. This involves supporting distinctively Christian music free from pagan. worldly influences. If you know of a young man or woman with musical talent and interest, support them emotionally, spiritually, and even financially to help them with their academic expenses in college or private music lessons.

b. Poisoning the well.

(a) Definition of Poisoning the well
This second technique in false reasoning and logic means to ***discredit a source in advance, as in pouring poison into the well before drawing out the water.*** Pouring poison into a well corrupts the water, making it undrinkable. This technique is used to attack a man as a source of unreliable evidence. When poisoning the well occurs in an argument, private or public, the person guilty of the fallacy is trying to intimidate his opponent by name-calling or prejudicing the issue.

(b) How Gamaliel used this faulty method
He used it in two ways: with Theudas and Judas. In Acts 5:36 he addressed the Sanhedrin with these words: **"Theudas appeard, claiming to be somebody."** Note how Gamaliel describes Theudas: a man **"claiming to be somebody."** This four word phrase clearly implies Theudas was proud, arrogant, boastful. When used by Gamaliel at the beginning of his Sanhedrin address, those four words are loaded barbs intended to dislike Theudas and prejudice their thinking against him.

He used the same technique with Judas (Acts 5:37) by saying **"After him, Judas the Galilean appeared."** Was Judas from the area of Galilee where Jesus lived in Nazareth? Yes, Judas was a Galilean. What is wrong? Calling Judas a **"Galilean"** was both 100% accurate, but also belittling, debasing him because Galilee had the reputation of low-life people, blue collar workers, uneducated, unrefined, inferior, primitive, from the other side of the tracks. When spoken, the speaker (Gamaliel) would tense his neck muscles, shift his head slightly, tighten the muscles around his vocal chords, and speak in a disgusting, guttural manner. It was often spoken in a disgusting way, as in **"O, he's a Galilean!"**

This technique of poisoning the well is often used in courtrooms, if permitted by the judge. A defendant will stand next to his lawyer and before the judge to face his charges. If the prosecuting attorney knows of this man's previous record on unrelated crimes, the prosecutor will want to bring out these previous crimes------even before the judge and jury hears the present case. A good defense attorney will immediately stand, address the judge, and say, **"Your honor, those issues are not pertinent to this case and will prejudice (prejudge) my client. I ask, your honor, the prosecutor be restricted from surfacing these past issues."** If the judge concurs he will announce "Sustained."----meaning, the judge agrees to the defendant's attorney.

(c) Guilt by association
When Gamaliel called Theudas as **"claiming to be somebody"** (proud, arrogant, boastful), he was inferring the apostles were like Theudas. When he called Judas a "Galilean" (primitive, uneducated, unrefined, inferior), he was inferring the apostles were also the same in character and temperament. Using this faulty technique, Gamaliel was able to infer the guilt of the apostles because of their association with Theudas and Judas. He

did not want the Sanhedrin to think objectively, justly, and clearly about the disposition of the Apostles and their teaching, so he masterfully planted negatively-charged words in their minds to prejudice them in favor of his counsel.

Today our nation is facing a most important election of a new president and administration. I have not heard recently, but I recall several years ago hearing a politician publicly refer to his competitor as **"My intemperate colleague,"** or **"My incompetent associate."** Those are nuclear-powered words exploding in the minds of people to prejudice them.

(d) Application of this faulty technique
Using such emotionally negative words clouds the reasoning process and nullifies any rational decision or conclusion, and too often Christians fall into this trap in conversations with other people when discussing music by using inappropriate terms or name-calling. Rather than calmly talking about the specific aspects of music (or any other subject), emotions become stirred, the tongue is unleashed, and words are spoken which hurt and offend others.

A good prayer to memorize and pray is in Psalm 19:14: **May the words of my mouth and the meditation of my heart be pleasing in your sight, O Lord, my Rock and my Redeemer."** Another excellent prayer is in Psalm 141:3: **"Set a guard over my mouth, O Lord; keep watch over the door of my lips."**

c. Appeal to force

(a) Definition of force
This third technique in false reasoning and logic is a motivation to fear, attempting to influence a person, as in **"If you do not convict this murderer, one of you may be her next victim."** This technique is also called ***"swinging the big stick."*** It is the use of potential force and fear as a motivation to act in a certain manner. Parents use this technique by saying to a rebellious child: **"If you don't clean your room, your father (or mother) is going to restrict your privileges."**

(b) How Gamaliel used this technique
How did Gamaliel use this appeal to force? The answer is recorded in Acts 5:39: <u>**"But if it is from God, you will not be able to stop these men; you will only find yourselves fighting against God."**</u> Here is Gamaliel-----the leading, and highly-respected Pharisee as a member of this religious council, the Sanhedrin, telling the 70 members to release the apostles because their ministry of Christianity may grow and you will suffer judgment from God by attempting to hinder them. That is "carrying the big stick." Who wants to fight against God? Certainly not the Pharisees and Sadducees! Gamaliel knew the hostile attitudes of the Sanhedrin prevented them from hearing a reasoned teaching from the Apostles about Christ, so he resorted to this false method of logic-----appeal to fear. The Apostles had already been imprisoned previously (Acts 4:1-21) and explained in brief then about Christ, but the Sanhedrin disbelieved.

(c) Absence of previous fear (1) Prior to the cross.
Before Christ died on the cross these same Pharisees and Sadducees opposed Him during His three-year earthly

ministry, never once thinking they were fighting God. Rather they were convinced Christ and His disciples were enemies of God.

(2) After the cross. But following the cross and Christ's resurrection, attitudes among the Sanhedrin radically changed. Now Christ has mysteriously resurrected and vanished from a sealed Roman tomb, they are unable to explain His supposed resurrection, they see the conspicuous growth of the New Christianity, and are beginning to consider that perhaps Christianity is true, and if so, there is the strong possibility God will judge them if they killed the Apostles and thwarted the work of God.

(3) Application to music. How does this false logic relate to the issue of this book? It applies to the reasoning process of objective thinking in affirming the truth or falsity of a statement, belief or behavior. At issue here is whether or not the Apostles are correct in claiming Jesus has risen and is in truth the Son of God who will judge all men (Acts 3:23). The Sanhedrin had not been previously convinced Jesus was the Christ, the Messiah, by the clear, reasoned arguments of the Apostles because the Sanhedrin was filled with intense hatred and prejudice. This technique appeal to force is an **EMOTIONAL APPEAL**, not a **MENTAL APPEAL.** It is an appeal to force through the emotion of fear. The previous error of poison the well of reasoning is also an **EMOTIONAL APPEAL.**

We must not use this method to convince other Christians about the weaknesses of much of CCM because it appeals to emotions; rather we make our clear, rational appeal why this music is poor in developing Christian maturity. Our reasoning must first be based on Scripture (the reason for this book) in combination with principles from recognized authorities on music to guide in music measuring up to the eight benchmark standards in Philippians 4:8, discussed in Chapter 6.

(d) <u>Guidelines in using appeal to force.</u> Is appeal to force always wrong? Definitely not! Sometimes it is necessary, as when a toddler slips away from his mother and wanders out into the street. She screams in horror: **"Johnny, get out of the street or a car will hit you!"** She is using sound reasoning plus the appeal to force as an emotion to motivate him. Or a teenage son asks for the family car; the request is granted with a curfew of 11 pm. He has used the car on previous occasions, but has missed curfew every time, so the father says , **"Jack, if you do not come home by 11 pm, then you will be unable to drive for six months."** That is a wise use of appeal to force as a motivating tool.

Does the Bible use appeal to force as a motivating tool? Certainly! Jesus Himself taught **<u>"Believe in me for eternal life, or perish forever in hell."</u>** Yes, pastors, Bible teachers must teach all the Bible----even the depressing facts of life without Christ forever. But there must be balance in our gospel presentations----balancing logical reasoning process of truth from a passage with a natural (not forced) emotional appeal to force when necessary congruency of emotion exists in the context.

d. Appeal to many

(a) Definition of the method

This fourth method in false reasoning is reliance on numbers to determine success, growth, and truth: the greater the numbers the greater success.

(b) Gamaliel's use of this method

In Acts 5:39 Gamaliel said, **"But if it is from God, you will not be able to stop these men."** He is using mathematics as a criterion of truth. He is in effect teaching: *"If this Christianity is really from God, then it will prosper, grow, expand, and succeed; therefore, measure truth and success solely by numbers. God's approval and blessing is based on large numbers: quantitative measurement. Little or no growth in numbers indicates God is not honoring the work because it is not from Him; if it was, it would grow."*

Gamailel knew firsthand the phenomenal growth of Christianity: how could any citizen in Jerusalem fail to see how that city and adjoining areas in Israel were being positively affected by the gospel message taught by these Apostles?

He also gave the reverse side of the numbers game when he said, **"For if their purpose or activity is of human origin, it will fail."** (Acts 5:38). Here Gamaliel stated lack of growth, or minimal growth will only lead to failure and thus prove the work was not from God. Is it true success is based on numbers? Definitely No! Yet that is the philosophy of Gamaliel ------and thousands of pastors, ministers of music, Bible teachers, and millions of Christians embrace this false philosophy. Theologically trained men who have studied the Word of God for years have unwittingly been "snookered," "duped," and "bought" a worldly philosophy of ministry which teaches: **"Big crowds means God is blessing; small crowds means God is judging."**

(c) Worldly philosophy

This philosophy of Gamaliel came from humanistic models of business success taught in every major Business Department of Universities. The business world wants to make a profit---- great profits; increased sales = increased numbers = increased profits. That is the American way of free enterprise in a competitive world, and the evangelical church has "bought hook, line, and sinker" into this secular, business model of "Church Growth." I have heard pastors say to large groups of other pastors: **"We are blessed by God. See all the numbers! We can hardly find places for people to sit. Our methods and CCM must be from God, or else we would not be growing so large and fast."** If this philosophy is true, then by sheer logical consistency we must conclude the cults are from God because they are growing and spreading. The false religion of Islam and terrorism must be true because both Islam and terrorism is spreading its tentacles world-wide.

Another way of restating this false error of reasoning is based on popularity: truth, beauty, and goodness is based on popularity. If something is true, beautiful, and good, then it will be popular and people will flock to it. Is this true? If it is, then logical consistency demands rock n roll concerts must be good, wholesome, beautiful, and true. These rock concerts are filled with thousands of devotees hearing rock bands screeching out their filth, vulgarity, indecency, and rebellion at ultra high levels of decibel sound.

Throngs of German citizens fully believed in the vision of a pure race of people advocated by Adolph Hitler who promoted the Death Camps in Poland, Germany, and France where six million Jews were sadistically terminated. These citizens considered him as a future world ruler. If you accept the philosophy that success, growth, truth, beauty, goodness, and morality is determined by numbers, then you must concur with the Third Reich, cults, and rock n roll concerts.

(d) Biblical philosophy of ministry

Scripture never promises we will always be successful in a monetary, physical sense, or have a mega church of 10,000 in attendance on a Sunday morning, but God has promised to bless all Christians in a spiritual sense of His character. Yes, He does bless and honor a few pastors and ministers of music with great pools of wealth and a 10,000 member church: that is the rare exception to only a few chosen vessels. Why does He honor certain men and women with unusual "success," growth, and wide influence? We do not know-----apart from His sovereignty: only God knows why He chose Abraham, Moses, Joseph, and Paul for leadership positions of greatness. What God has commanded to us is a word we don't like---------faithfulness! Serve God faithfully with the gifts He gives us, and He will reward us in heaven.

(e) Personal, painful illustration

Let me share a hurtful experience from my own battle with what Warren Wiersbe calls the **"damned demon god of success."** My wife, two children and I started a new church in our home with ten people. Each Sunday we met in our living room and the attendance began growing, spreading out of the living room into the kitchen. We outgrew our house and then rented a better local business for our services. Then we rented a larger facility. Progress was slow but consistent to the point we had about 45 people. I was working in the secular business world to support the family while the church was so small because it could not afford to pay me a full time salary. I attended a local breakfast meeting with many like-minded pastors, and as usual, the pastors began telling about their various events and growth in their churches. One pastor, whom I knew well and he knew me well also, leaned over the breakfast table and said with a telling smirk on his face: **"How's that little church of yours?"** At that point we only had about 30 people on Sunday, and I was discouraged with having to work in the secular business world during the day, rush home for dinner, shower, dress, leave the house to make some pastoral calls, then rise early at 4 am each morning to study and pray before heading out to work at my secular employment.

This question from a pastor friend crushed me! He had a large church with several people on staff, a generous salary, fringe benefits, and was well respected in the city. But that morning was a low point for me. I needed encouragement, not a demeaning question-----at least I felt the question was asked in a demeaning way with his use of "little church." Perhaps he did not intend the question in this manner, and perhaps I was being "too sensitive.." Either way, I still hurt.

I needed guidance and ideas for ministry on how to get a church growing into a "big" church-----just like the ones reported on in Christian magazines with the big name pastors who were advertised in the brochures as **"they know how to build a big church; they know how to get the job done. Come to this seminar and learn from these gifted men about creative programs and techniques to draw large crowds in your church back home."** So I began the seminar circuit-----attending pastor conferences to learn from these big name pastors. At each seminar excellent materials were made available so we could go back home "fired up" with these new programs and techniques. Well, I did-----month after month, focusing with discipline on following the printed instructions for these programs. I got discouraged-------so I would attend a different seminar with another big name pastor from _____ Church: only to face another attack of discouragement because somehow I could not attain the level of this successful pastor. I had to make a personal decision: don't attend any more pastor seminars. Why? Because each seminar added greater guilt in me by my failure to build a "big church."

These pastors are godly, definitely gifted men, and I never sensed any expanded ego nor insincerity in them. I was convinced their "programs," "novel techniques," and professionally-developed full color marketing materials did successfully "work" for them------but not me!

I cannot adequately describe the depth of discouragement in which I waded and slogged----all because I had sincerely, but naively "bought" into this worldly philosophy teaching success is based on numbers. I was fully trained in theology, counseling skills, musical abilities, graphic arts, and interpersonal relationships, but I could not build a "big church!" That time of discouragement and depression spanned four long years. I no longer pastor that church, so what is it doing now? **PREPARE YOURSELF**: it folded; disorganized; closed doors for ever---after several hard years of struggle and commitment by me, my family, and numerous other believers in the congregation.

Why did it "**fail**" or perhaps a better question is **"What went wrong?"** Every church fails or closes its doors for a variety of reasons too numerous and complex to answer here. Sometimes God raises up a church or other ministry for a given purpose known only to Him in His sovereignty, and when that purpose is accomplished God directs that church to blend in with another like-minded congregation or close its doors. Jesus said **"I will build my church and the gates of Hades will not overcome it."** (Matt. 16:18) The church He promised to build is His universal body of Christ, not every local congregation located at Main and First Street. The Body of Christ (Church) will never fail despite any attacks from Satan, but some local churches (like ours) may exist for only a specified time period known only to God.

Did our "little church" accomplish any good? We sure did! Several people came to Christ as Savior, other Christians greatly matured in their faith and practical obedience to God, and our fellowship was genuinely enthusiastic. One fine Christian woman led outstanding Bible studies with support from our congregation at another location from where we rented for our Sunday services. We financially supported local Christian college students involved in the church's ministry, a missionary in another state who worked with indigent people of low income, and a young pastor and his family who trained at a local Bible College and also immensely served in the church. A practical program our church instituted was a yearly event called, **A Hebrew-Christian Passover Observance**. This ministry occurred at Easter each year, and our rented facility would fill with many, many other people from other churches desiring to know more about the Hebrew Passover, its meaning for Old Testament believers, and especially its meaning and application to communion or the Lord's Supper. Yes, we did some good for God's kingdom

Am I an enemy of "big churches?" No----even though my verbal and written expressions may appear to sound that way. If, as you now read these words, think or feel I am an enemy, then I ask forgiveness in advance. I know my heart (Aren't you glad only you and God knows your heart?") and I was walking, or more pictorially slogging, through that sticky bog John Bunyan called the **"slough of despair."** This pit of gooey mud was self-generated all because I "bought" a worldly philosophy of success by measuring mainly numbers. The philosophy **"sounded good, right, logical,"** well-intentioned, supported and affirmed by many **"Successful, large, contemporary, cutting-edge congregations relevant to modern society with its consumer needs."** WOW! That's a condensation of many modern churches believing in PC (Politically Correct verbage non-offensive to anyone.)

How does this false method of appeal to many relate to the music theme of this book? Hopefully my previous explanations may have given you, the reader, insights of your own, but if I have failed, I will be very specific. The CCM movement (and other Christian ministries) quickly run to this passage in Acts 5 as proof of God's blessing and approval on using pagan music patterns (like the Egyptian pagan music at Mt. Sinai). I hear frequently on radio, Christian TV programs, and read many books by advocates of CCM words like these: **"Look at all the young people we are attracting with CCM,"** they proudly claim. **"Many of these young adults in high school, college, and young married families are finding Christ as Savior. You can't argue with success, you know. This modern music really works; it gets people excited and pumped up about worship."** I will discuss further in later chapters on specific applications of CCM, and provide a practical measuring chart in chapter six to evaluate Christian music. These sincere pastors and musicians err in embracing a false method of humanistic logic, (as I did in the past) and thus also embrace the false thinking of Gamaliel. True spiritual success, not merely numerical success, is based on faithful obedience to God's Word **AND** established rules and principles of musical melody and theological lyrics.

One final application of this false method of appeal to many. Gamaliel said if a work is not from God it will not grow and ultimately fail. If that is universally true (and that is the entire purpose of logical truth), then our **"little church"** was not in God's will (perhaps in your and Gamaliel's eyes) due to nine reasons and more: (a) to my own rebellion in starting the church; (b) poor preaching and teaching from me; (c) lack of pastoral concern; (d) inefficient management; (e) wrong class of people; (f) poor vision for ministry; (g) inadequate facilities, (h) wrong area of the city; (i) interpersonal conflicts; (j) absence of consistent leadership; (k) financial corruption---------and I could continue listing 100 other possible reasons for our church failure, while other people would be quick to quote 1,000 additional reasons for church closure. Think as you like! Rationalize any method of false logic you desire! I have wrestled long enough over my guilt feelings of unfulfilled accomplishments; God, through His Word, has freed me from this suffocating, stifling bondage of self-imposed guilt: He has liberated me! Halleluiah!

I know this for 100% certainty as I sit here today writing and reflecting about a historical event in the life of our church: my own heart was clean before the Lord when we had that first worship service in our living room with my dear wife playing the piano and our two teenage children dressed in their Sunday best; the dear Christians were fully committed to the work; all of us gave sacrificially of our income to support the financial obligations of a small "little church;" none of us (including me) were free of human warts, moles, and personality flaw, and sometimes we would "get on each others' nerves."

Because of this painful experience in church planting I have learned to identify more with Paul in I Cor. 4:4. The Corinthians were speedy to criticize the Apostle because in the minds of the Corinthians he did not measure up to the super apostles (false teachers who invaded the Corinthian church and convinced them they (false teachers) were more knowledgeable and spiritual than Paul.) He was, in their opinion, a second-class apostle lacking in knowledge. They were quick to judge Paul and his motives, but Paul graciously replied to these self-convinced "mature" Corinthian Christians: **"I care very little if I am judged by you or by any human court; indeed I do not even judge myself. My conscience is clear, but that does not make me innocent. It is the Lord who judges me."**

Gamaliel was ***PARTLY CORRECT*** by his counsel to the Sanhedrin, because truth, beauty, goodness, approval, blessing and growth is a ***FEW TIMES*** a sign of God's approval of success and growth, **BUT NOT ALWAYS**. Sometimes he prospers us in Christian ministry---- and sometimes not. Why? You tell me, because the Bible does not give us all the reasons for His sovereign plans: they are hidden from us. Yes, He did bless and honor the leadership of the Apostles in the early church because that was His plan, but with many pastors and missionaries God does not always honor with explosive growth in converts, financial support, and building grand architectural buildings.

` Gamaliel's counsel is therefore a **MIXED BAG** of errors and truth, and a mixed bag is far more difficult and dangerous to sift through the bag contents in determining the errors and discarding them, with truth and retaining it. An obvious truth and obvious error is easily detectable, but half-truths-----well, that's where the boys and men are separated. A perfect example of Jesus' teaching is Matt. 13:25-40 regarding the tares (weeds) growing beside the wheat. The tares with their simulated cluster of grain beads clutching the stalk look very similar to true wheat and often deceive us; only God knows the difference between a true believer (wheat) and a false believer (tares). He commands us to know and understand the difference between tares and wheat----and by implication between ***truth in sound logic and error in pseudo logic***. His words must be applied to the issue of church discipline in the kingdom of God, but by hesitancy and caution in removal of all unbelievers (tares) from the church (wheat). Jesus said, "**Wheat grows beside tares and since they look so like wheat, therefore, do not pull up the tares because you may also pull up the good wheat.**" Paul in I Cor. 5:1-13 gives further inspiration and teaching on church discipline in the Church age.

Gamaliel used the appeal to many as the standard of determining success; he was sincere, but sincerely wrong----because he was an unbeliever giving the best humanistic wisdom he could muster. If he is right, then many missionaries who have gone to foreign nations with the gospel of Christ have failed miserably because few converts were won to Christ. Many places of ministry in God's kingdom are more difficult than other areas; some areas are naturally fruitful----others are barren or shriveled. The words of Gamaliel: **"But if it is from God, you will not be able to stop these men,"** is false logic. But God's Word teaches: **"You will know the truth, and the truth will set you free,"** (John 8:32) and this is true logic---the spiritual truth of salvation in Christ. God wants us to be saved by true logic, and spurn false logic. True logic (clear, but unpopular thinking) leads to salvation, freedom, and mature worship; false logic (confused, but popular thinking) leads to damnation, bondage, and fleshly worship. The Corinthians were speedy to criticize the Apostle because in their minds he did not measure up to the super apostles (false teachers). They were quick to judge Paul and his motives. But I identify personally in my experience with Paul in I Cor. 4:4: **"I care very little if I am judged by you or by any human court; indeed I do not even judge myself. My conscience is clear, but that does not make me innocent. It is the Lord who judges me."** Someday in heaven someone, maybe Paul the great church planter, even the greatest Missionary, Jesus, will explain all the details with me; then, I will understand. Come on over to our chateau; we'll have cookies and milk, maybe strawberry short cake, and I'll tell you what I've learned-----if your interested.

(f) Additional affirmation of this appeal to many

Even secular sources confirm the importance of identifying, knowing, and applying true logic. There is Immanuel Kant, German philosopher in the 18th century: **"Seek not the favor of the multitude; it is seldom got by honest and lawful means. But seek the testimony of the few and number not voices, but weigh them." 1** C.S. Lewis, deceased Christian and famous English professor in England and author of the famed Chronicles of Narnia series stated noses may be a great method of running a government, but it is no necessary criterion for truth. A.J. Hoover in his book, Don't You Believe It, well said: **"You don't prove something is true, beautiful, or good just by showing that it is popular." 2** I am burdened about the professing evangelical church because sincere, God-loving leaders and laymen have bought into Gamaliel's worldly, humanistic philosophy of big numbers, flashy programs, novel gimmicks, jazzy music, pounding beat, driving rhythm, ditty tunes, and monotonous repetition of anemic "praise and worship" choruses.

e. Bifurcation

(a) Definition of bifurcation: The fifth technique in false reasoning means restriction to two choices. The term is composed of two Latin words: "bi" meaning two, and "furca" meaning a "fork" or "branch." Combined together the term means **"two-pronged"** or two choices, two possibilities exist, either/or. This fallacy presumes only two possibilities exist, either/or, and assumes only two choices are available, when in fact other alternatives exist. It limits choices to two.

(b) Explanation of bifurcation: Two statements are said to be contraries when neither is impossible for both to be true but possible for both to be false. If we say Jane may be rich or she may be poor, for example, we mean she cannot be both at the same time, but she may be neither. Two statements are said to be contradictories, on the other hand, when it is impossible for both to be true and also impossible for both to be false. Either the man is alive or dead. Either today is your birthday or it isn't. The fallacy of bifurcation arises when an either/or statement that actually contains two contraries is instead put forward as containing two contradictories.

(c) **What is wrong with bifurcation?** The answer is limited thinking. It forces us into limited thinking, restricting our choices to only two alternatives, when in reality there may be more choices available. Hoover in his excellent book, <u>Don't you Believe It</u>, well states: **"Thinking in extremes can be appealing, unfortunately, for it requires less mental energy than exploring all aspects of a problem."3** He continues by declaring often our prejudices blind us to see other alternatives, or we desire a simple solution to a complex problem.

(d) **How Gamaliel displays bifurcation** How is bifurcation displayed in Gamaliel? He only recommended two ways: (a) **TOLERATE,** (b) **EXTEMINATE.** In recommending toleration to release the apostles he was saying, **"Take a wait and see approach; then we can better judge their effectiveness or ineffectiveness. We need more time to see what develops and then act."** In extermination he was saying, **"Yes, go ahead and kill them; then we will be finished with this theological nuance of who is this Jesus."** Were there other choices? Yes, but they were never seemingly considered by the Sanhedrin and Gamaliel. There are seven other options they could have considered: investigate, emulate, repudiate, incarcerate, incorporate, inoculate, and excommunicate.

OTHER OPTIONS OF BIFURCATION

1. INVESTIGATE.

(a) Influential members Two prominent Jewish men were members of the Sanhedrin: Nicodemus and Joseph of Arimethea. Nicodemus said to the Sanhedrin in John 7:50, **"Does our law condemn anyone without first hearing him to find out what he is doing?"** Either he was not in attendance at the Sanhedrin trial of Jesus or there is no record of his protest. Joseph of Arimethea was a secret disciple of Jesus (John 19:38), wealthy (Matt. 27:57), and also a member of the Sanhedrin (John 19:50-51). Why did Joseph of Arimethea and Nicodemus fail to protest at the Sanhedrin council meeting where the Apostles were tried? We do not know, but perhaps both men quietly supported the Apostles but could not speak openly in the presence of the council.

(b) **Possible approach** These two men could have said, **"Let's investigate this matter further to determine the validity of this teaching from these Apostles of Jesus."** That precisely was the purpose of the Sanhedrin to conduct fair hearings on civil and religious issues in Israel. But this option would have stern opposition because the Sadducees were filled with hatred toward Jesus, His miracles, and the Apostles. The Sadducees could not refute the miracles of the Apostles (Acts 13:45), and were consumed with jealousy because the citizens of Jerusalem were following the teaching of the Apostles (Acts 5:19).

Acts 5:17 tells us these Sadducees were filled with jealousy. The Greek word for jealousy is only used here and in Acts 13:45, and means religiously motivated rage: a rage motivated by a desire to maintain purity of faith. At first the Sadducees were annoyed, agitated, and indigent toward the Apostles, but now this rage turns into a jealous emotional obsession toward them, thus preventing the Sanhedrin to honestly without bias conduct fair hearings. This religious council of 70 men were losing their support from the citizens of Jerusalem, and their sole desire was to them. We learn from this incident the important truth: **PRIDE BLINDS SPIRITUAL EYESIGHT;** therefore, investigation by the Sanhedrin was not a realistic option.

2. EMULATE

a. Definition of emulate

This second option of investigation open to the Sanhedrin is emulate and means to equal or surpass your opponent by comparison.. The Apostles were popular in Jerusalem with large crowds converted to the gospel message (Acts 4:4) making the 70 men on the Council jealous.

b. Process of development

The Sanhedrin could have adopted the choice to emulate or compete with the Apostles, thus showing the weaknesses of Christianity and increasing the certain failure and demise of this new faith. But they did not consider this option because they would have to match their miracle-working powers with the Apostles. In the business and commercial world new products are developed all the time as "better" than_____" (and you can fill in that blank: socks, shoes, house, suit, toothpaste, cars.) Even if the Sanhedrin had tried to emulate the Apostles, they would have failed because no program or idea can ever compete with the gospel of Christ.

3. REPUDIATE

a. Definition of repudiate
The third possible option for the Sanhedrin could consider is repudiation, meaning disown, cast off publicly. The Council could have issued a formal, written statement to the citizens of Jerusalem and all Israel in the entire nation, denouncing the Apostles as heretics and disloyal to Judaism This pronouncement would humiliate the Apostles in the eyes of the people, and hopefully discourage further conversations to this new teaching.

4. INCARCERATE

a. Definition of incarcerate
This fourth term of options means jail time. The Sanhedrin could lock up the Apostles in jail, but this action (Acts 5:17-18) has been taken already, but the Apostles escaped from jail in a miraculous way. I'm 100% confident the Sanhedrin said in unity: **WE ALREADY TRIED THAT METHOD----AND IT DID NOT WORK!**

5. INCORPORATE

a. Definition of incorporate This fifth term of options is incorporate, meaning to fuse the Apostles together with the religious leaders of the Sanhedrin. They could say: **"Let us join hands for the betterment of our nation and agree to disagree on some issues. We will both share equally in administering justice and fairness to all our Jewish people."** Does not this sound like politicians today? Can't we just get along? Well, the Council would never agree to this union because the Sadducees did not believe in the resurrection.

6. INOCULATE

a. Definition The sixth possible option for the Sanhedrin was to consider inoculation: meaning to introduce new ideas into the citizens to suppress the authority of the Apostles and cause their teaching to be minimized and even totally blocked. The term "Inoculation" is used in medicine for injecting a serum, vaccine, or antigenic into the human body to boost immunity against disease. We vaccinate or inoculate children with specialized serums or vaccines to prevent malaria, chicken pocks, mumps, polio.

b. Acquired knowledge These 70 men on the Sanhedrin were knowledgeable men of Old Testament teaching and knew its laws. Three years Jesus lived, taught, performed miracles and often quoted passages from the Old Testament. The Apostles continued the ministry of Jesus by further miracles, and often quoted passages from the Old Testament----interpreting them as being fulfilled in Jesus of Nazareth. In fact the first 4 chapters of Acts demonstrate clearly how Jesus is the Messiah and the one whom Old Testament figures such as Abraham, David, and Joel prophesized.

These 70 men no doubt hear these expositions of Old Testament law, but could not refute them. Now, in the presence of Gamaliel, the Sanhedrin could manufacture new interpretations of these passages and conclusively demonstrate their superior interpretations over the Apostles, but they could not, because **TRUTH CANNOT BE BROKEN=----=-regardless of what interpretations you may devise.** Yes, it can be twisted, but in time these distortions will not stand up and survive against close scrutiny of correct interpretation. The Apostles knew the truth: the Sanhedrin did not. Even had the Sanhedrin conjured up some new, novel interpretation to inoculate against Christianity, the new interpretation would be determined as false.

7. EXCOMMUNICATE

a. Definition The seventh possible option the Sanhedrin could have considered is excommunication: a formal, official exclusion from certain benefits; a punishment for wrongdoing resulting in a loss of privileges of an organization.

b. Authority The Sanhedrin had full authority to excommunicate and exclude any Jew from Temple worship or participation in Temple activities if the Sanhedrin deemed a Jew guilty of religious heresy or insubordination to traditional Jewish practices. Yes, such activity would instill fear in Jewish citizens of Jerusalem and warn them from following the Apostles, thus limiting the Apostles.

(f) Hasty Generalization

a. **Definition** The sixth technique in false reasoning is hasty generalization: drawing conclusions with insufficient information. It is jumping to conclusions without all the facts, misinterpretation of facts. Observation of all facts, not merely selected facts, is the start of sound inductive reasoning.

b. **How did Gamaliel fail?** He failed by using two instances of political insurrection in Theudas and Judas, then jumped to a wrong conclusion. This sixth technique of hasty generalization is linked with the first technique: false analogy. His use of only two instances of failed insurrection against Rome is summarized in two words: **SELF DESTRUCTION.** He falsely reasoned to a wrong conclusion in this manner:

Theudas and Judas attempted insurrection against Rome.
The insurrection failed.
The Apostles may (inferred as will) also fail in their ministry.

Can you spot the two errors in his logical reasoning process? First, there is the error of **False Analogy** (see the first error listed previously). Theudas and Judas led a political insurrection; the Apostles lead a spiritual movement. He is comparing apples to oranges: false analogy. Second, Gamaliel based his conclusion on insufficient facts: he only highlighted two insurrections of Theudas and Judas, when in fact the Roman Empire faced numerous insurrections from nations who did not want Rome to rule over them; some insurrections failed; some succeeded. Did Gamaliel know of these other insurrections? We do not know, but whether or not he knew, it is still unwise to come to dogmatic conclusions based on minimal evidence. His second error was hasty generalization: insufficient information leading to a premature, false conclusion. Furthermore, while Gamaliel did not declare the Apostles **WOULD DEFINITELY** fail, but he did infer it and thus guarantee his recommendation would be followed by the Sanhedrin.

I want to expand on these two serious errors in Gamaliel's reasoning: false analogy and hasty generalization. Conclusions are to be based on **ALL FACTS** before an accurate conclusion (called a universal truth applicable to all times). In this life all of us are trying to be wise and make good decisions, but we need facts rightly interpreted. History is replete with nations (not just the Roman Empire) who led insurrections because the citizens felt ill at ease: they felt enslaved, economically deprived, powerless to influence ruling authorities, victims of unfair, unjust treatment, and deprived of release to form their own nation. Normally a small band of citizens form, educate the people about potential freedom from tyranny, increase in numbers of concerned citizens, then revolt against a political power. Over a period of time the citizens many times become successful; sometimes they initially fail only to later succeed.

Here are three examples of insurrection. **FIRST**, the Exodus of the Jews out of galling Egyptian tyranny is the ideal example of political insurrection. They suffered 400 years under Egyptian rule and desired leaving to form their own nation. Finally after months of suffering and ten plagues sent by God, Pharoah released them-------then with his military followed them, but God provided a mass drowning of the Egyptian army. Gamaliel, as a leading Jewish Rabbi, definitely knew this greatest insurrection of all time.

SECOND, distant history records successful insurrection in the French Revolution (1789 – 1799) when common peasants rebelled against the abuses from the monarchy and abusive Catholic ecclesiastical clergy to gain more freedom and democracy. Our own United States of America rebelled against Britain and King of England. Colonists under the leadership of George Washington successfully gained our own independence as a sovereign nation resulting from the Revolutionary War of Independence of 1795-1783.

THIRD, recent history in the tiny nation of Cuba---90 miles south of Florida----also reveals successful insurrection. From December 1956 to January 1959 Fidel Castro, his brother Raul Castro, and Che Guevara combined forces of a few hundred dissidents against the government of General Batista because of the repressing injustices of the government. Despite the overwhelming strength of Batista's army and police force, Castro and his limited force successfully defeated Batista, and converted Cuba into an atheistic, Communistic, socialistic state-----which remains today as an enemy of America.

These three historical examples (and I could give more) disprove the logic error of Gamaliel: insurrections can and do succeed----not always, but many times. This is a universal truth. How does this last technique of hasty generalization apply to the subject of this book: music----especially Contemporary Christian Music? Leaders in the CCM movement make hasty generalization when they judge success based on numbers in the worship service----but they fail to check deeper issues of maturity and contamination of borrowing pagan music in worship to God. Check in the application section of this book where I go into great detail in answering this highly important question.

(g) Appeal to ignorance.

a. Definition The seventh technique in false logic is Appeal to Ignorance. This technique is based on the opponent's inability to disprove a conclusion's correctness, and thus shifts the burden of proof outside the argument onto the person hearing the argument, and such an argument becomes irrelevant. According to Normal L. Geisler and Ronald M. Brooks in their book LET US REASON states this appeal to ignorance assumes **"that something should be believed until it is shown to be false." 4** One who uses this fallacy says, **"Accept this because you can't prove it isn't true."** In other words, if you don't know something is wrong, you should embrace it. Geisler and Brooks gives an excellent illustration of a snake: "I can't prove that it is poisonous, so I guess it is safe to pick it up." Picking up such a snake can be deadly!

b. Example of appeal to ignorance

Gamaliel served as advocator of his conclusion and recommendation; the Sanhedrin (consisting of 70 Jewish scholars) served as hearers or opponents-----judiciously listening to his arguments and recommendation. They could not **DISPROVE** his assertions, nor his conclusion and recommendation; therefore Gamaliel took advantage of the ignorance of the Sanhedrin. In the context of Acts 5:35-40 there is an ***OBVIOUS ABSENCE*** of rebuttal from the Sanhedrin: no refutation of his assertion of the inequality of the **POLITICAL** insurrection of Theudas and Judas with the **SPIRITUAL** teaching of the apostles; no refutation of the failing results of any human origin with the seemingly successful results of God's work; no refutation to his recommendation of abstaining from any further punitive actions against the apostles; no refutation of his inference regarding success is always measured by numbers and popularity. They could not disprove his assertions; therefore, they agreed to his reasons and conclusion: his argument thus was an appeal to their ignorance.

A climactic word appears in Acts 5:40: ***"His speech PERSUADED them."*** The Greek word for "persuaded" is **PEITHO**, meaning to convince. This same Greek word is used in its root in Colossians 2:4 where Paul warns against being ***"deceived by persuasive words."*** In both passages the word can be translated into our common vernacular: **"being talked into something."** The Sanhedrin was persuaded, or "talked into" Gamaliel's reasons, his "fine sounding arguments." (Col 2:4)

c. Illustration of "persuaded"

Buying a used car rather than a new car requires more discernment—more questions to ask, and even knowing what questions to ask. The used car salesman may convince me the car only has 50,000 miles on it when actually it has 100,000 miles. He assures me the engine is original, when in fact the engine has been rebuilt because of a collision. I am being ***"sold a bill of goods,"*** but I am ignorant of the facts and am persuaded, convinced by the salesman's ***"fine sounding arguments."*** He appeals to my ignorance------and I am hooked! Only later after the purchase, do I realize I have been **"duped, tricked, hoodwinked, beguiled"** by a charlatan.

d. Reasons for the Sanhedrin's acceptance

Two reasons explain the blind acceptance of the Sanhedrin toward Gamaliel: ignorance of logic, and respect for leaders.

(1)   Ignorance of logic Why did this group of 70 men succumb to Gamaliel's logic? They were convinced by the ***"fine-sounding arguments"*** of Gamaliel----------all because they did not possess the skills to discern his false logic, or were fearful of exposing Gamaliel's false thinking. Geisler and Brooks observe **"fallacies.....might be psychologically persuasive, they are not logically correct. They cause people to**

accept conclusions for inadequate reasons."5 The Sanhedrin were **PSYCHOLOGICALLY PERSUADED**----but not **LOGICALLY CONVINCED**. These 70 Biblical scholars of the Old Testament law were not ignorant of doctrine, but ignorant of the false reasoning process, by smooth words, by false application of doctrine. We can easily find fault with these men, but we as Christians today are just as susceptible to "fine sounding arguments" of sincere, but misguided leaders, in the CCM movement. Ignorance did not die with the Sanhedrin: it remains alive and well today!

(2)   Respect for leaders The second reason why they did not attempt refutation of Gamaliel centers on their respect for this wise man. Acts 5:34 describes Gamaliel as a well respected, and highly honored man, a teacher of the law. The Sanhedrin was in a quandary about the apostles: imprisoning them had failed; beating them had failed; charging them to discontinue from teaching about Christ had failed. As a final attempt, they called on Gamaliel to give his advice. He was the "expert" in the law, a man of sound character, and wise in human relations. Yes, he was knowledgeable, but not a Christian: he gave the best human insight and wisdom-----but it was not distinctly Christian wisdom. There may have been a few men on the Sanhedrin who personally questioned the reasoning process of Gamaliel, but they remained silent, thinking, "Who am I to question and doubt this venerable, seasoned scholar of the law?"

Scripture is clear regarding respect for our leaders: pastors, Sunday School teachers, parents, congressmen and senators, president, police officers. But this respect must not cloud our ability to discern truth, morality, and questionable methods used to promote false philosophies. As Christians we are all priests before God, and must develop the skills of the Berean Christians who ***"searched the Scriptures daily to see if what Paul said was true."*** (Acts. 17:11) Paul was an apostle, respected among the Bereans, yet they did not allow this respect to keep them from matching his teachings with the Old Testament scriptures to determine the truth or falsity of his doctrine.

I have often instructed people to investigate Scripture at home to determine my allegiance to the Bible-----correctly interpreted and applied. I don't want Christians to respect me for any position I may hold, but for my loyalty to Scriptural teaching. Leaders in the CCM movement should be respected as sincere believers, but not at the cost of blind agreement to their false philosophy and false methodology of using a worldly music style-----sprinkled with Christian words. These leaders are incorrectly interpreting and misapplying Acts 5:34-40.

(3) Illustration of respect in Job An excellent example of respect is recorded in Job 29:21-25 where Job reflects on his life prior to his suffering. He claimed his opinions were sought, and men waited in silence to hear him speak (verse 21). After speaking, his audience remained silent as they pondered his wisdom (verse 22). They drank in his words as dry ground drinks in refreshing rain (verse 23). His visible presence was precious to them (verse 24), and he sat among them as their chief, as a king among his troops (verse 25).

Gamaliel also experienced this same quiet respect from the Sanhedrin: silence and admiration from hearing "wise words," little knowing they heard only **SEEMING and DECEIVING apparitions of truth**, not **SEERING and DEMANDING**

actuality of truth! He offered counsel, but it was darkened by **"words without knowledge."** (Job 38:2). This passage records God speaking to Job where God asks the question: ***"Who is this that darkens my counsel with words without knowledge?"*** The question was a blunting rebuke to Job and his three "friends"----Eliphaz, Bildad, and Zophar, for their inadequate, faulty knowledge of God and His ways. Gamaliel, like Job, was offering darkened counsel with words without knowledge. His recommendation to free the Apostles was truly in the sovereign will of God, but his reasons and rationale were faulty and misleading.

Later in Job 42:1-6 Job finally admits to God: ***"Surely I spoke of things I did not understand, things too wonderful for me to know.......Therefore, I despise myself and repent in dust and ashes."*** Job, as a believer, recognized he knew very little of God's working in this life, repented in dust and ashes, and so too should we Christians follow Job's example for our puny knowledge of God. Gamaliel, as an unbeliever, felt no need of repentance----nor the humbling of dust and ashes!

e. Examples of unwise counsel

(1)   Gamaliel These seven fallacies of logic by Gamaliel are demonstrated to be false and unwise. ***"But,"*** interrupts the average Christian, ***"he recommended the Apostles be released, and their life was spared to carry on the preaching of the Gospel."*** Yes, that is true, and we can give praise to God for their ongoing freedom and ministry to establish the early church. But we must distinguish between **RESULTS and REASONS.** God honored the **RESULTS** of Gamaliel's counsel (freedom and release of the apostles), but not the **REASONS AND FALSE PHILOSOPHY** of Gamaliel's argument. God is sovereign and uses even unbelieving, pagan rulers to accomplish His rule, (Proverbs 21:1) but He does not give card blanche to their false philosophies: He expects you and me to study the false thinking of these men, expose it, reject it, avoid it. Nebuchadnezzar was a pagan king, yet God used him in exalting Daniel to be Chief of the Magi (Daniel 2:48-49). Cyrus (Isaiah 45:1-3; cf Ezra 6:22) also was a pagan ruler yet God used him to return the Jews from Babylon to the promised land of Israel. These men illustrate how God in His sovereignty uses wicked men in accomplishing His purposes, but rejecting their false philosophies.

S. Morris Engle in his book, WITH GOOD REASON, AN INTRODUCTION TO INFORMAL FALLACIES, correctly states **the conclusion or recommendation may be true, but the reasons offered in defense of the argument are false or invalid.**[6] This was the case with Gamaliel's seven errors of logic: they were invalid and expressed unsound reasoning, even though the conclusion/recommendation may **"accidentally"** (Engle's word) be good and true: release of the Apostles. Engle observes this **"accidental"** true conclusion/recommendation comes from some other source other than the proposed arguments/reasons. Engle illustrates this common fallacy with cats:

a. **All cats are animals.**
b. **All tigers are animals.**
c. **Therefore all tigers are cats.**

Statements a and b are **INVALID REASONS** to support the conclusion, even though statement c is accidentally true: the conclusion is not based on the preceding invalid reasons.

Gamaliel reached a good, wholesome, right recommendation, but the recommendation was not soundly based on his seven errors of logic. The recommendation was true because it was God's sovereign plan to protect and preserve the Apostles in their ministry and continuing, explosive growth of the Church as recorded in Acts 6 when the Church formed deacons to release the Apostles to prayer and the ministry of the Word. Let me repeat this important truth: **God honored the RESULTS--RECOMMENDATION of Gamaliel's argument, but not the seven false REASONS.**

The argument of Gamaliel is called **INDUCTIVE LOGIC**---arguing from specific instances or analogies (such as Theudas and Judas) and forming a conclusion/recommendation based on these reasons. Such a conclusion/recommendation is only an **INFERENCE,** or **PROBABILITY**---but not a guaranteed **PROOF. Probability** *means likelihood; chance stronger than possibility but failing short of certainty.* Probability also allows for exceptions or potential failures, events failing to attain desired results.

My sincere attempt in starting a new church eventually ended in the church dissolving. We had some **PROBABILITY** of success, but no guaranteed **PROOF.** Countless churches and mission endeavors, like ours, have also experienced this emotional let down when noble aspirations did not materialize into success. This is the same in the business world: every new business venture does not succeed----in fact only a few business ventures become large and financially successful like Microsoft, Apple Computers, Dell Computers, General Motors, Ford Motors, Aetna Life Insurance Company, American Air Lines. Failure does not always stem from wrong marketing methods alone, but from many mysterious factors known only to God.

PROBABILITY (a subjective judgment) is measured in degrees, as observed by Geisler and Brooks, **7** and adapted in the following chart:

TYPE	EXPLANATION	DEGREE	EXAMPLE
VIRTUAL CERTAINTY	Overwhelming evidence in its favor	99%	Law of gravity
HIGHLY PROBABLE	Very good evidence in its favor	90%	No two snowflakes are alike
PROBABILITY	Sufficient evidence in its favor test	70%	Most medicines have to pass this
POSSIBLE	Either no evidence or equipollence	50%	The chance your team will win the coin toss is 50%
IMPROBABLE	Insufficient evidence in its favor	30%	No one believes except the few for whom it worked
HIGHLY IMPROBABLE	Very little evidence in its favor	10%	Theory Jesus spent His early years studying with a Hindu guru
VIRTUALLY IMPOSSIBLE	Almost no evidence in its favor	1%	The existence of unicorns is at this level.

Where in this chart would you place Gamaliel's probability of success for the apostles? In my opinion I believe Gamaliel gave them a "Highly Probable" chance of success and growth----allowing for a 10% chance of failure and demise of Christianity. Of course Christianity did grow and expand to all the world, despite some setbacks, but this venture by the Apostles was based on the sovereign will of God-----not on cute, contemporary, contrived methods which dazzled the sinner and appealed to his self-centered sense of self-importance. He honored the Apostles with a world-wide ministry because of His sovereignty-----not because of their methodology.

Another important element of **INDUCTIVE LOGIC** involves **INDUCTIVE LEAP:** reaching out beyond the evidence to make, what Geisler and Brooks labels "broad, general statements."**8** Gamaliel unwittingly presented two analogies in Theudas and Judas to demonstrate their failure of political insurrection against the Roman government; therefore, he reasoned, the Apostles also may fail. This conclusion is the **INDUCTIVE LEAP**---- extending the example of Theudas and Judas to the Apostles. "Usually, inductive conclusions cannot be called universally true, though, because they are **generalizations, and exceptions are always possible.** (emphasis mine) Rather than being true or false, they are more or less possible."**9**

What causes these analogies to form a weak conclusion/recommendation/generalization? Answer: the examples of Thedas and Judas do not correlate accurately to the Apostles: Theudas and Judas were leading a political insurrection while the Apostles were leading a spiritual infusion of Christianity. Theudas and Judas were seeking to overthrow the Roman Government; the Apostles were not attacking the Roman Government, but teaching Jesus is the Messiah. The inductive leap was weak------yet God still used Gamaliel's conclusion/recommendation/ generalization to release the Apostles for further spread of the gospel. Gamaliel generalized the Apostles also may fail----like Theudas and Judas, or they may succeed: therefore, he took a "Wait and see" approach.

The main issue the Sanhedrin had with the Apostles was not their **METHOD** of preaching, teaching, and evangelism, but their **MESSAGE** of Jesus as the Messiah, the Son of God. The Apostles were not using modern music styles contemporary with the first century; nor were they advocating novel techniques to lure people into the synagogue; nor were they using a projection screen in the synagogue to display words from the Psalms in their worship services. No, they simply believed and taught Jesus was the Messiah, the Savior, the Son of God------- resulting in anger from the Sanhedrin.

TESTS OF PROBABILITY. What factors determine the probability of a conclusion/recommendation or the likelihood the analogies of Theudas and Judas would apply to the Apostles? Geisler and Brooks list four **10** essential factors applicable to all forms of inductive logic: (1) number of cases; (2) representation of evidence; (3) scrutiny of evidence; (4) application of evidence

(1) NUMBER OF CASES. This factor asks the question: "How many cases are examined?" We want a broad number of cases across a wide spectrum, but Gamaliel only listed two examples of political insurrection, when in fact there were other instances of political insurrection against the Roman government. The greater number of cases studied, the greater is the chance the probability will be increased, but Gamaliel failed in this first factor with insufficient number of cases.

(2) REPRESENTATION OF EVIDENCE. This factor asks the question: "How representative is the evidence?" We want a broad spectrum of people with a wide social, racial, economic and religious experiences to insure proper evidence, but Gamaliel failed in this second factor with limited representation in Theudas and Judas.

(3) SCRUTINY OF EVIDENCE. This factor asks the question: "How carefully was the evidence examined.?" Did Gamaliel critically examine the evidence in Theudas and

Judas, their followers, conditions prompting their insurrection, and isolate the causes from the results? The context of Acts 5:38-40 suggest minimal explanation of these questions; therefore, we conclude he also failed in this third factor with seeming cursory, selective evidence.

(4) APPLICATION OF EVIDENCE.
This factor asks the question: "How does the evidence gained apply to the greater body of knowledge we already have in general?" Does it contradict anything of which we are certain? Does it help better explain things? Specifically the application of evidence revolves around growth and success based on either human or divine origin: "For if their purpose or activity is of human origin, it will fail. But if it is from God, you will not be able to stop these men." Theudas and Judas, we assume, were convinced their movement of insurrection was from God-----but obviously they failed. The apostles, likewise, were convinced their movement was also from God. Does Gamaliel's recommendation of "wait and see" or extended time add to the general body of knowledge regarding institutions of "human" and "divine" origin? The answer is no! Our common, historical knowledge shows mixed results: some human institutions and movements do grow and succeed: others do not. Some divine institutions and movements grow and succeed; others do not. So, the application of evidence to the wider field of knowledge of universal growth and success here in the context of Acts 5:38-40 shows **IMPROBABILITY**----based on the analogies of Theudas and Judas. His reasoning process of Theudas and Judas and the four tests of probability, in my opinion, lead to **IMPROBABILITY.**

Conspicuously absent from Gamaliel's arguments in Acts 5:38-40 is any reference to the explosive growth of Christianity, yet I am certain he knew of its fast, wide-spread growth: the whole region of Jerusalem was alive to this new Christianity. He was not a spiritual ostrich with his head in the ground! He was well aware of the threat of this new religion to traditional Judaism.

There appears to be a contradiction between the **IMPROBABILITY** and the **PROBABILITY** of Gamaliel's conclusion/recommendation. The improbability is based on his faulty reasoning process absent from knowledge of Christianity's amazing growth, but the probability is greatly increased with his knowledge of the number of conversions and miracles among the citizens of Jerusalem.

Gamaliel's recommendation to set free the apostles was not guaranteed **PROOF** Christianity would succeed, but rather his counsel was a **PROBABILITY**---a strong likelihood this new Christianity would grow and prosper because he had already witnessed the spectacular events of 3,000 conversions in Acts 2:41, the miracles of Peter in Acts 3:1-10, the increased number of 5,000 followers in Acts 4:4, and the continuing miraculous signs and wonders of the apostles in Acts 5:12. He desired to "squelch" this movement-----but he could not: he was powerless. Therefore, he counseled a "wait and see" approach: maybe this new movement might stumble, weaken, and finally dissolve------like the insurrection of Theudas and Judas.

Many people in the evangelical church today misinterpret and misapply the seven false reasons into majoring on "modern methods," "modern music," "fun-filled worship services" as the central ingredient to "big church growth." Sincere Christian leaders overlook the fact that growth, success, and spiritual maturity comes---**not from modern music, or "flashy methods," nor from "relevant, entertaining worship services"**----but from the sovereign will of God. Yes, modern music, modern methods, and "relevant" techniques may initially produce big crowds and seemingly "landslide of conversions" in evangelism, but is this emphasis of **PRAGMATISM** clouding the greater emphasis on loyalty to the truth of God's Word? We must not blind ourselves to wholesome, culturally pertinent methods in reaching our post-Christian culture, but never must we compromise allegiance to God's Word and teaching of His Word. We must be faithful in these tasks------and trust God for growth-----in His sovereign timing.

Gamaliel's reasoning process was not **WICKED**, but **FAULTY:** on the surface the rationale seemed convincing, so "right," so logical, yet so deceptive as itemized previously by the seven logic errors. Proverbs 14:6 provides a cutting contrast between the unbelieving mocker and believing disciple: ***"The mocker seeks wisdom and finds none, but knowledge comes easily to the discerning."*** The unbeliever may claim he seeks wisdom, but his immoral lifestyle refutes his assertion. But the believer who has the knowledge of God will over time gain discernment. Is this true of all Christians? No, definitely not! Few Christians possess this spiritual discernment, for it only is attained by a **"meat"** rather than **"milk"** diet of God's Word (Heb. 5:12-14). The knowledge in this proverb refers not to minimal, but maximum knowledge of God and His ways. Discernment is deep insight which severs **PRETENSE from PROBITY; DISGUISE from DISCLOSURE; APPARATION from ADMISSION; CREDULITY from CERTAINTY.** The discerning Christian can see through the fog of Gamaliel's false logic and know why he could only offer the best humanistic wisdom to the Sanhedrin.

(2) Pharisees Matthew 15:1-14 gives sharp words of Jesus to the legalistic nature of the Pharisees causing them to be "offended." He then summarizes their behavior as "***blind guides. If a blind man leads a blind man, both will fall into a pit.***"(Matt. 15:14). Gamaliel was a Pharisee----chief of the Pharisees, a blind guide leading other blind men----into a pit of false logic. Can these words apply to Gamaliel, or must we restrict them to the Pharisees in general, and exclude Gamaliel? After examining in detail the seven false logic reasons of Gamaliel, I believe we can legitimately consider him a "blind guide." And who are the followers of Gamaliel who follow him into the pit? They are the leaders in the CCM movement and any other believers who misinterpret and misapply Acts 5:34-40.

(3) Wise counselors of Zoan Isaiah 19:11-14 records God's judgment sent on the wise counselors of Zoan---a city in northeast Egypt in the Nile delta. These wise counselors of Pharoah gave **"senseless advice"** to him, and God promised to pour into them a **"spirit of dizziness"** to make Egypt stager in all she does, as a drunkard staggers around in his vomit. The term **"spirit of dizziness"** is a Hebrew word meaning **perverted, mixed, distorted**. These pagan counselors would mix good and evil advice together, and only the discerning man can distinguish between this mixture. A drunk man can not walk straight, but staggers, or weaves from side to side, and this staggering is reflected in Gamaliel's false logic. Did these wise counselors of Zoan inculcate in their logic an appeal to ignorance like Gamaliel? We do not know; all we know is their counsel was **"senseless."**

Just as God sent a **"spirit of dizziness"** into the counselors of Zoan, so God allowed a similar **"spirit of dizziness"** into Gamaliel's rationale causing the non-discerning Christian to stagger and weave in misinterpretation and misapplication of methods of worship and humanistic philosophies God's Word never intended. Gamaliel's advice here in Acts 5:32-40 is a **"mixed bag"** of **"dizziness"** filled with ***seeming truth and submerged error*-----often misinterpreted and misapplied. Clear, analytical thinking is required to keep from staggering and weaving through this passage.

(4) Counselors of Rehoboam I Kings 12:10-19 records the request of the Israelites to Rehoboam to reduce the galling taxation imposed on them by Solomon, but Rehoboam would not listen; instead he followed the counsel of his selected friends who advised an even heavier tax burden: ***"I will make it even heavier. My father scourged you with whips; I will scourge you with scorpions."*** This advice and resulting action resulted in the kingdom being split into the ten northern tribes of Israel ruled by Jereboam and the two southern tribes of Judah ruled by Rehoboam. Did these counselors of Rehoboam use an appeal of ignorance? Again, we do not know, but their counsel resulted in a divided kingdom------as churches today are sadly being split by worldly music------- endorsed by a misinterpretation and misapplication of Acts 5:34-40.

God had previously prophesized through Ahijah the prophet the future divided kingdom between Israel and Judah (I Kings 11:29-40). Ahijah took hold of the new cloak worn by Jereboam, and tore it into twelve pieces (I Kings 11:30), pronouncing the ten northern tribes would be ruled by Jereboam, and the two southern tribes ruled by Rehoboam. This prophesy was not a **verbal,** but **visual** announcement of God----a memorable "visual aid."

Now in I Kings 12:10-19 God will fulfill His prophecy of dividing the kingdom of Israel by allowing Rehoboam to believe and follow the **unwise** counsel of his young, selected friends, rather than the **wise** counsel of elders from Solomon. God did not give approval to the unwise counsel, the **REASONS,** but He approved the **RESULTS** of a divided kingdom. This incident in Rehoboam's life illustrates again God's sovereignty in building His kingdom. Nor did God approve of Gamaliel's **REASONS**, but He did approve of the **RESULTS**------ release and freedom of the Apostles to spread the Gospel.

e. Visual summary of false logic

The following line graph bar is adapted from Stephen Naylor Thomas**11** in his book , Argument Evaluation. It visually displays the **degrees of validity** of all forms of logical thinking. The bar graph depicts weak and moderate arguments that are classed as **"invalid,"** and strong arguments classed as **"valid."**

Valid reasoning is defined as reasoning which is true and would justify believing or expecting the conclusion to be true. Invalid reasoning, the truth of the statement(s) given as the reason(s) (supposing they were true) would guarantee, or make extremely likely, the truth of the conclusion. **Invalid reasoning** are reasons, even assuming or supposing they were true, still would not justify believing or expecting the conclusion to be true. The conclusion is a false conclusion based on true reasons.

Sound reasoning means the steps of reasoning are valid and all relevant reasons are true. **Unsound reasoning** means reasons in which either one (or more) of the relevant reasons is false, or the step of inference is invalid, or both. **Deductively valid** means there is no conceivable or imaginable way in which the reasons could be true and yet the conclusion be false. Truth of the premises would totally guarantee the truth of the conclusion. It is logically impossible for the reasons to be true and the conclusion false. **Strong** refers to the likely hood of the conclusion. If the reasons were true, they would make the truth of the conclusion extremely likely, certain beyond any reasonable doubt, **"virtually a sure thing,"** but not totally guaranteed. (How likely is "extremely likely?" Likely enough to make it reasonable to stake something of great value on the truth of the conclusion if the reasons are true and likely enough to serve as a definitely reliable basis for actions.)

DEGREES OF VALIDITY

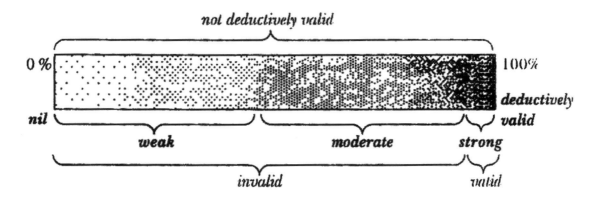

Summary of Degrees of Validity
(or "Degrees of Confirmation")

In view of the seven avenues of false logic used by Gamaliel in Acts 5:34-40, (1) false analogy, (2) poisoning the well; (3) appeal to force; (4) appeal to many; (5) bifurcation; (6) hasty generalization; (7) appeal to ignorance, where would you place his arguments on this bar graph? Some of these arguments are stronger than others, but I personally consider all of them as **INVALID** and disconnected from the **"sovereign"** true conclusion/recommendation. The

68

conclusion/recommendation of Gamaliel is not based on his arguments or reasons, but solely on God's sovereign will. The seven reasons or premises are supposed to lead to and support the conclusion/recommendation of Gamaliel, but they fail because they are inherently **INVALID**. His recommendation, therefore, must be **DIVORCED** and severed from his arguments, as shown in the following bar graph.

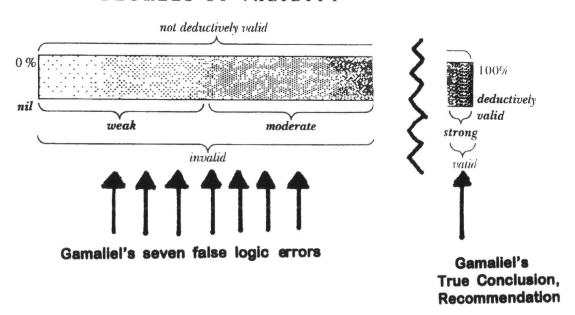

How do we know God's sovereign will was at stake? Because of His command in Acts 1:8 addressed to the apostles to spread the gospel first in Jerusalem, second in Judea, third in Samaria, and fourth to the ends of the earth. At this point in Acts 5:32-40 the apostles had already reached the first goal in Jerusalem. Had Gamaliel recommended execution for the apostles, then the work of God may have terminated, and God's command in Acts 1:8 would have been thwarted. Release of the apostles, however, permitted further spread of the gospel into Judea, Samaria, and into the Roman world----affirming God's sovereign will in Gamaliel's recommendation. Gamaliel never realized he was the instrument, despite his faulty logic, was used by God to further spread Christianity.

Specifically, much of the CCM movement with its emphasis on fleshly music style, like Gamaliel's arguments, is based on faulty reasons: **CASUISTRY, PRAGMATISM, UTILITARIANISM**, discussed thoroughly in Chapter 7, Application #9.

CHAPTER 6

Standards in Music Selection

**"Whatever is true, whatever is noble, whatever is right,
Whatever is pure, whatever is lovely, whatever is admirable---
If anything is excellent or praiseworthy---think about such things."
Philippians 4:8**

Previous chapters have demonstrated an exposition of Exodus 32:17-8; Leviticus 10:1-8; Acts 5:40; and Colossians 2:4,8,23 in presenting a **NEGATIVE** example of selecting worldly, pagan music with its evil philosophy. Exodus 15:1-18 and Deut. 32:1-44 presented a **POSITIVE** example of contemporary music used by Moses. In this chapter we will explore in depth the criteria for selecting good, wholesome, edifying music in worship by examining eight standards revealed in Philippians 4:8. Hopefully these eight standards will help each Christian in knowing **"how to select worship music,"**----music pleasing to God, is Christ-centered, focused on God's holiness and majesty, and free from worldly, pagan overtones of evil associations. You may not know all the technicalities and theory of music; you may not even be able to read the musical notes on a sheet of music, nor consider yourself as a good singer, but as a Christian you can apply the eight words of Philippians 4:8 to any kind of music and discern whether it is poor, sensual, entertaining, jazzy, self-centered, good, or excellent. You have the Holy Spirit and He will guide you into all the truth of this one verse.

The issue of Contemporary Christian Music (and other areas of knowledge as well) **SIGNALLY HINGES** on a correct interpretation and application of this single verse; therefore, this discussion will describe in detail categories of benchmarks under eighteen areas: **(1) Number, (2) Sphere, (3) Definition, (4) Distinction, (5) Elevation, (6) Preparation, (7) Instruction, (8) Correlation, (9) Duration, (10) Personalization, (11) Confirmation, (12) Progression, (13) Subjectivity, (14) Maturation, (15) Categorization, (16) Defection, (17) Demonstration, (18) Illustration.**

(1) Their Number

Eight bench marks, or measuring standards, are recorded by Paul in Philippians 4:8 for evaluating music and other fields of knowledge. Eight words summarize the procedure for music selection: **(1) True, (2) Noble, (3) Right, (4) Pure, (5) Lovely, (6) Admirable, (7) Excellent, (8) Praiseworthy.** This verse in Philippians is not directly addressing music, but encompasses all realms of knowledge, ethics, morals, and behavior. Spiritual discernment is the **GENERAL TERM** for expressing value judgments, and Paul provides here in Philippians 4:8 the **SPECIFIC TERMS** in making these value judgments. In Moses we see the **PRACTICE** of discernment at Mt. Sinai: ***what is discerned;*** in Paul we see the **PROCEDURE** of discernment at the church in Phillipi: ***how discernment is performed.***

(2) Their Sphere

These eight words are **NOT DISTINCTLY** Christian terms, but rather function in the **SECULAR or SOCIAL** sphere of life. Paul adapts these terms from the Greek-Roman culture of his day because they describe virtuous ideals and values every man, woman, and child should pursue. In the Greek-Roman school systems of Paul's time, each child memorized these eight words or values and expended mental and emotional effort to attain these social virtues in their conduct and decision-making to become a **"good, well-respected citizen."** Even though the social culture of Philippi and its surrounding area was pagan in religious worship, yet there remained good, positive values in the Greek culture, and Paul, being the great teacher, used these terms as ideals for Christians also as they worked in the social system of that time.

(3) Their Definition

These eight words and their abbreviated meaning are as follows:

TRUE	right and genuine; real; sterling; unfeigned; absence of pretense or illusion; ultimate reality rather than false, temporal, shallow, superficial, and apparent reality
NOBLE	worthy of respect; dignified; reverent; sublime; august; anything which wins and charms by its dignity and reverence.
RIGHT	meeting the standards of God, not merely the standards of man
PURE	morally pure and upright; commanding awe and respect; sexually chaste
LOVELY	pleasing, agreeable, amiable, anything which inspires love and graciousness, like a welcome fragrance "which gives pleasure to all and causes distaste to none." **1**
ADMIRABLE	well-sounding; attractive; appealing; whatever is kind and likely to win people, and avoid giving offence
EXCELLENT	inspires and measures the highest moral goodness in man
PRAISEWORTHY	conduct which wins the praise of man

These eight words are divided into three categories: **(1) INTRINSICALLY ETERNAL, (2) INTRINSICALLY MORAL, (3) EXTRINSICALLY REPUTATIONAL.** The first word, ***TRUE***, is a standard of **intrinsic eternality**, the foundation for the remaining seven words, and measures ultimate in contrast to temporal reality. Is cancer, automobile accidents, incest, rape, child abuse, adultery true? Definitely yes; they exist in our sinful world, but Paul does not command us to think on these things because they are **_TEMPORAL REALITY_** and will be replaced by **_ULTIMATE REALITY_** in heaven when these sins and injustices are replaced by righteousness and justice. Cancer and child abuse are not illusions; they are real-----but temporary. We are to think on things of eternal value as Paul instructs in Col. 3:2: **"Set your mind on things above, not on earthly things."**

The next five words (Noble, Right, Pure, Lovely, Admirable) are **intrinsically moral**----measuring the inherent qualities composing the substance of anything: music, literature, sculpture, art, carpentry, gardening, dress standards. We are to think and look for these five moral qualities in any area of life to discern value.

The last two words, (Excellent, Praiseworthy) are **extrinsically reputational** and form a general summary of the previous six words. After examining the intrinsic qualities of true, noble, right, pure, lovely, admirable, we must step back and discern the general reputation of these qualities: are they excellent and praiseworthy in the minds and values of moral, knowledgeable, refined men and women? Do these six traits in music receive acclaim, honor, and accolades from mature Christians? See the following chart depicting the arrangement and organization of these eight virtues.

The first six virtues are **SPECIFIC** in nature----detailing precise qualities to examine in all issues; the last two **(Excellent, Praiseworthy)** are **GENERAL** or **SUMMARY** of the previous six---meaning **EXCELLENCE and PRAISEWORTHINESS** in truth, nobility, righteousness, purity, loveliness, and admirableness. The standards are extremely high because their absence is tragic in consequences: moral, ethical, behavioral corruption and mediocrity in all areas of life.

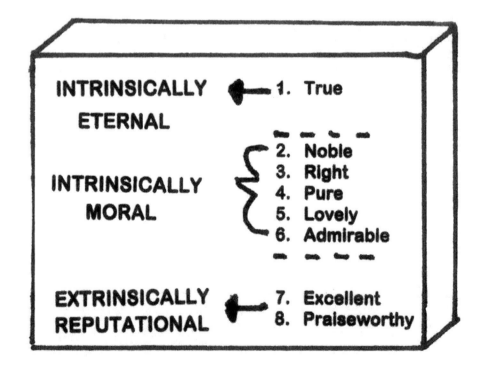

(4) Their Distinction

How are these traits distinct? How are they contrasted? These positive traits are here contrasted with their negative opposite:

POSITIVE TRAITS	NEGATIVE TRAITS
True..................<>................	**False**—artificial, superficial, temporal
Noble..................<>................	**Ignoble**---disgraceful, morally low; lacking in reverence; ignoble; vulgar
Right..................<>................	**Wrong**---wicked, unjust
Pure..................<>................	**Impure**---dirty, defiled
Lovely..................<>................	**Ugly**---unsightly, offensive
Admirable..................<>................	**Despicable**---detestable, depraved
Excellent..................<>................	**Inferior**---substandard, mediocre
Praiseworthy..................<>................	**Dishonorable**---shameful, embarrassing

In the city of Philippi (and in our modern cities today also) these negative traits exist in music, art, sculpture, literature, drama, conversation, clothing styles, interior decoration trends, and business transactions. We as Christians living in a secular society must refrain from adopting and inculcating these negative traits into our values, ethical standards, and conduct.

(5) Their Elevation

Paul uses these eight virtues and **ELEVATES** them from the **SOCIALLY DISTINCT** level to a higher standard---God's level of **DIVINE DISTINCTION.** This is called in the field of education the ***law of apperception: going from the known to the unknown, or acquiring future knowledge based on present experiences.*** He and the Philippians already knew the eight virtues as ideals for good citizenship in the Greek-Roman culture of that day, so he started where they were in their thinking and built on this social knowledge to advance them to a higher standard of God's requirement. Paul used this same educational law in Acts 17:10-34 in the city of Athens where he started his discourse of the **"unknown god"** and proceeded to tell his listeners about the **"knowable God----Jesus Christ."** Every good teacher, like Paul, will begin where the students are in their understanding, build on this knowledge, and elevate their knowledge to a higher standard.

An informed Greek-Roman citizen would judge and discern these eight virtues based on **SOCIAL STANDARDS;** Paul introduces and elevates these virtues to a much higher level: **GOD'S STANDARDS.** Truth, Nobility, Righteousness, Purity, Loveliness, Admirableness, Excellence, and Praiseworthiness are now measured by God's, not man's, standards. He and the principles of His Word determine these qualities-----not the biased opinions of self-centered man. ***Humanism is dethroned; God is enthroned!*** Apperception is thus achieved when I judge nobility and loveliness on God's higher standards. He, through the Holy Spirit, gives discernment to the Christian to **"judge all things." (I Cor. 2:15).** The following diagram depicts two standards of judging these eight virtues: **Social Standards or God's Standards.** Note the eight words remain the same in both columns, but the standards are on a higher level under God's Standards

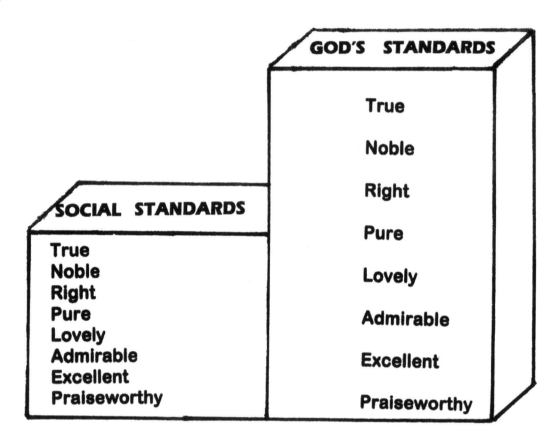

Yes, we must consider society's view on these virtues, but as Christians we march to the beat of a higher Drummer: God! We determine truth, nobility, rightness, purity, loveliness, admirableness, excellence, and praiseworthiness by God's standards revealed in His Word. How do we know these eight virtues must be interpreted by God's, not man's, standards? Because of the context! Paul's list is surrounded by references to rejoice in the Lord (verse 4), be gentle to all men because the Lord is near (verse 5), avoid anxiety and pray (verse 6), God's peace will guard you (verse 7), and God's peace will be with you (verse 9).

(6) Their Preparation

These eight virtues can not be isolated and extracted from the context in Philippians 4, but must be integrated and harmonized with truth from the preceding verses. Four commands and one promise precede verse 8: the commands are to **(a) "rejoice in all circumstances,"—4:4; (b) "be gentle toward all people,"---4:5; (c) "pray about everything;"--4:6; (d) "give thanks to God;"---4:6;** and the resulting promise will occur: **"God's peace will guard your hearts and minds in Christ Jesus;"---4:7.** Obedience to these four commands and reception of God's

74

calming peace are necessary to **"think on the eight virtues"** of verse 8. The following circular diagram illustrates the harmony of verse 8 with the context of verses 4-6. Note two promises surround the command in 4:8 to **"think on these things:"** God will give His peace **PRIOR** to thinking on eight virtues (4:7), and give His peace **FOLLOWING** thinking on these virtues (4:9).

CONTEXTUAL COMMANDS

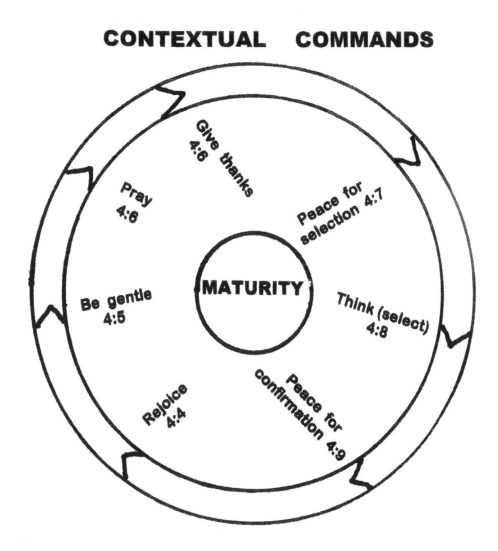

God's peace calms our minds in preparation for ***SELECTION*** in verse 8, and God's peace will give ***CONFIRMATION*** of selection in verse 9: **"God's peace will be with you."** The principle is clear: ***God's tranquility both precedes and follows my selectivity.*** A worried, anxious, depressed, conflicted Christian cannot think straight and clear: his lack of tranquility prevents him from selecting things that are true, noble, and lovely. His judgments and discernment are marred by an unsettled mind and turbulent emotions. But when he rejoices, shows a gentle, teachable spirit toward other people, prays about everything, thanks God for everything------- then God's peace will calm his thinking and feelings. He will be qualified to discern all eight virtues, and his preparation of verses 4-7 enables him to receive instruction of verse 8. If you desire to make the best choices, then first gain God's peace and tranquility.

(7) Their Instruction

Four important elements are present in Paul's instruction: __(a) the definition, (b) the kind of action, (c) the target audience, (d) the leveling influence.__ **(a) FIRST, the definition.** What exactly does Paul mean by **"think on these things"?** The Greek word for "think" is **LOGIZOMAI** and means to think critically, not mere casual thinking. This Greek word is used in the commercial world of business issues as unemotional reckoning of business affairs, such as tabulation of bank records, legal documents, and real estate transactions. In business relationships emotional feelings must be discarded; careful, analytical thinking is demanded. **2** The purpose of such careful thought is to gain factual information in determining the difference between what is good, better, and best.

Such thinking is Paul's answer to his request for the Philippians in 1:9-10: ***"And this is my prayer: that your love may abound more and more in Knowledge and depth of insight, so that you may be able to discern what is best....."*** Note, he did not pray the Philippians would discern good things, nor even better things, but what is best! Discernment is knowing the difference between good, better, and best.

How can such critical thinking occur? Bombard issues, events, music, philosophies with critical, scrutinizing thinking. Analyze in minute detail what you read and hear in conversations to determine the truth or falsity of projected ideas. Distinguish between negative and critical thinking: negative thinking looks for unwholesome, despicable traits; critical thinking looks for ultimate truth in contrast to temporal truth and error. For example, aging is a natural process of degeneration: I become slower in my walk, lose my hair and eyesight, gain weight, and ultimately die. But Paul does not mean to think critically about such issues because while they are true, they are temporal truths. Ultimate truth looks to the future when Christ will change my body at the resurrection to a perfect, never-dying body. Paul gives Col. 3:2 as an apt commentary on critical thinking: **"Set your minds on things above, not on earthly things."** Don't think about cancer, abortion, homosexuality, death, mortgage bills, crime rate, disease, terrorism. Do these things exist? Yes, of course, but these are temporal truths. Rather, think critically on eternal truths which will aid us in becoming more Christ-like.

(b) SECOND, the kind of action. Paul commands: "think on these things." The Greek grammar is incisive here emphasizing ***continuous, ongoing action:*** "keep on thinking on these things; don't stop thinking on these things." Another translation of Paul's words are "let your mind dwell on these virtues." The purpose is to discern or judge between what does and does not measure up to these values, and every Christian each day faces discernment in all eight categories. The listing of the **POSITIVE** virtues automatically implies the **NEGATIVE** traits, and Paul would command: "Don't' think on these negative traits of falsehood, ignobility, wickedness, impurity, ugliness, despicability, inferiority, and dishonorableness; don't let your mind dwell on them; don't even expose yourself to these corrupting influences; run fast from them; don't associate with people who display these vices in their character and conduct."

Biblical thinking is a rarity today in the Church,------substituting emphasis on emotions or feelings, and pragmatism or what works. Pastors and music directors no longer ask, **"Is it true, noble, right, pure, lovely admirable, excellent, and praiseworthy?"** but rather **"Will the**

76

music and sermon make the people feel good and gain a spiritual high experience," or **"Will the music and sermon work----meaning, will it entertain and motivate people to return next Sunday and put more money in the offering plate?"** In marketing strategy the emphasis is on the consumer-----meeting his felt needs: making sure the customer is happy. Pastors, music directors, leaders of denominations, and Bible teachers in seminaries have adopted this marketing strategy for the church as a means to gaining bigger and bigger attendance in the Sunday morning worship service.

Paul did not embrace this **"consumer"** mentality of making Christians **"feel good;"** He demanded a higher standard: Biblical, critical thinking about doctrine and truth as it applies to all areas of life. Sadly, much contemporary Christian music today fails to promote this serious, analytical thinking because many of the popular choruses use trite, insipid words repeated over and over in monotony to tunes devoid of a naturally flowing melody, and many sermons are more correctly categorized as a spiritual **"pep talk," or "motivational speech"** using humor, anecdotes, dramatic vocal flourishes, expressive gestures------but little Biblical explanation, teaching, and thinking. The Christian may depart from such services **"feeling good"-------but mentally empty!** He is not challenged to think, and walks out into the business world naïve and gullible to the persuasive logic and philosophy of pagan values. The emphasis is no longer **CLARITY OF THINKING,** but **EUPHORIA OF FEELINGS!**

Emotional and spiritual experiences. Distinction must be made between an emotional and spiritual experience. Kimberly Smith comments on this distinction: "An emotional experience does not necessarily mean we've had a spiritual experience." **3** She illustrates this observation by attendance at a football game, a symphony, or at the Veteran's Memorial in Washington, D.C. In all three locations our emotions may be moved by the roaring crowd at a football game, pleasurable music at a symphony concert, or somber reflection at the memorial to deceased soldiers, but divorced from a genuine spiritual experience. Our emotions often are affected by hormones, lack of sleep, or eating pizza late at night, yet these elements are distinct from our spiritual nature. Experiencing an emotional upsurge from some fleshly music in church does not automatically mean we have had a deeply spiritual experience------it may be deceptive, deluding us into a false thinking of worship.

Two examples illustrate this distinction between emotional and spiritual experience. The first example is in Mark 4:1-20 where Jesus gives teaching on the four kinds of soil (hard, rocky, thorny, good),and four responses to the seed sown on the soil. No response is seen from the hard, compacted soil, and the birds devour the seed. An emotional response is present in the rocky and thorny soil. The emotions of people quickly respond in the rocky soil, but the shallow response quickly dies----resulting in no growth in fruitfulness. Emotional response from the thorny soil seems genuine, but weeds and thorns grow, choke out the good seed, resulting in loss of fruitfulness. In both rocky and thorny soil there is stirring of emotions motivating commitment to Christ-----but it is shallow and selfish. Only seed sown on good soil produces fruit of thirty, sixty, and a hundred fold. This soil alone represents a genuine spiritual experience.

The second example is in Matthew 8:18-22 where Jesus records the words of a would-be disciple who claimed: "I will follow you wherever you go." Apparently the emotions of this man were stirred but he lacked spiritual commitment because he made excuses or conditions to following Christ. Jesus promised him, "Foxes have holes and birds of the air have nests, but the Son of Man has no place to lay his head." This man failed to count the cost. How can we tell the difference between emotional and spiritual experiences? **By observing on-going fruitfulness, maturity, and discernment in the life of a believer.**

This diagram shows distinction between man's emotional and spiritual response to music, reading of God's Word, or preaching. Our emotions are on the surface, but our spiritual level is much deeper. Fleshly music may target our emotions to ultimately reach the deeper level of spiritual commitment, but this strategy can be deceptive because we are easily influenced by immediate, temporal change of attitudes in the worshipper. Will this seeming, positive change in attitudes last a month, year, five years, fifteen years, thirty years? Is the response rocky, thorny, or good soil? Using fleshly, worldly music or pop, entertaining, story-telling preaching may stir emotions and produce "good feelings" in the listener, but this approach falters in reaching the deeper level of true spiritual commitment. Godly music and clear exposition of Scripture which measures up to the eight virtues of Philippians 4:8 will not target Level #1---our euphoria of feelings, but Level #2---clarity of thinking at the deeper level of spiritual commitment, and produce abundant fruit.

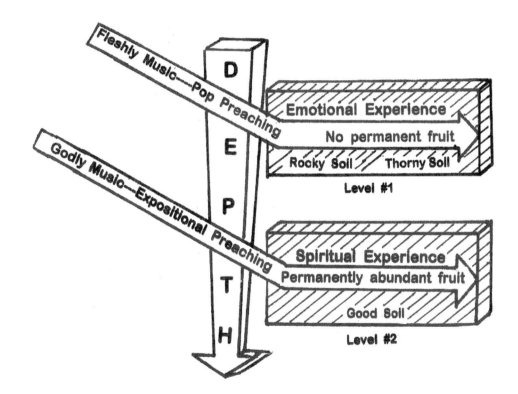

(c) THIRD, the target audience. The word **"think"** is an imperative verb----a word of command----and is in the **PLURAL** not **SINGULAR** person---meaning Paul is not addressing one individual, but a group of individuals----the Christians in the Church at Philippi. They as a group, as a community of believers, must together keep thinking of these positive virtues and adopt them into their **CORPORATE** and **INDIVIDUAL** lives. These eight benchmark values, therefore, are **CORPORATELY**, not solely and **INDIVIDUALLY** determined. Yes, I as an individual have a part in determining the things that are true, noble, right, pure, lovely, admirable, excellent, and praiseworthy, but I must submit and blend my **INDIVIDUAL** judgment to the combined thinking and judgment of the **CORPORATE** body of believers; I must consider and evaluate their judgment too. **INDIVIDUAL** judgment and discernment can be biased and skewed by personal preferences, immaturity, and lack of knowledge, but consideration to the **CORPORATE** body of believers serves as a safeguard against this personal bias and immaturity.

(d) FOURTH, the leveling influence. CORPORATE determination of these virtues prevents the *"lone ranger"* mentality present in the common thinking of Christians who say to themselves, **"I'll decide for myself what is true, right, and pure. No one is going to tell me what to do. I know how to judge and I don't have to listen to anyone!"** This arrogant, defiant, self-centered spirit is not new; it reverts to the key verse in the book of Judges: *"everyman did that which was right in his own eyes." (Judges 17:6; 21:25)* Then and now the **"lone ranger"** Christian rides his horse named **"Pride"** and refuses to listen to the seasoned, experienced, knowledge of other people. He is a law unto himself!

Whether the area is music, architecture, building design, interior decorating, cooking, financial investments, or how I dress, I must listen and consider the knowledge of other people who are well trained in their respective fields. I don't have all knowledge; no one does-----except God-----and He has given guidance in His Word instructing me to be humble and seek wisdom from other people who are experts in their field. That is smart thinking!

Everyone has certain personal tastes, likes, and dislikes in music. That's normal. But few of us are thoroughly trained in the large field of music theory, music history, music performance, music composition, music types. We must consider the seasoned judgment of these highly trained professionals and their views on musical standards. Will all of them agree on each detail of music? Of course not, but there will be an overall consensus among them regarding the proven principles contributing to music which is true, noble, right, pure, lovely, admirable, excellent, and praiseworthy. **SECULAR CORPORATE** judgment is needed as a leveling influence, and it must combine with **SPIRITUAL CORPORATE** judgment of seasoned Christians in the Church who gain their spiritual maturity from God's Word. This dual **CORPORATE JUDGMENT** will starve the **"lone ranger"** Christian.

An illustration of teach-ability is seen in house construction. I may build my house in all sincerity, but overlook needed details in laying the proper foundation----failing to dig deep enough for the concrete blocks. **"I know what I'm doing,"** I claim, but refuse to listen to knowledgeable contractors and engineers. After the house is completed, cracks begin forming in the walls; doors become jammed; the brick chimney begins pulling way from the wall---------because of insufficient foundation and poor grade mortar. The foundation was only the surface reason; the deeper reason was *personal pride* in the builder: lack of a teachable spirit. Jesus in the Sermon on the Mount identifies this man as building his house on sand, instead of rock.

(8) Their Correlation

Is Pàul giving a new command about our thought lives? Definitely not, because Solomon in Proverbs 4:23 taught the same principle: **"Guard your heart (mind, emotions, will), for**

it is the wellspring of life." Our mind, will, and emotions is compared to a well of water in the ground requiring a guard rail constructed around it to prevent any contamination from entering the well. From this well we can bring forth pure or corrupted water: right thinking thus produces right behavior.

(9) Their Duration

Application #7 above **(INSTRUCTION)** discussed the on-going, continuous nature of thinking on things true, noble, right……. Why is this duration of thinking prolonged? Why must we continually reflect on these eight virtues? The answer swings on **THREE** elements: **(a) Nature of the object, (b) Nature of mankind, and (c) Nature of spirituality.**

(a) Nature of the object. Two words summarize these eight virtues: **QUALITATIVE DURABILITY.** Excellence and praiseworthiness is not always immediately detectable, but is only judged over a period of time. We as humans want **CURRENT IMMEDIACY;** Paul stresses **TESTED DURABILITY.** We are enamored with shiny new shoes which fit comfortably on our feet-------and at a rock-bottom sale price, so we make the purchase and pride ourselves on **"getting a good deal"**-------until two weeks later when the stitching separates the vamp from the sole, and we learn the sad, costly lesson: they are shiny, but not long-lasting. We got **"stuck"** with poor quality because we failed to thoroughly examine the shoes, reputation of the manufacturer, and testimony of customers.

Years ago the world-famous Louvre Art Museum in Paris, France loaned the priceless painting, **The Mona Lisa,** by Leonardo da Vinci, and painted in the 16th century, to the New York Metropolitan Museum of Art; people lined up for hours to get a look at this historically famous painting. This magnificent art work is perhaps the most famous painting in the world, and acclaimed by art connoisseurs and laymen as the ultimate standard of art design. Bullet proof glass was placed in front of the painting and security guards stood at attention on each side. One by one, Americans walked slowly by and paused briefly before this acclaimed piece of art. One sincere man blurted out in disgust, *"So that's the famous Mona Lisa! I don't see anything so great about this painting!"* One of the security guards replied in a tactful, but pointed manner, *"Sir, the Mona Lisa has proved herself for centuries; she is not on trial. You are on trial!"* Great art survives; it endures the test of time; it stands up under the close scrutiny of art collectors. Its excellence has proved itself and met all eight tests of Philippians 4:8.

Great music, architecture, landscaping, painting, writing, and wood-working craftsmanship, like **The Mona Lisa,** will survive the test of time and prove its magnificent worth. It will demonstrate **QUALITATIVE DURABILITIY.** The writings and plays composed by William Shakespeare, called the Bard of Avon, England are still acclaimed today as great literary masterpieces: they have endured through all these years. Our responsibility as Christians in our worship of God and Christ is to discern this value in all areas.

(b) Nature of mankind. We as humans are by nature impatient------we want to make quick decisions and move on to some other interest, but judging and discerning the eight values of Philippians 4:8 often takes time---------examining the historical style of music, its effects on people, its reputation among knowledgeable Christians and trained musicians. These eight qualities are not instantly acquired, and our appreciation must be cultivated by repeated exposure to the issue being examined. You may listen to a hymn, classical piece of music, or view famous art and be **"turned off"** by it. You may be like the sincere man standing in front of **The Mona Lisa**: you see no great value in the painting nor in certain hymns or classical music. For a variety of reasons you do not like it, but if you persist in **"continual thinking"** or listening you may in time learn to appreciate the beauty, harmony, unity, structure, and flow of the music or noble qualities of a painting or sculpture. You will conclude, ***"Yes, this music, art, literature, sculpture, construction work, business management, financial investment measures up to Philippians 4:8!"***

   (c) Nature of spirituality. Philippians 4:8 is set in the broader context of the chapter focusing around the issue of spiritual maturity or spiritual stability----traits measuring the marks of spiritual maturity, and one central trait is ***DISCERNMENT*** : assessing, evaluating, and judging between **GOOD, BETTER, and BEST**----or between **MEDIOCRITY and MAGNIFICENCE.** The discipline of continuous, prolonged thinking produces a two-fold benefit in Christians: skill in judging issues, and skill in developing spiritual maturity. ***Discerning judgment and development of spiritual maturity both require extensive time.*** That is why Paul taught the **DURATION** of thinking.

(10) Their Personalization

   The eight **ABSTRACT, THEORICAL** values of verse 8 become **CONCRETE, PRACTICAL** values in Philippians 4:9 when Paul says: **"Whatever you have learned or received or heard from me, or seen in me----put into practice. And the God of peace will be with you."** Paul used himself as a living, personal model of the eight values he had just commanded the Philippian Christians; he spent protracted time thinking on things that were true, noble, and right, and displayed these values in a practical way in his own life. That is why he said, **"All the things you have learned from me, received from me, and seen in me-----put these same values to practice in your own life."** His life was transparent; he hid nothing from the Philippians.

   He began the book of Philippians in 1:9-10 with a prayer for these Christians: **"My prayer is that your love may grow more and more in knowledge and depth of insight so you be able to discern what is best....."** And how can Christians determine what is not merely good, or mediocre, but best? The answer is in his command in Philippians 4:8----**"think on the things that are true, noble, right........"** He begins the book with a **prayer** for **EXCELLENCE** in decision-making, and ends the book with a command on the **procedure** for gaining **EXCELLENCE----thinking on eight virtues.**

   Paul was a tentmaker by trade-----making and selling tents to support him in the ministry while planting churches. I Cor. 4:12 and I Thess. 2:9 record Paul's physical labor of work while planting a church in Corinth and Thessalonica in order to prevent being a burden to the people. He was from Cilicia, known for their high quality goat-skins used in making tents, and various kinds of leather. Since he was a Jew his parents taught him the trade of making tents: selecting the best goat-skins, drying them properly, sewing them together to make various sizes of tents well-secured by good ropes. Though not directly stated, Paul was a living example of making only high-quality goatskin tents and leather goods during his church-planting ministry in Philippi. How do we know? Because he displayed these eight virtues of excellence in his life-----and the Philippians knew it; they knew he never made poor-grade tents. Some of the Christians in Philippi may have purchased from him a goat-skinned tent or leather good from him and could vouch he made excellent tents.

Yes, excellence applies to music------and goat-skin tents! Paul's example of demonstrating these eight values is a command to you and me as well: Live out these eight virtues so other people can see we are not satisfied with poor, nor even mediocre music, but excellence in music, car repair, house cleaning, interior decorating, sewing, building, carpentry, electrical repair, plumbing, dress standards.

Aaron and the Israelites did not choose the best music----they chose worldly, pagan Egyptian music; Paul chose the best music. Aaron could not honestly say, **"whatever you have learned or received or heard from me, or seen in me----put into practice;"** but Paul could say it. Can you say to others: "Talk like me, dress like me, act like me, listen to the kinds of music I hear, think like me, respond like me, build houses like me?"

(11) Their Confirmation

Making decisions in any area of life involves consideration of different courses of action, advantages and disadvantages of each option, and some decisions are more difficult than others. Paul gives words of encouragement to the Philippians and us today in this process of deciding what is true, noble, right: **"God's peace will be with you."** In verse 7 he promised God's peace would **PREPARE** *us in advance* for judging things that are true, noble........; now in verse 9 he promises God's peace will **CONFIRM** *us in and follow us* in selecting the best choices. **CONFIRM** means establish, assure, strengthen, encourage. That is precisely what God does as we think on these eight virtues: He gives us an inner assurance and encouragement we are making the best decisions----we gain God's calming tranquility.

(12) Their Progression

How, in a practical manner, can Christians obey Paul's command to **"think on these things"?** One simple word summarizes this obedience: ***EXPOSE!*** Expose yourself to great art, great music, great sculpture, great literature, great opera, great architecture, great interior decorating, great carpentry, great engineering, great teachers, great orators, great scientists, great authors, great families, great husbands and wives, great fashion styles. Frequently visit art museums; read outstanding, classic books; listen continually to music which has been acclaimed for centuries; attend home shows to see how designers arrange and color-match furniture; examine closely the craftsmanship of fine carpenters and detailed wood makers; enroll in classes where master teachers ply their teaching skills in challenging students to think; walk through creatively designed gardens and landscapes to enjoy the arrangement of colorful flowers and layered landscaping effects; find and observe great families where the husband and wife lead their family in wisdom and godliness. Continual exposure to these varied avenues of greatness will in time mold your own thinking, refinement, and discernment. You will absorb and model the eight virtues Paul commands.

EXPOSURE, however, must be continuous----ongoing. Paul did not command, **"think one time, and expose yourself one time"** to things which are true, noble, and pure; but rather he commanded continuous exposure. **"Keep on attending music concerts, keep on examining skilled carpenters, keep on visiting art museums, keep on consulting interior decorators, keep on walking through colorful landscaped gardens."** This ongoing exposure over time will help you discern what is true, noble, pure, lovely, and you will become a **CHRISTIAN** who has developed **"good taste"** in your values, ethics, conduct, music, manners, clothing styles.

(13) Their Subjectivity

All eight virtues are **SUBJECTIVE,** not **OBJECTIVE** in nature-----meaning there are no outward or scientific standards in discerning these values. **SUBJECTIVE DISCERNMENT,** therefore, relies on seasoned, tested **INTERNAL** values, and the one word which encapsulates all eight words is **REFINEMENT, meaning delicacy or elegance of language, speech, manners, polish.** The opposite of refinement is crudeness, primitiveness, coarseness, harshness. God wants men to be **"Christian gentlemen,"** and women to be **"Christian ladies,"**--------in their manners, values, and in their dress.

SUBJECTIVE JUDGMENT is built on **OBJECTIVE FACTS.** A building contractor can say a house is **"well-built"**; that's his subjective judgment, his opinion----but it is based on many objective facts: deep foundation; high grade mortar; well insulated; high quality framing; fine carpentry in the intricate moldings; plumb (straight) walls; plumbing which exceeds standard building codes; colorful and precise painting. All these objective details justly give the contractor the right to pronounce his judgment of **"well-built."** His opinions can be trusted. All eight virtues in these benchmarks are **SUBJECTIVE,** but, like the building contractor, are based on many detailed **OBJECTIVE** facts.

How do these eight, **SUBJECTIVE** words apply to the issue of discerning music? Shown here is a chart designed to help you discern and evaluate music used in worship of God, and weigh each trait. Three steps are necessary: **(1) Form** a team of four people, and score each of the eight traits by circling 1 to 5 on the scale measuring **"STRONGLY DISAGREE"** to **"STRONGLY AGREE."** **(2) Add** all four scores and divide by four to get an average number. **(3) Discuss** among the team why each member scored each of the eight items. This team approach will help reduce personal bias, lead to increased discernment, and elevate standards of worship music in your church. An ideal score would be 40 points (5 x 8), meaning the music you are evaluating would rank a number "5" on each trait. Your goal is not to aim for 40 points, but an honest, thoughtful, discernment of each trait quality of the music and words. This tool is not designed to **evaluate music in general,** but a **specific song**----whether a psalm set to music, hymn, gospel song, anthem, or praise and worship chorus. Select any song used in the worship service of your church, and evaluate it by this chart.

	STRONGLY DISAGREE				STRONGLY AGREE
TRUE	1	2	3	4	5

1. The music and words sound morally right and genuine rather than shallow, superficial.
2. The music and words present a majestic view of God and Christ?
3. The melodic tune creates thoughtfulness, divine idealism, beauty, holy aspiration, and quiet reverence.

NOBLE	1	2	3	4	5

1. The music and words are worthy of respect, dignified, sublime, august.
2. The music and words rise above the level of mediocrity, cheapness, ignobility.
3. Absent from the words are any hint of triteness, shallowness, insipid expression.

RIGHT	1	2	3	4	5

1. The words and melody meet God's standard of high moral rightness.
2. The tune itself is clean, reverent, holy, humbling.
3. No worldly, jazzy spirit, nor sexy sound found in saloons and rock concerts is present in the music.

PURE	1	2	3	4	5

1. The flow and rhythm of the music emphasizes moral purity and cleanness.
2. The words and music commands awe and respect by expressing grand truth of doctrine in a majestic manner.
3. The tune and beat does not promote any bodily gyrations or sensual movements.

LOVELY	1	2	3	4	5

1. The music sounds pleasing and agreeable to the ears with its blended harmony, and balanced dynamism of loud and quiet passages.
2. The music inspires love, graciousness, and classic beauty like a welcome fragrance.
3. Absent from the music is any sound of harshness, wildness, overpowering volume, dissonance, or monotonous repetition.

ADMIRABLE	1	2	3	4	5

1. The music and words are attractive and harmonious in sound to win praise from people without giving offence to anyone.
2. The music is well-sounding and appealing to inspire reverence and holy worship.
3. Nothing in the music borders on a rock, soft rock, jazzy spirit, or sensuous tone.

EXCELLENT	1	2	3	4	5

1. The music inspires the highest moral goodness among knowledgeable, mature Christians.
2. Knowledgeable people would rate this music as superior, not inferior, magnificent, not mediocre.
3. Nothing in this music emphasizes self-centeredness or personal fleshly feelings.

PRAISEWORTHY	1	2	3	4	5

1. Knowledgeable, mature Christians of high moral conduct praise and extol this music.
2. This music gains wide, high reputation from mature, trained musicians.
3. This music earns the title of "permanently durable," rather than "trendy," from its long years of usage among knowledgeable, mature Christians.

Shown here is a guide in rating your individual and team scores:

50 – 40 Magnificent music
39 - 30 Mediocre music
29 - 19 Marginal music
18 - 9 Poor music
8 - 0 Unsuitable music

Remember you alone determine the first six qualities of true, noble, right, pure, lovely, and admirable; the last two, excellent, praiseworthy, are determined---not by you----but by mature, knowledgeable Christians and non-Christians well trained in music. How do they evaluate the music? What is their opinion regarding its value? Do they consider the music as having lasting, durable value because of its intrinsic moral qualities, or do they view the music as **"trendy"** for the month----merely a musical **"flash in the pan,"** a popular, catchy piece of music satisfying consumer needs for the present? You may be unable to evaluate these last two qualities because you do not know the reputation of this music among mature, knowledgeable Christians and trained musicians. If this is the case, then investigate and solicit the combined judgment of team members and other non-team members regarding their judgment and discernment skills. Ask them their opinion of the music.

Several companies each month produce CDs (Compact Discs) of new "praise and worship" choruses, featuring the **"IT"** chorus of the month-----the most popular song as judged by leaders in the CCM movement. The next month a new **"IT"** chorus, followed by another novel **"IT"** song the following month. Will some of these **"IT"** choruses survive the trends and endure for years as a qualitative, Biblical song of reverent worship? Time will tell. The overwhelming majority of these entertaining, emotion-pleasing songs do not gain the excellent, praiseworthy reputation of mature, knowledgeable Christians.

ILLUSTRATION OF THE HALLELUJAH CHORUS. George Frideric Handel wrote the world famous **MESSIAH** in 1741, with its famous triumphant, stirring chorus **THE HALLELUJAH CHORUS**, heard most often at Easter and Christmas. This majestic chorus sung by choirs each year has earned the reputation of one of the greatest pieces of music ever composed. For over 250 years the chorus and greater **MESSIAH** oratorio has proven itself superior, monumental in the studied judgment of Christians and non-Christians. You may not like this majestic music because it is classical, heavy, "high-brow," not entertaining: you prefer more popular songs as **FROSTY THE SNOW MAN, JINGLE BELLS, or RUDOLPH THE RED NOSED REINDEER.** That is your prerogative. But these popular Christmas songs are not considered by knowledgeable people as equal in value and durability to the **HALLELUJAH CHORUS.** *Great music endures; "trendy" music is "catchy"----until replaced next month!*

The goal of this evaluation chart is to aid you in selecting durable music for your soul and spiritual maturity. Do you desire a "catchy" superficial tune this month, a diet of warm milk, or a theological meal of sound doctrine served with excellent music to develop spiritual muscle and deepen your worship of God and Christ?

NATURE OF DISCERNMENT:

1. Discernment is subjective. Total your score, then consult with a team of three other Christians who have also evaluated the same music. Add the four scores and divide by four to gain an average score for the music. Question each team member on why they evaluated each trait. There may be disagreements in the group; that is normal and to be expected, but this process will stimulate your thinking on discernment and give you insights on prejudice and bias.

2. Discernment is gained by inches-----not yards. You can not develop discernment into music by giant leaps, but by baby steps of inches, because discernment is an outgrowth of spiritual maturity. This maturity comes from deep, wide knowledge of Scripture, broad experiences of living the Christian life for many years, consistent prayer for God's discernment, and practical instances of developing an uncanny sense of moral judgment. You may evaluate a jazzy, sensuous, beat-dominate, loud selection of Christian music and consider it as **SUPERB:** that is how you perceive the music at this point in your Christian life. But how will you score this same music five, ten years from now? Will your discernment remain on the same level, or increase in spiritual insight? Hopefully your level of discernment will grow, develop, and blossom into Biblically penetrating insight into appropriate and inappropriate worship music.

(14) Their Maturation

These eight benchmarks are given to the Philippians, not the Corinthians! Out of all the churches planted by Paul, the Philippian church was by far the most mature, while the Corinthian church was the most carnal, self-serving, self-absorbed with a lengthy list of church problems. The only problem in the Philippian church was a disagreement between two women---Euodia and Syntyche (Philippians 4:2). Paul could not say to the Corinthians: **"Think on things that are true, noble, pure, right, lovely,"** because they could not correctly interpret these things. Because of their narcissism and self-absorption, they would interpret true as temporal reality instead of ultimate reality; noble as morally questionable; right as wicked; pure as defiled. The immaturity of the Corinthians would listen to the Egyptian pagan music and say with confidence, **"It sounds good to me! I like it! I like the jazzed up beat: it gets me motivated! I don't see anything wrong with it!"** Their obvious immaturity prevents them from correctly applying these eight standards of conduct and values. These Corinthians, like the 3,000 Hebrews dancing and cavorting around the gold calf, would consider modern pagan music as a **"useful, new tool in worship."**

The problem is not with these eight words, but with a false, immature grid of evaluation. Aaron considered himself as a "qualified worship leader," but he was self-deceived, as are many contemporary pastors and "worship leaders" who likewise consider themselves mature and see "nothing wrong" with the modern music styles emphasizing a heavy, driving beat, syncopation, screeching hot guitars, jazzy sound from the night club scene, and trite, repetitive lyrics of "praise and worship" songs.

Immaturity is illustrated in a 16 year old teenage girl who dates boys of questionable character and dress, despite the objections of her parents. **"I am mature and resent you telling me whom I can date,"** she blurts out to her parents. **"My opinion is just as good as yours,"** she asserts. She is Corinthian in her maturity level: definitely unable to correctly apply these eight words of measurement.

This diagram reveals an arrow with its shaft of **KNOWLEDGE** consisting of two components in the Christian life: **DISCERNMENT** and **MATURITY** seeking to penetrate, evaluate, judge, weigh, and discern worship music. But the penetration level is correlated to the degree of discernment and maturity. A young Christian (bottom arrow) may be at level number two in his maturity, his discernment failing to exceed his maturity in Christ. Every Christian is at a different maturity/discernment level. What increases the maturity/discernment level is a growing knowledge of Christ and His Word. Knowledge, however, means far more than intellectual attainment by knowing doctrine: it must include holy living matched to doctrine. If two Christians, one at level two and one at level ten (top arrow) of maturity/discernment, seek to discern the eight standards of Philippians 4:8 regarding a specific selection of appropriate worship music, there will be obvious disagreement------they are on two different levels of Christian maturity. The young, immature Christian, possesses minimal discernment/maturity and can only discern to level two of a selected piece of music. The older, more mature Christian, can penetrate and discern to a deeper level of ten. Each Christian sees things differently! In this real life scenario the responsibility weighs on the shoulders of mature pastors, directors of music, and pastoral staff to accurately discern musical standards by rejecting worldly, fleshly pagan music styles, and adopt worship music which measures up to the eight virtues of Philippians 4:8. The example of Aaron in Exodus 32:17-18 is instructive, for he considered himself as **"the qualified worship leader"** and **"mature"** in discerning music---------but he was tragically wrong: he was self-deceived. Pastors and directors of music also must trust God to give insight to young Christians who desire music which is worldly in nature------hoping they will advance in their faith to a greater maturity/discernment level.

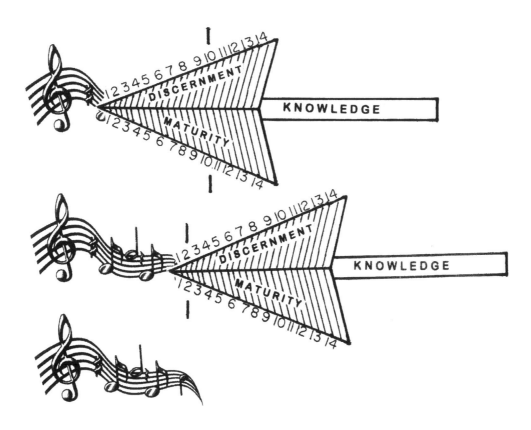

Interpretation and application are vitally related, but correct application can not be performed by immature Christians: they do not yet have this skill. Hebrews 5:14 states this skill of maturity comes through "constant use" to Christians who have **trained themselves to** **distinguish good from evil."** Note that word **"trained."** It is the Greek word **GEGUMNASIUM,** from which we get our English word "gymnasium." A gymnasium is a place we go for physical training: lifting weights, stretching, repetitious exercises, sweat, and all done on a daily basis for months and years. The mature Christian has spiritually trained himself through long years of teaching and application to the point where he can properly distinguish between good and evil, and he alone can correctly apply the eight words of Philippians 4:8 to all areas of life in forming correct judgments of values.

Discernment distinguishes between good and evil. The word "evil" (Greek word **KAKOS**) does not mean "bad" in its strict sense as in a definite crime, but is also used in a broad sense to mean bad thinking, feeling, acting---anything that injures the mind or body. The milk Christian may not commit overt acts of crime such as murder, adultery, stealing, but he engages in activities and thoughts that are questionable and worthless, and these worthless thoughts and activities harm his ability to discern: they dull his senses. His reading material may not be strictly "bad," but worthless; his recreation may not be overtly immoral, but "questionable;" his time management may not be "sinful," but "self-absorbed." Such activities harm his ability to discern; they affect his ability to discern between "bad" and worthless; "bad" and "questionable; "bad" and self-centered.

These milk, immature Christians have trained themselves to be ***MENTALLY FLABBY***; unlike the mature, meat Christians who have trained themselves to be ***MENTALLY SHARP*** and ***DISCERNING***. The mentally flabby Christian listens to poor music; reads poor literature; practices self-indulgence; displays undisciplined living; dislikes anything which challenges his self-centered lifestyle. He is like the man who spends major time in his easy, reclining chair with the only exercise given to his finger as he surfs the TV stations using his hand-held remote. He is ***MENTALLY FLABBY*** because he does not exercise his mind in the gymnasium of the Christian life.

The "strong meat" in the context of Hebrews 5:12-14 is the doctrine of the Priesthood of Christ, and its sequel is Philippians 4:8 and its eight virtues. Both the ***DOCTRINE*** of Christ's Priesthood in Hebrews and the ***PRACTICE*** of disciplined thinking in Philippians 4 require maturity, critical thinking, and discernment: virtues unknown and undesired by the ***MENTALLY FLABBY, MILK, SELF-CENTERED, FEELING-ORIENTED*** Christian.

The Greek word for "unskilled" in Heb. 5:13 is **APEIROS,** meaning lacking in experience, untried, ignorant. Such an "unskilled" Christian cannot properly "think on these things" of Philippians 4:8: he will interpret these eight virtues in an unskilled, self-centered, pleasure-dominated manner. Yes, Philippians 4:8 is definitely **MEAT----NOT MILK!**

The mature Christian has trained himself to be discerning, and though not stated in the context, yet implied, the immature, milk Christian has likewise trained himself to be nondiscerning between good and evil: he thinks and practices mediocrity, unwholesomeness, and evil-----without realizing these three traits hinder him from discerning excellence instead of mediocrity, unwholesomeness instead of healthiness, evil instead of godliness. He can be compared to a man who has trained himself to enjoy sandy soup: chicken noodle soup containing two tablespoons of sand. At first he objects to the harsh, sharp sand, but through persistence learns to enjoys the taste of the soup as well as the undissolved grit of the sand. **"I like it,"** he states, even though the sand wears away the enamel from his teeth, injures soft tissue in his mouth, and has no nutritional value.

At first the sandy soup may have been objectionable, but through constant training he has learned to endure, accept the sand, and enjoy the gritty texture. In a similar manner many

Christians at first may find objectionable the worldly, jazzy, pagan, rock music patterns presently practiced in Christian music, but through continual use and exposure they accept it as **"normative"** and **"I like the new sound."** When these Christians begin to obey Paul's command to think on things true and noble, they are unable to discern what is good, better, and best because they like sandy soup and reject any music without a worldly, jazzy, night-club sound to it. Their discernment has been dulled! I call this common experience ***DISCERNMENT DESENTIZATION***----inability to discern due to sandy soup syndrome.

MUSICAL SWITCHING. Dr. John Diamond, an Austrian physician and psychiatrist, is the acclaimed author of YOUR BODY DOESN'T LIE. He states we hear music, not only with our ears, but our bodies as well-------even when the ears may be blocked, our bodies still feel the pulses and driving beat of the music. He explains this impact of rock music on our bodies by using a term called **"SWITCHING"**-----the loss of symmetry or harmonious balance between the two cerebral hemispheres of the brain, resulting in the entire body being thrown into a state of alarm or imbalance. Shown here is a diagram of the human brain with its left and right hemispheres. Note each hemisphere revealing the major functions of each lobe. The brain is extremely complex and mystifying, yet we know the right lobe receives and processes wholesome music with its melodious harmonies, dynamic fluctuations in volume, and natural rhythms combined to create healthy balance of bodily systems, normalized blood pressure, and a general calmness of mind and emotions. The medical term describing this healthy balance of bodily systems is **HOMEOSTASIS:** Greek words "homeo," meaning same, and "stasis," meaning position. An inability to maintain homeostasis is called **HOMEOSTATIC IMBALANCE.** Exposure to high heat, such as in a desert, can overload the human body and lead to heat exhaustion, even death. Rock, hip hop music can upset this balance, overload the brain, and in some unknown way **"SWITCHES"** the two hemispheres of the brain causing imbalance, tension, apprehension, and alarm. **4**

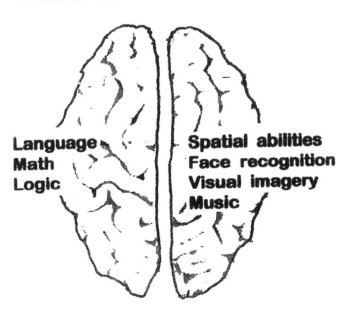

LEFT HEMISPHERE   RIGHT HEMISPHERE

Language
Math
Logic

Spatial abilities
Face recognition
Visual imagery
Music

Repeated, ongoing listening to rock, jazz music styles creates this switching in brain waves through an **ANAPESTIC BEAT**-----*a weak--weak--strong pulsation,* or a da-da-**DA** sequence known in poetry. The word "anapestic" refers in metric timing to two short syllables followed by a long one, or two unaccented syllables followed by an accented one. Such a beat emphasizes addictive conduct, our sensual nature, aggressive behavior, and inability of the body to discern between what is harmful and healthy. This beat pattern is evidenced at football games where crowds of people intone the pulsating words: **"We will, we will, rock you."** Wholesome music, like a waltz or a good hymn, uses the opposite *strong--weak--weak pattern* or **DA**-da-da pulsation which reflects the stabilizing heartbeat and normalizing rhythm of your body. **5**

Classical music sometimes uses this anapestic beat, such as the Presto section of Franz Schubert's "Fantasy in C Major (Wanderer Fantasia)", Op. 15, D. 760. But this section is only a small part of his greater work which gives more balance, harmony, relaxing resolve, and natural pulsations. Rock music, however, majors on the anapestic beat pattern throughout a single piece of music and does not vary its unnatural, driving, pulsating patterns.

The hymn, **MAN OF SORROWS**, illustrates this strong—weak pattern. The first stanza records these words: "Man of sorrows!" what a name for the Son of God who came." When sung the strong pulsation occurs on the first word, "Man;" the weak pulsation occurs on the second word "of;" followed by another strong pulsation on the first syllable "Sorrows," and completing the weak pulsation on the second syllable "Sorrows." The famous Christmas carol, **"O COME, ALL YE FAITHFUL,"** also shows this strong—weak—weak beat pattern. The first stanza records these words: "O come all ye faithful." When sung the strong beat occurs on the word "Come," followed by two weak beats of "all ye" then a subsequent strong pulsation on the first syllable word "faithful."

How does this **"SWITCHING"** of the brain result in musical desires? Frank Garlock observes: "We learn to like the wrong kinds of music, and reject the right kinds of music." **6** He illustrates **"SWITCHING"** by an experience with a client. He was driving his car and had a tape playing of majestic hymns by the London Philharmonic Choirs and accompanied by the National Philharmonic Orchestra. The client/passenger observed, **"That music gives me a headache!"** He apparently was used to listening to unwholesome music, and felt the pain of a headache when exposed to good music. Garlock concludes: **"If that which is good gives a headache and that which is gross and perverse is enjoyable, then could it be that the very thing to which one has given his ear and attention has altered ("switched") his thinking?" 7**

How does **"SWITCHING"** manifest itself in other areas of life apart from music? Diamond in his research and medical practice observes in children a decreased performance in school, hyperactivity, and restlessness. Among adults he observes decreased work output, increased errors, general inefficiency, reduced decision making capacity on the job, and a nagging feeling things are not right----"in short, the loss of energy for no apparent reason." **8** These negative factors stem from listening to rock music. In addition to harmful, irregular beats in rock music, and its close association of soft rock, shrill frequencies prove to also be harmful to the body. Using CCM in worship services may not always result in these extreme, overt, obvious behavioral symptoms, but the **"SWITCHING"** will display itself in more subtle behavior of reduced skill levels on discernment, corresponding superficial view of Biblical worship, and inverted motives, as displayed by the Israelites at the Golden Calf. **SWITCHING,** therefore, is not new: it existed over three thousand years ago at Mt. Sinai.

Diamond concludes: ***"It is as if his body no longer can distinguish what is beneficial and what is harmful. In fact, his body now actually chooses that which is destructive over that which is therapeutic."*** **9** Regretfully many Christians, through constant exposure to CCM in worship services, have lost their skill of discernment, and have embraced this fleshly worship music as **"normative-----I like the contemporary sound." Their mind has been "SWITCHED,"** or **"KIDNAPPED"** as Paul taught in Colossians 2:4,8 through a false, heretical philosophy and pagan musical style. They lose their desire for good hymns and other wholesome music with their **strong--weak—weak beat,** and prefer worldly music styles of the **ANAPESTIC BEAT** with its **weak--weak—strong beat.**

Another illustration of ***DISCERNMENT DESENTIZATION*** is ***AUDITORY DESENTIZATION***-----impairment of hearing due to chronic exposure to loud noises over a period of time, such as a chain saw, lawnmower, or leaf blower. Working or living in an environment where loud noises are common can lead to permanent damage to the inner ear. Such loud noise contributes to **presbycusis,** or age-related hearing loss, and tinnitus, which is a ringing, buzzing, or roaring sound in the ears. Loud noise can permanently damage the inner ear creating an inability to hear certain high or low frequency tones: the individual may hear certain music but cannot honestly discern euphoric high notes or rich bass notes. His range of hearing is thus greatly reduced and impaired. He is unable to adequately discern music that is true, noble, right, pure, lovely, admirable, praiseworthy, excellent because his ears have been desensitized.

These eight measurements can only be properly applied by mature Christians. Yes, they can and must be taught to all Christians, but unskilled, immature Christians will misapply them: they will come to the wrong conclusions because they have not been trained in the "gymnasium" of the Christian life. They have spent little time studying the Word of God, few hours in prayer, and embrace a pagan philosophy of culture which teaches truth is measured by personal feelings: what makes me feel good!

The command to "think on these things" is preceded by the previous verses (4:2-7) to (1) rejoice always; (2) be gentle to everyone; (3) don't be anxious about anything; (4) present your requests to God. Can an immature Christian obey these commands? Yes-----but not fully, because he is still dominated by self-centered desires and temporal view of values. Experience reveals these four commands are most appropriately applied by the mature Christian who has been in the Christian "gymnasium."

What is the significance of the fourth command to present our requests to God? Is it referring to all requests in general? Yes, but in the context the specific requests are four: **(1) "Father, teach me to rejoice at all times; (2) lead me to be gentle to all men; (3) prevent me from anxiety; (4) give me guidance in thinking critically and unemotionally on things true, noble, right, pure, lovely, admirable, excellent, and praiseworthy."**

Evidence of the maturity level of the Philippians is further illustrated in Philippians 3:15 where Paul identifies himself and the Philippians believers as "mature." Will mature Christians disagree on issues? Yes, of course, and Paul recognizes this fact, but he adds in 3:15-16: **"And if on some point you think differently, that too God will make clear to you. Only let us live up to what we have already attained."** Mature Christians who think on things true, noble, right will not always agree on what is good, better, best, but in time God "will make clear to you." He will, in time, create a unity of thought among all believers.

(15) THEIR CATEGORIZAION

The categorization of Philippians 4:8 is seen in two ways: (1) examination of the commands, and (2) examination of words. First, we gain a categorization by examining the 24 commands in Philippians as listed below:

2:2 Make my joy complete	3:1 Rejoice in the Lord
2:2 Be like minded	3:2 Look out for dogs
2:2 Have the same love	3:15 Think on those who are mature
2:2 Be one in spirit	3:16 Walk in your level of maturity
2:3 Do nothing out of selfish ambition	4:2 Agree with each other
2:3 Consider others better than yourselves	4:3 Help these women
2:4 Look at the interests of others	4:4 Rejoice in the Lord
2:5 Have the same mind of Christ	4:5 Let your gentleness be known
2:12 Obey in my absence	4:6 Do not be anxious
2:12 Work out to the finish your own salvation	4:6 Present your requests to God
2:14 Do not murmur or complain	4:9 Put into practice
2:18 Rejoice with me	4:21 Greet all the saints

The command of Philippians 4:8 is purposely absent from this list because it is in a different category. These 24 commands are **REACTIVE COMMANDS** calling for quick action followed by **IMMEDIATE CHANGE** of conduct. The command of 4:8 ("think on these things") is a **REFLECTIVE COMMAND** calling for quick action of reflection followed by **DELAYED CHANGE** of conduct. The 24 **REACTIVE COMMANDS** target a change of conduct; the **REFLECTIVE COMMAND** targets a delayed change of values and skill: *DISCERNEMENT.* **Conduct comes quickly; discernment comes slowly**----after prolonged thinking on things true, noble, right, pure……. The thrust of Paul's command is to continually think on these things until correct discernment and values is achieved----and this process requires much time. That's maturity.

This distinction in **REACTIVE** and **REFLECTIVE** commands are illustrated in the following diagram. Note in the top diagram illustrating **REACITVE** commands, the initial act of quick obedience (shown by the 0) is followed by successive acts of obedience (shown by repetition of 0s) and change of conduct. In the bottom diagram illustrating the **REFLECTIVE** command of 4:8 the initial act of obedience is followed by a slow, gradual increase in discernment gained over time. Note the rising level of attained degrees of discernment. In the area of music, sculpture, art, carpentry, sewing we are commanded to think on these areas and slowly but certainly gain an increasing discernment of excellence. The greater the discernment, the greater is our ability to distinguish ultimate reality from temporal reality, the pure from the impure, the tawdry from the majestic, the lovely from the ugly, the admirable from the questionable, the spiritual from the sensual, the musical mediocre from the musical magnificent.

REACTIVE COMMANDS		
QUICK OBEDIENCE 0	CONTINUED ACTS OF OBEDIENCE 0 0 0 0 0 0 0 0 0 0 0	RESULT Change of conduct
REFLECTIVE COMMAND		
QUICK OBEDIENCE 0	INCREASING DISCERNMENT	RESULT Change of values

Second, we gain harmonization from examining the words "think." Two different Greek words are used in Philippians for "think:" **PHRONEO** and **LOGIZOMAI. PHRONEO** (from which we get our English word "phrenic" meaning "mind;" mental) is the common word for think---meaning earthly, normal thinking and appears ten times in Philippians 1:7; 2:2 (twice); 2:5; 3:15 (two times); 3:19; 4:2; 4:10 (twice). **LOGIZOMAI** (from which we get our English word "logical") is used one time in Philippians 4:8 and means careful, unemotional thinking which weighs the value of any thing. Paul is saying here: **"Lay aside your prejudices and bias in order to think deeply and carefully for the purpose of critical evaluation and discernment on things that are true, noble, pure."** Of the two Greek words, **LOGIZOMAI** is a much stronger word demanding more serious judgment.

V. P. Furnish aptly comments on the significance of **LOGIZOMAI** in stating the word does not refer so much to a critical evaluation of heathen culture and its standards of morality, but rather to a careful discernment and reflection on the eight positive traits in order to shape our conduct by them.**10**

(16) Their Defection

Did some of the Philippians defect and turn away from such careful discernment of things true, noble, pure? We are not sure, but perhaps some did as stated by Paul in Philippians 3:17-19 where he commands the Philippians to mark, take note of other Christians who follow Paul's example of maturity (which would include thinking on noble things). But many veered from this command and live as enemies of Christ: **"Their destiny is destruction, their god is their stomach, and their glory is in their shame. Their mind (PHRONEO) is on earthly things."** Is Paul referring to unbelievers or believers? We are not sure, but the word "destruction" **(APOLEIA)** is used in Philippians 1:28 probably for unbelievers and their eternal destruction. But believers can experience premature death if they continue to resist the will of God (Acts 5:1-11; I Cor. 11:30; I John 5:16).

If Paul is referring to believers, he is identifying these Philippians as **ANTINOMIANS** (against all objective standards of righteousness) and describes them in Philippians 3:2-3 with three traits: (1) **SENSUAL APPETITES: they give free reign to their sensual appetites and do not restrain the flesh;** (2) **SHAMELESS PRIDE: they take pride in things that should cause them shame;** (3) **MATERIAL PLEASURES: they give themselves over to physical and material things and the enjoyment of life, to the exclusion of spiritual matters.** These antinomian believers (if they were actually true believers) were not perhaps members of the Philippian church, but itinerants who would visit the church on occasions and seek to influence the Philippian Christians. Gordon Fee describes these people as "probably ….itinerants, whose view is such that it allows them a great deal of undisciplined self-indulgence……In any case, they have not appeared heretofore in the letter, and do not appear again. They have served their immediate purpose of standing in sharp relief to Paul's own 'walk' and to his heavenly pursuit, so crucial to this letter."**11.**

Antinomianism is belief in rejection of any objective standards of righteous living, following only personal desires of selfish living, or as Paul states in Philippians 3:19, **"Their mind is on earthly things."** Many Christians pursue "earthly things" rather than follow Paul's example of godly living in thinking on noble things. Their desire is not for discernment, but self-indulgence and undisciplined living. In the realm of music, their standard is **"what makes me feel good; what gives me a 'holy' buzz; what stirs my emotions; what gives me a sensual delight; what will attract the crowds; what is entertaining."** These Christians have trained themselves to like fleshly, self-centered, worldly music with its nightclub sound, and thus have dulled their senses of spiritual discernment. They may initially "think" on things true, noble, pure, right……..but reject any sense of righteous discernment because it clashes with their self-centered "feelings." They may initially listen to great music, great hymns, or observe great art, great sculpture and conclude: **"I don't like it; it doesn't speak to me; it doesn't make me feel happy and motivated; it's boring; it doesn't inspire me to clap my hands, wave my arms, or gyrate my body."**

TASTE AND PREFERENCE IN MUSIC Often our musical taste is based on repetition. Authors Fishman and Katch observe: "repetition increases preference. Therefore, the more we hear something, the more we tend to like it."**12** This fact only reinforces Paul's command to think on things true, noble, pure. Music may be rock, soft rock, jazz, hip hop, country western, blue grass, country western, popular, classical, semi-classical, heavy metal, rhythm and blues. Repeated exposure to any one type of music increases the desire, taste, and preference for that music. Thus people will honestly say, ***"I can't help it; I can't deny my feelings: I like rock, soft rock, hip hop, country western, blue grass, jazz."*** They are truthful-----but misinformed about the reason for their taste or preference: they have acquired a taste because of repetition to the wrong kind of music. The issue is not taste or preference in music, but God's command: what kind of music best pleases Him in worship? Paul commands in Colossians 3:2: **"Set your affection on things above, not on things on the earth."** This command expressly teaches we **DETERMINE** what we like: we select the things (music) which we fill our minds to experience enjoyment.

This self-centered indulgent Christian is equal to the "milk" Christian of Hebrews 5:11 who is "slow to learn" or dull in hearing about the priesthood of Christ. The Greek word for "slow" is **NOTHROS,** meaning slow, dull, sluggish, and is used of the numbed limbs of a sick lion. This immature, worldly Christian finds the teaching of the Priesthood of Christ as **"boring; abstract; unattractive; not entertaining; not stimulating; not relevant; too intellectual; not practical to my business career."**

This attitude is evidenced in the following diagram adapted from the previous diagram termed "Reflective Command." It shows an initial act of thinking on these eight virtues, but due to their worldly taste and preference for "Egyptian pagan music," they reject any music which does not conform to their worldly, jazzy, nightclub style of music with its sensuous, breathy sound. Many Christians do not pass the first level of discernment because their selfish, sensual mind which thinks only on earthly things, and returns to their "Egyptian pagan music." Worldly, jazzy, heavy-beat music is what they know and they judge all music by these earthly, sensual standards.

REFLECTIVE COMMAND

INITIAL OBEDIEINCE TO "THINK"	NO CONTINUED PRACTICE OF "THINKING"	RESULT
		No Discernment

(17) Their Demonstration

Yes, these eight benchmarks are **SUBJECTIVE,** but combined together they form an unbreakable bond in evaluating music, interior decorating, architectural design, sculpture, painting, carpentry, oratory, and all other fields of knowledge and skill. A common kitchen sieve or strainer demonstrates these eight words. A sieve is a utensil with many small meshed or perforated openings of a size allowing passage only to liquids, finer particles, or loose pulverized mater. A housewife may sift her flour to allow the fine flour to pass through the meshed wire while the larger lumps are trapped and discarded. The following three wire mesh strainers visually demonstrate a common kitchen strainer showing a coarse, medium, and fine strainer----- each one allowing fine particles to pass through the wire mesh. Fine flour will pass easily through all three strainers, but only strainer #3 is best in demonstrating the eight words of Philippians 4:8, because it only allows finer material to pass while trapping and discarding the larger, inferior particles. Unfortunately many Christians, like strainer #1 or #2, allow pagan values, standards, ideas, music, and philosophy to pass through their **"broad-minded," "tolerant," "liberated"** thinking-----like the Israelites----to their own spiritual corruption. What pagan values, worldly standards, and sensuous, jazzy music is trapped in your strainer for discarding?

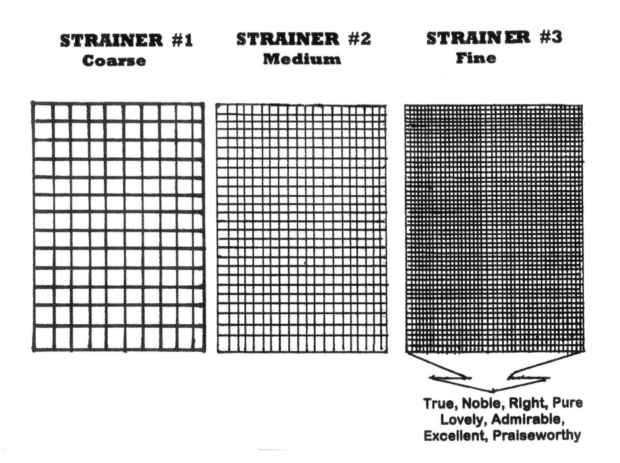

STRAINER #1 Coarse   STRAINER #2 Medium   STRAINER #3 Fine

True, Noble, Right, Pure
Lovely, Admirable,
Excellent, Praiseworthy

What kind of strainer are you using in judging music, carpentry, art, literature, painting, architectural design, clothing styles? What material are you allowing to pass through the strainer, and what material are you trapping and discarding as unsuitable?

(18) Their Illustration

Making a cake is a good illustration of this straining process. The cook sifts the flour with a fine sieve to remove the larger lumps of flour, but suppose she used Strainer #1. Yes fine flour would pass through the wide mesh, but so would hardened clumps of flour, some small stones, or glass shards which inadvertently found their way into the bag of flour. These foreign materials would be mixed with all the ingredients, baked in the oven, and finally topped with a lustrous, tasty strawberry frosting----including real strawberries crowning the edges of the cake. Yes, the cake might initially look tempting and taste delicious-----until your teeth clamped down onto a small stone or sharp piece of glass. Injury, then, not taste, becomes paramount! Who wants to risk their teeth, tongues, and jaws on such a **"liberated, broad-minded, tolerant, flexible, non-judgmental"** cook?

Like this **"broad-minded cook,"** we may allow certain music into our ears and lives because **"it sounds good to me; it makes me feel good; I like the beat; I like the popular sound,"** but like the hardened clumps of flour, small stones, and shards of glass, what spiritual injury occurs in our spirits, our conception of God, the nature of true worship? The strawberry cake may taste good, but is it good for me?

The eight benchmarks are the sieve or strainer. Every day in school, on TV, on radio, in the office, at home our minds and ears are constantly exposed to language, music, jokes, pictures, paintings, conduct, and we must, like the strainer, filter out detestable things, and permit the "true, noble, right, pure, lovely, admirable, excellent, and praiseworthy" things to pass into our hearts. **What we allow to pass through the strainer determines what kind of person we become!**

Moses used the strainer of God's commandments and his training in music to reject the **"pagan, contemporary music"** of the Israelites at Mt. Sinai. This kind of music did not measure up to the eight benchmarks of Paul in Philippians 4:8.

CHAPTER 7

Application of Principles

1. Discern through spiritual maturity what is true worship music.

Aaron was wrong in his interpretation of what he heard: he was self-deceived and a weak leader. Exodus 32:25 teaches Aaron ***"had let the people get out of control."*** His failure to stand up to the Israelites and forbid them to make the golden calf reveals his lack of spiritual maturity and bold courage. We could call Aaron the first **"worship leader"**----but he was a poor one. Thankfully Moses had the spiritual eyesight and discernment to properly identify the false music used in this new "worship service." Acts 7:22 tells us Moses ***"was educated in all the wisdom of the Egyptians, and he was mighty in his words and deeds,"*** -----an education equipping him to be an Egyptian prince. The Egyptian culture was the most highly literate people and nation of its time, and Moses received education in all the wisdom of Egyptian culture: math, science, agriculture, philosophy, religion, and **MUSIC**-----giving him the benefit of properly evaluating music and its effects. Aaron lacked this skill------and he reaped the consequences of his ignorance.

2. Expect the wrong type of music to produce wrong behavior.

The Israelites used this **"worship"** music but its effect resulted in sensuality----stimulating, pleasing the flesh and their lower evil nature. It produced drunkenness, revelry, a party spirit. Revelry means boisterous, loud merrymaking. Accompanying this revelry was dancing: not a tamed ballet or pirouettes, but according to historic Egyptian records this dancing involved a twirling, leaping, and bending of the body to the driving beat of the music.

Distinction must be made between controlled and uncontrolled joy. The Psalms command us to worship with joy and enthusiasm, but the dancing and revelry of the Israelites was an uncontrolled fleshly flight into erotic dancing: this is what provoked Moses to rebuke them. Egyptian history reveals women moved by this driving music would dress in semi-transparent garments and bend and contort their bodies. The Israelites observed these secular and religious dances for 400 years, and may have adopted this pattern of behavior as they danced around the golden calf. **Today some of the CCM may not produce outward drunkenness and wild revelry, but it stimulates a jazz spirit, a heavy, dominating beat which is sensual in nature, and a syncopated rhythm conducive to sexual drives, fleshly pulsations, and self-absorbed focus on emotional feelings.**

Wrong behavior is external; wrong emotions are internal, and the internal, in time, will consent to the external. Happiness and joy are two related, but distinct, emotions, and some of the CCM played and sung in evangelical churches targets the **"happiness"** goal----not the **"joy"** center. Happy feelings of glee and surface excitement may result from the new **"style"** of worship music, but it is not joy, because joy is not dependent on lucky happenings, chance events, or **"good feeling music."** Rather Biblical joy is a deep emotion of quiet hope in God produced by the Holy Spirit and is not dependant on **"happy sounding music."**

Often Christians will depart a worship service where this **"new style of Contemporary Christian Music"** is played/sung, and people may remark, <u>**"Wow! Wasn't that a great worship service? I feel so excited; I feel happy; I feel so close to God. It gave me a real buzz."**</u> Note in this commonly-heard statement those words "feel." The emphasis is on **"how I feel; what can I get out of worship."** <u>**This is pure narcissism: self-worship falsely parading under the banner of "worshipping God."**</u> And where in God's Word are we ever commanded to worship our feelings? Never! Rather we are to forget our feelings and major on exalting the character and holiness of God and His Son Jesus Christ.

Did the Israelites feel <u>**"happy, giddy, excited"**</u> in their worship of God through the golden calf? Certainly! They apparently gained a "holy buzz" of emotions----whatever that term means in today's narcissistic culture. But their worship was false-----an <u>**ILLUSION**</u> of true worship! They were sincere, but sincerely wrong!

3. Recognize music is more powerful than the words.

No where in the context of Exodus 32 are recorded the words of the music the Israelites were singing. They were not worshipping a false god, but the true God---- in a false way. We can safely assume they were singing words of <u>**"praise and worship"**</u> to the true God Jehovah, but with the wrong kind of music. Moses was outraged, not by their words, but by the type of music and its effects on their emotions and behavior! Perhaps they were singing, <u>**"God, You are great and wonderful, full of compassion. You delivered us from Egyptian bondage."**</u> They may have sung the words learned three weeks prior at the Red Sea----the grand words of Exodus 15:1-18----deliverance by God from the Red Sea. The words may have been doctrinally true, but wedded to wrong music. Their revelry, drunkenness, and partying spirit was not caused by the "biblical" words, but by **UPBEAT, UPTEMPO, REPETITIVE, HYPNOTIC, DRIVING** music.

From later records in Exodus 32:28 we learn about 3,000 combined Hebrews, and mixed multitudes formed the large group cavorting and singing around the golden calf. That's an impressive choir accompanied by musical instruments of lyres, harps, flutes, coronets! I can imagine the loud volume made as Moses descended the mountain, yet Moses commanded the Levites to go through the camp and kill all 3,000 people---------just for singing the wrong kind of music! Today in our pluralistic, relativistic value system Christians in the Sunday morning worship service would charge Moses with being inconsiderate, narrow-minded, opinionated, judgmental, factious!

CCM advocates believe music is **AMORAL**-----totally neutral in its effects on people, and illustrate this modern philosophy by using middle C on the piano keyboard. Strike the key and middle C is sounded. Regardless of which instrument is used (piano, organ, guitar, flute, trombone, violin, harp, trumpet) middle C will always sound the same. <u>**"What's so moral or immoral about the middle C?"**</u> these CCM advocates ask. The logic seems so *"reasonable, so right,"* but that middle C can be formed into different chord structures, major or minor key, loud or soft in volume, diminished or augmented, carried by a flowing or halting melody, consistent in its natural rhythmic pulsations or pulsed with a heavy or syncopated off beat. That one simple note of middle C is **AMORAL,** but it can definitely become **MORAL** by how that one note is developed into a myriad of music possibilities and its resultant effects on the listener in his body and emotions.

Another example illustrates this difference between **AMORAL** and **MORAL.** Use the letter **"e".** This small letter **"e"** by itself is **AMORAL--**-a neutral letter in the alphabet. Now compare the following two statements:

"I prais**e** God."

"I hat**e** God."

What is the difference in meaning? How does the one letter "e" affect the interpretation? The answer is obvious: one statement is positive; the other is negative. The 26 letters in our alphabet are all **AMORAL,** but in combining them into words, sentences, and paragraphs they become **MORAL** in communicating either positive or negative information to us, making us feel positive or negative, depressed or joyful, dour or excited, withdrawn or outgoing, tense or relaxed, expressive or inhibited. Music, like letters in the alphabet combined into words, make music **MORAL.** All music (classical, popular, jazz, rock and roll, country western, secular, sacred) has a definite effect on our bodies in making us feel a certain way and in our minds in causing us to think on certain thoughts.

Paul gives two important commands about heretical philosophy in Colossians 2:4,8----commands which are broad to cover all areas of life, especially in music philosophy. He further explains in detail the results of this heretical philosophy in Colossians 2:23.

FIRST COMMAND: (Col. 2:4) *"Don't be deceived by fine-sounding arguments"* This phrase, "fine-sounding arguments," occurs only here in the New Testament, and is used in other sources outside the New Testament for the words of the law court and refers to the lawyer's persuasive speech and its power to influence an audience towards an unjust verdict. The arguments in the context regards false teachers in the church distorting the true nature and essence of Christ---seeking to motivate the Colossian Christians to abandon Christ and replace Him with a deeper mystery from God. One application is philosophy of music: do we get our philosophy of music from the Bible, or from the secular musical world? CCM has yielded to the philosophy of the world regarding music-----the fine-sounding argument that music is **AMORAL**----that music is neutral, and therefore we can use any kind of music-----as long as the words are Christian.

SECOND COMMAND: (Col. 2:8) *"Don't be taken captive through hollow philosophy, which depends on human tradition and the basic principles of this*

world rather than on Christ." The word **"philosophy"** (only used one time here in the New Testament) simply means love of wisdom and knowledge, and all of us have a philosophy or opinion of how something should be done, but note in this verse our philosophy must be based on Christ and the Word of God, rather than on human, man-centered, market-driven, results oriented, consumer-pleasing, attendance-building, money-increasing, strobe light-flashing methods of this carnal world.

RESULTS OF HERETICAL PHILOSOPHY.

We do not know precisely the nature of this "philosophy" present among the Colossians Christians. Some scholars think it was the heresy of Gnostism, some conjecture it was a mystery religion in Colosse, others theorize it was a form of Cynic belief. But we do know three factors of this heretical philosophy: we know its (1) ***PURPOSE:*** lead believers away from the sufficiency of Christ. We know its (2) ***PREMISE:*** human tradition and the basic principles of this world rather than on Christ. Distinction must be made between **HUMAN TRADITION** and **APOSTOLIC TRADITION**. Apostolic tradition means the teaching handed down from the apostles (II Thess. 2:15; 3:6) which formed the basis of New Testament revelation, and is commanded to all believers to maintain this revelation from God. Human tradition, however, is not divine revelation, but the accumulation of man-made practices, values, philosophies, and worldly thinking produced by man-centered concepts. The philosophy present in Colosse was based on a false human origin and misinterpretation of truth, rather than on the truth in Christ.

We know its (3) ***PRODUCT:*** **"an appearance of wisdom, with their self-imposed worship, their false humility......and lack any value in restraining sensual indulgence," (Colossians 2:23).** This philosophy involved asceticism-----the doctrine that rigid denial of the body and human pleasures leads to spiritual and intellectual attainments (Colossians 2:21-22). Paul remarked about this emphasis on rigid rules: ***"These are all destined to perish with use, because they are based on human commands and teachings."***

This "philosophy" talked about worshipping Christ, but it resulted in **FALSE, INEFFECTUAL, ILLUSORY WORSHIP.** This false philosophy may have made the Christians in Colosse "feel good with stirred emotions and a sense of connecting with God," but the worship was an illusion---an unreal, deceptive, or misleading appearance; an erroneous perception of reality. True worship of Christ leads to true, not false humility, and demonstrates divine power in controlling sensual urges. These three passages of 2:4; 2:8; and 2:23 do not directly address the issue of music, but the principle of false philosophies apply to all areas of life: music, theology, political views, historical assumptions.

Much of CCM uses language about "worshipping Christ," but, like the pagan philosophy rampant among the Colossian Christians, the worship is superficial, an illusion. Why? Because the music is based on the human tradition of worldly, sensual, emotionally-stimulating, beat-dominating music styles. The experience of Aaron, the golden calf, and pagan Egyptian music in Exodus 32:17-18 clearly teach God cannot be worshipped with the wrong kind of music------even if sacred, Biblical words, are used. Advocates of CCM may point to proof texts such as Gamaliel's counsel in Acts 5:38-42, but their interpretation is based on a faulty exegesis of the passage. Or they may invoke the musical practices of Martin Luther and John Wesley, but fail to accurately explain their rejection of using secular tunes and musical styles suggestive with evil associations.

In the music realm, many Christians have **EMBRACED** this worldly philosophy of church music in a sincere effort to build big churches and big budgets. They have purchased the **"fine-sounding arguments"** of the world because, **"It just seemed so logical, reasonable, convincing, persuasive. And besides, this CCM 'gets the job done.' It gets results. It makes people feel happy and excited."** Their minds have been taken captive: they are prisoners (though they think themselves as "liberated") locked into a worldly philosophy of music that says Christian music in our churches should reflect the secular tunes, beats, gyrations, dress, sensual breathing techniques of the local clubs surrounding the church, and the music styles prominent on MTV.

For centuries musicologists have consistently believed music is definitely moral----producing either positive or negative effects, yet only in recent years has a new music philosophy come to the stage claiming music is **AMORAL**------meaning neither moral or non moral, but neutral; therefore, with this new amoral philosophy, any kind of music can be used with different words. Last year a famous pastor in a large church in Texas claimed, **"We will take any worldly method, baptize it, and use it in our church services."** Knowledgeable musicologists are not making these claims of music being **AMORAL,** but by Christian leaders in the CCM movement as a justifiable reason for using secular rock music, soft rock, jazz, and sensual mood music in worship services. The rationale is a consumer, market-driven motivation: give them their kind of music; they can identify with it; our church attendance will increase; we can evangelize them.

Musicologists for centuries have agreed the wrong kind of music can produce the wrong behavior------despite the presence of biblical words in the music, because the music is more powerful than the words. Marshal McLuan, famed Canadian professor of Communication Theory, is right in his assessment and cogent statement: **"The medium is the message."** This famous quote simply means the method of communication (singing, vocal, instrumental, visual) is the central message retained by the listener-----not the actual words. The advertising business uses this foundational rule in all advertising media by focusing viewer attention-----not on a product (such as a car, toothpaste, exercise equipment, or beer)----but on the visual image of a scantily-clad woman. The advertising mantra is true: **SEX SELLS!** The product (car, toothpaste, exercise equipment, beer) is purchased because of the motivating medium: the sexually enticing woman, or well-sculpted man with muscular shoulders and "six pak" abs!

Neil Postman of New York University states in his book, **AMUSING OURSELVES TO DEATH, "The form in which ideas are expressed affects what those ideas will be. It is naïve to think that something that has been expressed in one form can be expressed in another without significantly changing its meaning, texture, or value."** **1** We as human beings are more influenced by the medium (the method---kind of music, kind of advertisement, kind of commercial) than the message (the words.) CCM advocates maintain music is neutral: neither moral nor immoral. Therefore, they contend, any kind of music can be used with Christian words to further worship and evangelism.

Examine the logic of CCM regarding the **"NEUTRALITY"** of music styles. If this logic is true (which it is not), then why do TV producers program certain kinds of music to fit the scene displayed on the screen? The TV may show a woman walking down a dimly lighted street and the music heard in the background is a quiet, depressive, ominous sound designed to make the viewer feel like an assailant is ready to attack, strangle, and rape the unsuspecting woman. The music sets the stage; it creates the mood. Now if music is totally neutral, neither moral nor immoral, then why not substitute a joyful kind of music, such as the Hallelujah Chorus, to fit this same crime scene? The answer is obvious: The Hallelujah Chorus does not create the same mood as a sinister piece of depressive music.

Two clear examples in the Bible affirm music is **MORAL** not **AMORAL.** The first example is found here in Exodus 32:17-18 where Moses orders the death of 3,000 sinning Hebrews-----all because they used pagan Egyptian music to worship the true God, Jehovah. Keep in mind the educational level of Moses: he was trained in all the academic areas of Egyptian history, knowledge, and culture----including the realm of music. He knew the difference between sacred and secular music; between average and excellent music; between appropriate and inappropriate music. Perhaps some "brilliant" Hebrew smugly said to Moses, **"Moses, you are out of touch with changing times. You are opinionated and totally subjective in your judgments. After all, music is merely a matter of taste, and is immune from any standards of objective musical measurements!"** (Sounds familiar to today, does it not?) WOW! Had this happened I would not be surprised if God did not immediately strike him dead-----before the other 3,000 people! Moses knew music was moral----capable of influencing either wholesome or unwholesome emotions, thoughts, and behavior.

The second example of music being **MORAL** is found in I Samuel 16:14-23 where Saul has learned he will be rejected as King over Israel. An evil spirit comes on him producing despair and depression, resulting in Saul issuing an order to his servants to search for a capable man to play music for him. A young shepherd boy, David, is found, brought to the king's chambers, and plays his harp----resulting in Saul's better emotional state and discharge from depression. Verse 23 tells us, **"Whenever the spirit from God came upon Saul, David would take his harp and play. Then relief would come to Saul; he would feel better, and the evil spirit would leave."** If music is **AMORAL**---remaining neutral, then how could David's harp playing create such positive psychological health in Saul?

In addition, if music is neutral, neither moral nor immoral, then why will Mick Jaggers and the Rolling Stones and other popular rock and roll groups not play tunes such as **"Nearer My God to Thee," "Crown Him with Many Crowns,"** or **"All Creatures of our God and King"** in their concerts? The answer is obvious: these tunes will not produce the same sensual effects in concert-goers as the rock and roll songs. These rock musicians know hymns are **"out of place"** at a rock concert. Why then do Christian leaders think rock, soft rock, jazz, and sensual music sung in a breathy manner with its wild, screaming guitars, heavy beat, syncopated rhythms, ear-piercing volume, fragmented tunes, and repetitive words are "appropriate" in church? It is sad when rock musicians have more insight into appropriateness than Christian leaders! Jesus well said: **"The people of this world are more shrewd in dealing with their own kind than are the people of light." (Luke 16:8)**

4. Don't rely on family heritage in making important decisions.

Aaron, the high priest, was the brother of Moses, and had the responsibility to lead in the spiritual functions of worship and teaching the Israelites the commandments of God. The commandments had already been given by God to Moses, clearly forbidding any idolatry. Aaron knew this command, yet he permitted the Israelites to make the golden calf as perhaps a **"useful tool"** in the absence of Moses who was still on the mountain communing with God. Perhaps he did not consider in his mind the calf was an idol; he may have **"redefined"** in his thinking what was and was not an idol.

He and the Israelites **"borrowed"** the popular musical style of the Egyptians and incorporated it into the worship of Jehovah. He could not consult Moses, so he relied on his family heritage, human wisdom as brother to Moses, and decided on his own to allow the golden calf. Your father or grandfather may have been an outstanding preacher or teacher of God's Word; maybe your mother or grandmother were godly women. These are excellent traits to have in your spiritual and family heritage, but that is no guarantee you will always make good decisions concerning spiritual issues. Important decisions must be based on the clear teaching of God's Word, and close communion with God to gain the subjective, yet vital, virtue of spiritual discernment.

5. Seek spiritual counsel on important decisions.

Aaron failed to seek advice, and 3,000 Israelites were killed because of his sincere, but misguided judgment. None of us will ever be so spiritually mature as to be above guidance by older, wiser Christian servants of God. Aaron's sin was presumption: presuming and assuring himself he could make decisions apart from consultation with other people. Conspicuously absent in the context of Exodus 32 is any disagreement of Aaron with Moses regarding Moses' evaluation of this new "worship" music accompanying the golden calf.

Aaron could have said **(AS IS THE PREVAILING MOOD TODAY)**, *"Moses, my opinion is just as good as yours. Who are you to claim this 'music' is terrible? After all, 'good music' is a totally subjective judgment, and I have every right to form my own judgment on what is and is not good music. Besides, I am the High Priest; I'm the worship leader, and it is my responsibility to lead these people in meaningful, relevant worship. All your formal training in Egypt has made you legalistic, rigid, and inflexible. In order to meet the needs of these people we must give them a 'style' of worship that appeals to them, maintains their interest, and is relevant to their lifestyle here in the desert. We must incorporate newer methods to attract the younger generation of teenagers in each of the twelve tribes if we want them to grow in spiritual maturity. We are out here alone in the desert and there's not much entertainment available except in our worship services. If we don't give people what they want in a relevant worship service, then most of them will remain in their tents. Our attendance and offerings will suffer----and God knows we need increased offerings to meet the needs of all the four million Israelites!"*

Had Aaron evidenced such an arrogant, impudent, insolent, contemporary mindset, God may have immediately struck him dead there on the spot! Thankfully, Aaron submitted his personal opinion to the spiritually-mature discernment of Moses.

6. Detect superficiality in the church.

Two types of superficiality exist in the Church and in all other organizations: superficiality from **lack of education,** and from **lack of commitment.** A young child may be sincere, but superficial because he lacks teaching; an adult Christian may also be sincere, but superficial because he lacks teaching from God's Word: he is, like the child, immature. An adult may regularly attend worship services, but not be genuinely converted to Christ: he lacks the needed commitment for conversion. He, like the **"mixed multitude"** of the Egyptians, may be attracted to the church because of the benefits of church attendance: personal friendships, social respectability, business connections, cultural betterment, self-improvement. These **"benefits"** attract him, and he goes along with the program----but he is not a true Christian: he is superficial.

Who led the Israelites to complain against God and influence them to adopt a **"new worship music style"**? It was this **"mixed multitude---this rabble"** (Numbers 11:4) Even Aaron, the High Priest, the worship leader, succumbed to the "logic" of this **"new worship music"**. He **"bought in"** to this thinking-----to his and Israel's detriment.

Normally problems and confusion in the Church today do not begin with spiritually mature Christians----but with superficial Christians who are not fully taught in God's Word or with unconverted people who attend the church for its "benefits." These two classes of people are in every church, and we must detect and resist their cunning influence seeking to alter true worship music of God's people.

The Bible tells us Satan will attack the Church either as a roaring lion, or a cunning, sly snake. He attacked Israel in Egypt as a roaring lion through 400 years of forced slavery and the powerful threats of the Egyptian Pharoah. Now in the desert he attacks Israel as a cunning, sly snake through the corrupting influence of superficial, pagan Egyptians. Their **"logic"** sounds good, seems reasonable, and their pagan music **"makes me feel good."** But they are wolves in sheep's clothing. Watch out for them; detect them; resist their worldly logic regarding music.

Scripture makes a clear distinction between divine and human wisdom in Colossians 2:4,8: **"let no one deceive you by fine-sounding arguments........See to it that no one takes you captive through hollow and deceptive philosophy, which depends on human tradition and the basic principles of this world rather than on Christ."** The term in verse 4 (**"fine-sounding arguments"**) means **PERSUASIVE SPEECH BASED ON FALSE LOGIC.** Our English idiom communicates the same idea: _**"talk someone into something."**_ Aaron **"bought into"** this persuasive speech and false logic of the pagan **"mixed multitude."** They **"talked him into it."**

The phrase in verse 8 (**"take you captive"**) is used of kidnapping-----stealing someone without their consent. And how is this "kidnapping" accomplished? Paul gives the answer: **"through hollow (empty) and deceptive (trickery) philosophy."** Aaron was **KIDNAPPED-----**by the pagan mixed multitude! No, they did not physically assault his body-------but his mind: they used persuasive, convincing arguments based on false logic and tricky philosophy which seemed plausible------so convincing!

Today spiritual kidnapping is rampant in the Church by superficial Christians who follow a worldly philosophy of music instead of the Biblical principles of music! Pastors, ministers of music, ministers of youth, teachers in seminaries willingly allow themselves to be kidnapped in their mind-------by false logic, false philosophy. Aaron, the first worship leader is dead, but his willing descendants in the Church today are victimized in their mind--------but they don't know it! They consider themselves **"liberated"** and **"contemporary"** in their thinking-----**"free from a narrow-minded, out-dated mentality."**

An excellent example of trickery is a magician who can make rabbits and doves appear out of seemingly thin air. We are entertained by a good magician even though we don't know the professional "secrets" of his trade. We are amused, clap, and express wonderment at his deceptive trickery. Aaron and the Israelites were tricked---but they did not realize the deception, and in the Church today sincere, godly men and women are also tricked by false logic, persuasive speech, and a worldly philosophy of life.

7. Don't rely on advanced age as an automatic qualification in making right decisions.

Aaron was 83 years old when he was with Moses before Pharoah in Egypt during the time of the plagues (Exodus 7:7). Now here in Exodus 32 Aaron is about 93 years old, and we would think a 93 year old man is old enough and wise enough to make sound decisions. But Aaron failed: his advanced age did not qualify him to make a right decision on the issue of worship. **Spiritual decisions must be based on spiritual maturity, not physical age**. True Biblical worship and the music to accompany it are spiritual decisions requiring spiritual maturity and knowledge of musical appropriateness.

8. Deflect human logic alone in making spiritual decisions.

Two human issues prompted making the golden calf: (1) impatience, and (2) relevancy. The Israelites came to Aaron complaining about the long absence (40 days) of Moses on the mountain: they were impatient with his absence and ready leadership. He had faithfully led them through the ten plagues in Egypt, across the Red Sea, supplied them with water and food, and now he is absent for a long time. **"We need to do something now,"** they clamored to Aaron. **"We can't wait any longer."** Aaron concurred with this human thinking. Their solution involved making a golden calf as a visual aid to worship, a golden object that would be more relevant than the unseen God Jehovah. Again, Aaron concurred: he **"bought"** into the philosophy of human logic.

Moses was gone, God was invisible, and therefore irrelevant, reasoned Aaron and the children of Israel. The golden calf would solve these two dilemmas: (1) provide immediacy and (2) relevancy in worship. God had given them commandments about **spiritual worship; they wanted sensual worship**: **worship which appeals to our human, sensing, feeling nature**. Making the golden calf would bring God "down" to their level, instead of having to "rise" upward to God in worship. The issue was spiritual versus sensual worship. Today evangelicals, like the Israelites, are **"impatient"** because they do not see the spiritual worship and growth of churches as they would like, so they cast about for different methods of making God more **"relevant,"** more **"user-friendly"** to modern man----especially the younger generation.

People have adopted contemporary secular, rock and roll, jazz music as the new "method," the new "drawing card" that will bring God down to our human level, make Him more appealing, more understanding. **"Since contemporary, jazzy, rock and roll music is the popular medium,"** this philosophy states, **"we will merely add Christian words to the popular music style people already like."** Such thinking is attractive, convincing, and many pastors, music directors, churches, and seminaries have **"bought into"** this philosophical thinking. Human logic, man-centered philosophy must be evaluated and judged by God's Word. Aaron and the children of Israel failed to test their thinking by the commandment God had already given. They may have known the commandment regarding idolatry, but they did not understand its spiritual implications and applications.

Leaders in CCM justify use of borrowing secular music and transporting it into the church by citing two historical Christian leaders: Martin Luther and John Wesley. **"Both men used the secular tunes and melodies of their time and added Christian words to tunes already popular in that culture,"** claim many people in the CCM movement. **"If these men of God did it with success, then so can we!"** Is this accurate? Do historical facts support this claim? Is it true? The answer is: **IT IS A HALF TRUTH.** A half truth is often worse than a clear lie because a half truth is so deceptive. What are the facts about Luther and Wesley in using secular melodies and adding Christian words to existing music? I will give only a brief explanation, but a much fuller, in depth, documented treatment is found in the book by John Makujina, **Measuring the Music.2**

Luther and Wesley desired to teach gospel truths to people through music and did borrow some, not all, selected melodies from secular ballads and folk songs and then added Christian words. People already knew the melodies, so the new Christian words would facilitate a faster learning among the common man. But both men were highly scrupulous in their selections and demanded the secular tunes must conform to high musical standards because Luther and Wesley did not want people to associate the songs with evil ideas and effects.

John Wesley was not the gifted musician; his brother, Charles, was. Charles composed 6,500 hymns, but many of them were poor in lyrics and melody, and these never were incorporated in early hymnals. Often Charles would compose a new melody or adapt an existing secular melody and add his new Christian words, but John, though not gifted in music composition, yet possessed a greater spiritual discernment and forbid Charles from using certain tunes-----because of their evil association.

German-born George Frederic Handle was the most popular musician in England at this time and was considered as one of the greatest composers of all time, writing forty-eight operas. He composed three tunes for Charles Wesley, but the Wesleys used many tunes and choruses from Handle's operas.

During Luther's time he composed thirty-seven chorales; fifteen of them were original melodies; thirteen were melodies from Latin hymns, four were melodies from German hymns and *Leisen,* (religious German folksongs); two were pilgrims' songs; two were of unknown origin; and one was parodied from a secular folksong. Yes, like the Wesleys, he did borrow some secular melodies from contemporary folk songs but these melodies were similar to church music, because in that medieval period there was little difference between the secular and sacred, for music was predominantly ecclesiastical in origin and orientation. He rejected some secular melodies because of the sinful images they communicated, and adapted other melodies by discarding negative elements of the tune while retaining the positive melody. On some secular songs he changed the rhythm because it was too heavy, too intense, too dominant and would detract from the spiritual message of the words.

When Luther began composing religious songs, he adopted the broadside ballad----a narrative or story in the style of the secular Hofweise----court songs sung by musicians. Specifically he adopted the "barform" structure of the texts. "Barform" is an old musical form used by minnesingers of the 12th to 14th century in Germany by composing the lyrics of each stanza to form a pattern of AAB. Such a poem contains three stanzas (or more). This method is seen in "The Star Spangled Banner" where the first stanza repeats the same time structure (AA), and then the remainder of the song is structured in a different sequence (B). He did not copy the musical melody, but the "textual" pattern, as observed by Robin A. Leaver in her comprehensive book, Luther's Liturgical Music: Principles and Implications. She asserts: "Again and again statements have been made that imply that Luther made extensive use of popular music. In support of the use of such music he is even quoted as asking the rhetorical question, 'Why should the devil have all the good tunes?'-----words that cannot be found anywhere in his voluminous writings. Certainly Luther was aware of such tunes, especially by those who seek to justify their own use of secular styles in contemporary worship."**3**

Did Luther and Wesley borrow and adapt secular music to Christian words? Yes----but only the best musical tunes, the most excellent method of writing lyrics. They did not accept and embrace any secular tune just because **"it was popular and fashionable."** Rather, they selected music which met the eight standards of measurement found in Philippians 4:8.

All great music is not solely Christian; many secular songs have proven their value over the years by their enduring, inspiring quality, and Christians must search for wholesome music and use it as did Martin Luther and John and Charles Wesley. I have often heard outstanding secular music performed by an orchestra, pianist, or vocal soloist and said to myself, **"Someone needs to write Christian words to fit this beautiful piece of music."** I kept waiting--- several years-------- for someone else to rise to the need. No one did, so I decided to compose sacred lyrics to this world-famous, great music. God expects all of us to use discernment in the music we hear and select, and we see this Biblical discernment in Martin Luther and John and Charles Wesley.

9. Avoid judging success by results.

Were Aaron and the children of Israel successful with their results of the golden calf? Definitely: 3,000 Israelites joyfully worshipped around the golden calf accompanied by lively music. Seemingly the results gave confirmation about the rightness of the method: the golden calf and Egyptian music. There is no pastor or church who would not want 3,000 people in their worship service each Sunday morning. **"What can we do to have big crowds?"** is the common question, and the answer is simple: give them a golden calf and a 'pop' music style; give the people what they want! **Today, Contemporary Christian Music is the new "golden calf."** It gets results: bigger crowds, more **"lively"** music, more **"joy,"** more **"fun-filled"** services, enthusiastic hand-clapping, fresher **"worship"** experiences, and newer **"worship"** songs and **"praise" choruses.**

Three big words lie dormant and undetected behind this new golden calf: **(1) CASUISTRY, (2) UTILITARIANISM, and (3) PRAGMATISM. CASUISTRY** is technically defined by the dictionary as **"the solving of special cases of right and wrong in conduct by applying general principles of ethics, and deciding how far circumstances alter cases."** It is also used disparagingly of **"subtle but evasive reasoning in questions of duty."** Note the first definition: deciding how far circumstances alter cases. Casuistry is the art of using human logic to evade duty and moral principles, or in common words: **"the end justifies the means."** **"If the end results are good, then the methods must be good to produce those results,"** claim the modern disciples of utilitarian, casuistic thinking. In this logic, the golden calf was good----because it produced good results: 3,000 devoted worshippers singing lively songs! Why argue with **"success?"**

UTILITARIANISM is a related word coming from the word **"utility"** simply meaning useful, practical. If a method is good and useful and it gets good results then that method is utilitarian. Many churches and pastors would disavow with their tongue any agreement with casuistry or utilitarianism: **"Oh no! I definitely don't believe the end justifies the means,"** they exclaim, yet that is precisely the philosophical underpinnings of the new golden calf of Contemporary Christian Music. Yes, 3,000 Israelites became enthused with their new "worship" style, dancing, joy, handclapping, and revelry-------but examine their final results: they were all slaughtered with the sword by the Levites. The lesson is obvious: we can not worship God any old way we choose; He has not given us this freedom. His Word never teaches: **"Worship in any style you desire; use any music you find pleasing; incorporate any entertainment which will build big attendance; add any light shows to give dramatic flare; preach any sermons which are 'user friendly' and will not offend anyone; appeal to the emotions of people so they will enjoy the worship service and return next Sunday."**

PRAGMATISM means what is practical, what will work, what will accomplish the objective. It is synonymous with **UTILITARIANISM.** Of the three words, **PRAGMATISM** is used the most in describing much ministry efforts in the church today, and pastors are constantly looking for methods, techniques, programs that **"will work---get the job done."** Biblical truth takes a back seat to pragmatism. Pastors want big congregations, big choirs, big youth programs, big budgets, big church staff, big building programs in order to be **successful,** and they look for **"any thing that works"** to accomplish this goal.

Yes, certain methods, programs, and kinds of music may **"work;"** they may get results----but at what cost to Biblical truth? Three thousand Israelites used pagan Egyptian worship music; this method **"worked,"** but at the expense of disobedience to God's commands. Recently in our community I noticed a large, professionally printed sign in front of the church building:

CHOOSE YOUR WORSHIP STYLE:
CONTEMPORARY OR TRADITIONAL

The sign listed the different times for these two distinct worship services, and could well have been printed first by the Israelites at the base of Mt. Sinai, inviting the 2 million Israelites to choose their worship style: contemporary (from Egyptian practice) or traditional (from Biblical commands). Regretfully, they chose the "contemporary" style with its pagan music and sensual beat. Five illustrations may clarify this philosophy of **PRAGMATISM and CASUISTRY.**

FIRST, a pastor in a Southern church planned to preach a series of sermons on **RED HOT SEX**, and designed a color brochure informing the community of this series. Each week for a month a different salacious title emphasizing a new phase of **RED HOT SEX** was printed on the color brochure, along with a picture of a man and woman in bed, covered with a sheet, showing only their feet extending out of the sheet. Over fifty thousand of these attractive brochures were mailed out to homes in the surrounding community to arouse interest and influence new people to come hear these sexy sermons!

Many people in the community were offended by these unsolicited mailings and called the church to complain. Often children were sent to the mailbox to get the day's mail and asked their parents, "Daddy, what are these people doing?" Such questions prompted unease among parents.

The pastor, however, justified the sexy brochure by replying, "We had 87 people saved as a result of that brochure and series of sermons." This pastor may never have heard the words **CASUISTRY, UTILITARIANISM, or PRAGMATISM,** but he was definitely a follower of this philosophy! His total focus was not obedience to God's Word, but results: what methods will give me the best results, the biggest attendance, the most "converts"?

What should be our response to such "evangelistic success"? Must we take at face value 87 people were genuinely converted, or should Biblical discernment enter our minds and spirit----causing us to question the permanent validity of such "conversions"? Did these 87 people truly repent in the full Biblical meaning of the term, trust Christ alone apart from any good works on their part, or were the "conversions" seed scattered on rocky and thorny soil?

Jesus gives clear teaching on the parable of the seed and the four kinds of soil, teaching some people quickly respond to the gospel, but they don't last long because their soul is "rocky soil". Others respond but their life is "thorny soil" and the cares of this life and deceitfulness of riches choke out the seed, and it dies.

SECOND, another church designed a special church service around a popular TV game show on improving marriage relationships. The MC (Master of Ceremonies) interviewed husbands and wives about their spouses and how well they knew each other. The audience swelled in attendance to see and hear these couples being interviewed on stage. The wives were kept in another room while the husbands were asked questions. Some non-threatening questions were asked of the husbands about how well they knew their wives, but the main, final question was bold, blunt, and embarrassing: "What part of your wife's body do you enjoy the most?" One husband was reluctant to answer while the people in the auditorium clapped, cheered, and screamed in approval of the question. Finally, the first husband replied, "Her _____!" Again the audience hooted and hollered in approval.

The second husband replied in a sheepish, embarrassed manner: "I'm a _____ man!" More cheers and squeals of approval from the Christians in the audience!

Did this TV impersonation method get people to attend? Definitely! Did the audience seem to enjoy the event? Certainly! Why then object? Because a moral issue is involved: privacy, appropriateness, sexual suggestiveness and titillation---------endorsed by this church as "good, wholesome."

THIRD, Cornerstone Church in Chandler, Arizona rented a large billboard showing a man and woman in bed under a sheet with just their feet extended from the edge, and in large red letters advertising the church are these words: **BRINGING SEX BACK.** I do not know the marketing results, but I assume many new people would attend this church for at least one time to get the inside scoop on sexuality. And perhaps some "conversions" take place because of this sexy marketing method. If the method works, then God must be blessing the method-----at least that is the logic of the argument! But I'm not a disciple of this worldly philosophy!

FOURTH, the pastor of a church in Georgia recently completed a series of sermons with a poker/gambling theme entitled "All In". The sermons were not warning of the dangers of sin or gambling, but embraced poker and gambling metaphors. The platform of the church was designed like a casino in Las Vegas with eye-catching color, giant poker cards, flashing lights, and an entertainer/singer who dressed like Elvis Pressley-----complete with hip gyrations and pelvic thrusts like the King of Rock and Roll. The pastor was dressed like a card dealer at a casino table shuffling his deck of cards during his "sermon." This "sermon" (if you want to call it that name) was a non-biblical message teaching the value of being a risk taker. Jesus was barely mentioned (but the pastor did talk a lot about himself), and the message gave the impression a sin is committed if we are not risk takers. There was no mention of sin, Christ Crucified for sinners, repentance or the gospel.

The "sermon" could have been presented at a business conference, in a group therapy session, or a Tony Robbins infomercial and it would not have sounded out of place.

The pastor claims the church is growing by "leaps and bounds." Sounds like his methods "work," "gets the job done," "attracts the unchurched." Why argue with success? Or maybe we should! Yes sir! Argue Biblically, strongly! Does the end justify the means? Not according to the Bible, but then in today's success-driven, bigger-attendance-record evangelical church, the Bible **"gets in the way"** of relevant ministry. Among a hoard of self-proclaimed evangelical pastors the Bible must be "reinterpreted" in our modern culture; exegesis, exposition, organ music, hymns are outdated; eisegesis, entertainment, jazzy pagan music, flashy strobe lights, screeching wild electric guitars, and pop-psychology-self-help sermons are in.

FIFTH. A church in a large southern city has shifted its sermons from Biblical content to movies being shown in local theaters. The pastor spent several weeks speaking on the spiritual lessons contained in the Hollywood movies. With his emphasis the pastor does not need to go to seminary, learn exegesis, or the Biblical languages; instead, he can make up any spiritual lesson from any movie, and no one will challenge him because "feelings" are sacred. New people are attracted to this church because the "sermons" are so "relevant" to the movies they viewed during the week, and the people can leave the service with no guilt feelings over sin. This pastor's Hollywood review method works, but at what cost to Biblical truth and the gospel message?

Just imagine all the good the Apostle Paul could have accomplished if he had the entertainment accoutrement of the mega churches today! If he had screeching electric guitars, hot keyboards, thudding drums, eye-popping strobe lights, and a praise team of sensual, breathy-voiced singers and hip-thrusting women on Mars Hill, he may have had a better evangelistic "conversion" record and spent less time in jail! Poor Paul-----he was shackled with an old "preaching" style in his time. But now pastors are liberated!------to worldly methods which "seem so good." Marketing the church-----not Biblical preaching/teaching----is the modern focus.

BIBLICAL SUPPORT FOR THIS GROWTH?

A favorite Biblical passage often interpreted to support church growth and success is Acts 5:25-43----the account of the Apostles before the Sanhedrin. The apostles were preaching and teaching in Jesus' name to the consternation of these Jewish leaders who wished to kill these apostles. Seeking advice, the Sanhedrin asked Gamaliel, the most prominent Jewish rabbi of his time, what to do regarding these bold apostles. He was head or leader of the Jewish Sanhedrin and in the Talmud bears the title "Rabban," meaning "our teacher," a title higher in honor than rabbi, meaning "my teacher." He was the most respected Pharisee of his day. The Mishnah, a collection of commentaries on the oral laws of Israel published toward the end of the second century A.D., contains the following statement about him: "Since Rabban Gamaliel the elder died there has been no more reverence for the law; and purity and abstinence died out at the same time."

He begins his discourse with the Sanhedrin by referring to two **PAST HISTORICAL** events of insurrection: (1) an unknown man named Theudas and his 400 followers who rallied around him in opposition to the government of Rome. Theudas was killed and his followers dispersed; (2) Judas the Galilean also led a band of people in revolt against Rome, but he too was killed and his followers scattered. Gamaliel's unstated but inferred logic is: *__human effort alone will lead to failure.__*

His advice is found in Acts 5:38-39: **"Leave these men alone! Let them go! For if their purpose or activity is of human origin, (like the efforts of Theudas and Judas) it will fail. But if it is from God, you will not be able to stop these men; you will only find yourself fighting against God."** Note his logic: human activity will fail; Godly activity will succeed. Put another way we can restate: **"If your work is not endorsed by God, it will fail; it will not succeed and grow. But if your work is endorsed by God then it will grow, prosper, and**

succeed." Finally an even more dogmatic belief is asserted by people using this Acts 5 passage: **GROWTH IS AFFIRMATION OF OUR METHODS, AND THUS A PROOF OF GOD'S BLESSING.**

The logic Gamaliel uses is called inductive reasoning: a process of reasoning in which the premises of an argument are believed to support the conclusion but do not ensure it. Gamaliel used two examples (Theudas and Judas) to support his conclusion and recommendation to release the apostles and take a "wait and see" approach to discover the results of their teaching. He infers their teaching will end in ruin (like Theudas and Judas), but time will tell. He further adds motivation to accept this recommendation with an appeal to fear (also known as scare tactics): "you will only find yourself fighting against God." This appeal to fear motivates the Sanhedrin to agree to Gamaliel's claim of toleration toward the apostles and their teaching. Who wants to fight against God? That is a strong motivation to agree with Gamaliel's claim, but such motivation is not relevant to the truth or falsity of the claim.

Gamaliel's second statement: "But if it is from God, you will not be able to stop these men" is an allusion to well-known rabbinic principle as stated bou Josephus: "Any assembling together that is for the sake of Heaven shall in the end be established, but any that is not for the sake of Heaven shall not in the end be established."[4]

In Acts 5:40 Luke uses a most interesting word about the Sanhedrin after hearing the speech and counsel of Gamaliel: it is the word "persuaded"----"His speech persuaded them." The word "persuaded" is a Greek word **(PITHO)** meaning persuasive speech. The word is used in the papyri in a court case of those who sought persuasive words to keep the things obtained by robbery. The terminology used here is practically equivalent to our English expression, "to talk someone into something."[5] This same word is used in Col. 2:4 "fine-sounding arguments." This persuasion or logic can be based either on true or false logic.

The previous five illustrations of churches and pastors believe strongly their methods are from God because the methods get results: larger attendance, more conversions, greater offerings in the offering plate, new programs of ministry, increased church staff, expanding building programs. If this logic is true, (which it is not) then consistency of argument must equally apply to the religion of cults and Islam, because they are growing in vast numbers and amassing large revenues in their treasuries. The false religion of Islam is spreading like a prairie fire across the globe.

Is the advice and counsel of Gamaliel true? No, it is false! He was not a Christian, and therefore could not give spiritual counsel; he was a learned, respected Jewish rabbi who knew well Old Testament law, but not a follower of Christ and therefore unable to provide true Christian counsel. He gave the best human counsel he knew, and from this human, worldly viewpoint it did appear as sound.

What motivated him to give such counsel? Four elements: **(1) jealousy, (2) fear, (3) cowardice, (4) pragmatism. (1) Jealousy** is expressed in Acts 5:17 tells "the high priest and all his associates, who were members of the party of the Sadducees, were filled with jealousy." They were jealous because the apostles were gaining more and more influence and conversions of the common people in Jerusalem, while the Sadducees had little esteem in the eyes of the people. **(2) Fear** is highlighted in Acts 5:26 where the temple guards seize the apostles, but do not use force against them "because they feared that the people would stone them." The crowds supported the apostles and the guards were fearful of a rioting crowd if the apostles were mistreated. This fear extended to members of the Sanhedrin and Gamaliel too.

(3) Cowardice or lack of moral courage dominated Gamaliel. He knew of the resurrection of Jesus, the miracles performed by the apostles in healing people (Acts 5:12-16), the supernatural release of the apostles from jail (Acts 5:17-24), and the growing influence of their teaching in Jerusalem. These supernatural actions clearly did not indicate a movement of human, but divine origin, yet he remained a skeptical unbeliever. He was a moral coward---- unwilling to face the obvious facts of this new Christian movement; nor did he courageously recommend the Sanhedrin honestly examine the claims of the apostles regarding Jesus Christ and the veracity of people who had been miraculously healed by the apostles.

(4) Pragmatism led him to make a decision based on political compromise to accomplish three benefits: (1) avoid crowd riot, (2) retain personal prestige, and (3) extend corporate power. Examine the potential of crowd riot. The people in Jerusalem were already following the teachings of the apostles, and would certainly riot against the Sanhedrin if the council issued the order to kill the apostles. Examine the personal prestige of Gamaliel. He was a widely respected rabbi for his knowledge, piety, and wisdom; but if he recommended death to the apostles as the Sanhedrin desired, his wisdom would be questioned by the citizens of Jerusalem and the Sanhedrin, and his prestige would be marred. His long years of earned prestige would be dashed by this single decision. Examine the corporate power of the Sanhedrin: it was the official ruling body over the religious affairs of Jews, and consisted of both Sadducees and Pharisees, with the Sadducees serving as the majority but ruled by the minority of Pharisees. The Sadducees were concerned with political stability with Rome and opposed the new Christian movement of the apostles because it represented a threat to established peace, but the Pharisees were more concerned with spiritual values and obedience to Old Testament law. The average citizen of Jerusalem disliked the Sadducees, and favored the Pharisees, and Josephus records in his Antiquities XVIII, 1,4) almost nothing could be accomplished without the Pharisees, and the Sadducees often went along with the Pharisees in order merely to be tolerated by the masses and maintain their corporate power in the Sanhedrin.

This explains Acts 5:40: Gamaliel's speech persuaded them (the Sadducees). Did the Sadducees of the Sanhedrin fully believe Galaliel's counsel, or did they (as they often did) merely outwardly agree to maintain their corporate power in the Council? We know the Sadducees desired to kill the apostles, but perhaps went along with Gamaliel's counsel----not necessarily because they were convinced of his logic, but to maintain unity in the Sanhedrin and extend their corporate power and influence.

Were good things accomplished by Gamaliel's counsel? Definitely! Four benefits were attained: (1) the citizens of Jerusalem did not riot; (2) Gamaliel retained his personal prestige; (3) the Sanhedrin maintained its unity and corporate influence; (4) the lives of the apostles were spared. That is the nature and meaning of pragmatism: practical benefits ensuing from certain polices or methods. But the greater question is what moral and ethical issues are violated in order to attain these "benefits"?

And neither does God approve and endorse the human-centered, worldly advice of Gamaliel. This knowledgeable Jewish rabbi was sincere, but wrong in his spiritual judgment. I can begin robbing banks and give all the money to my church for its support of missionaries and the new building program. The church prospers, the budget increases, the gospel is advanced through increased income of the church. Does this growth and success of the church mean God is blessing my bank robbing ministry? If you believe Gamaliel's counsel was true, then by sheer logic alone you must also condone bank robbery as a legitimate method of raising money for God's kingdom.

Improper interpretation of this passage in Acts 5:25-43 leads advocates of Contemporary Christian Music to claim allegiance to Gamaliel's counsel as they point with pride to him and his recommendations to the Sanhedrin. Often they will say, **"This music must be of God because He is blessing its ministry. Young people are flocking to our churches and concerts, and many people are being saved because the music is relevant to their time and age. It communicates; it excites them; they get turned on by it."** This kind of thinking (embraced by thousands of pastors, youth directors, music ministers) is pure, unadulterated **PRAGMATISM**: what ever works! It also reveals **CASUISTRY**----the end justifies the means (if a method "works" and gets "results" then the method must be of God.)

10. Follow four criteria to gain spiritual discernment.

This criteria is: **(1) time, (2) knowledge, (3) experience, and (4) communion.** How did Moses gain spiritual discernment in properly judging the new **"worship music"** of the Israelites, and why did this virtue escape Aaron? **FIRST,** Moses spent large amounts of time with God. For 40 years he tended sheep in the barren desert of Midian and during this time he learned much about Jehovah God. While Aaron and the Hebrews were waiting on Moses, he was communing with God for 40 days! No where in Scripture do we find Aaron spending 40 days or 40 years in deep communion with God and learning His ways. How much in-depth time do you spend with God and His Word?

SECOND, Moses gained knowledge of God on Mt. Sinai when God revealed not just the ten commandments, but all related laws to him. Moses not only knew objectively the law, but he understood the spiritual principles behind each commandment. Furthermore, Moses was brought up in Pharoah's palace in the land of Egypt and gained the choice education as an Egyptian prince. Stephen in Acts 7:22 states Moses was **"instructed in all the wisdom of the Egyptians, and he was mighty in his words and deeds."** He knew philosophy, business management, economic theory, music, governmental administration, agricultural procedures, history, mathematics, and engineering. His broad, in-depth education prepared him for leadership. Aaron knew objectively the ten commandments, but he definitely did not understand the spiritual insight behind them, or he would not have allowed the Israelites to make a golden calf.

THIRD, Moses **"walked with God"** as a friend; he experienced a deep fellowship with God and learned how to sense His presence and recognize His ways; we do not find Aaron walking in such close fellowship with God. Walking with God is a figurative expression implying constancy, dialogue, and intimacy. It involves listening for God speaking in His Word and your spirit, and honestly telling Him your needs------and frustrations. This virtue is not cultivated in a morning devotional time of ten minutes, but an on-going conversation with God throughout the day.

FOURTH, Moses communed with God through fasting and prayer a total of 80 days and nights on Mt. Sinai. The first time on the mountain (Ex. 24:18) he spent 40 days and nights communing with God and receiving the law. The second time on the mountain (Ex 34:28) he spent an additional 40 days and nights in communion with God. No record is given of Aaron spending this protracted time with God in prayer and fasting. When did you last fast? How long? One meal-----or a whole week?

Because Moses had the benefit of these four criteria, he could accurately discern the **"new worship"** music surrounding the golden calf. Yes, it is valuable to have an in-depth knowledge of God's Word, but I must also have understanding of other fields of knowledge too. I may have spiritual insights into God's Word, but if I don't know much about engineering, then I am unable to adequately discern and design proper tensile strength for a massive swinging bridge over a wide river. If I do not have knowledge of music theory, music history, and the effects of various kinds of music, then I can easily be attracted to philosophies of music which conflict with God's Word. If I do not understand the various secular philosophies rampant in our culture today, then I will be unable to spot and identify them with their attendant methodologies of presentation.

True spiritual discernment comes from spending protracted time with God, in-depth knowledge of God's Word wedded to broad knowledge in secular fields, multitude of experiences with God, and much prayer and fasting. The result is a mature man or woman of God capable of discerning not just between good and evil, but according to Philippians 1:9-10 discerning what is "best." Paul teaches in I Cor. 2:15: **"The spiritual man makes judgments about all things, but he himself is not subject to any man's judgment."** Moses was this spiritual man who made judgments about style and music of worship, but he was not subject to Aaron's naïve opinions and uninformed judgment.

I give thanks to God for honoring His Word in allowing me to be born into a godly line extending back several generations. In my own family I see this long line of Riggs generations who have loved God and His Word; I take no personal credit for this act of God's grace, but rejoice in honoring some godly ancestor in our family tree---some unknown man or woman who determined to honor God above all cost, and I am humbled for God's gift to me. (Exodus 20:7)

LIBERTY IN WORSHIP. Liberty is not removal of boundaries, but the power to move easily among established boundaries, as illustrated in driving rules. Would we really be liberated by dismantling all stop signs, yield signs, one-way direction signs, and all speed markers? Of course not, for that would mean pure bedlam and mounting accidents. True liberty in driving means recognition of these traffic markers, and operating safely within these guidelines.

11. Accept Christ-honoring Contemporary Music.

The sieve or kitchen strainer serves two purposes: **(1) NEGATIVELY:** trap and discard unwanted material, and **(2) POSITIVELY:** permit desired material to pass through the wire mesh. The eight bench mark words of Philippians 4:8 serves both purposes in Christian music: reject any music (sacred or secular) failing to measure up to the eight tests, and accept any music meeting the eight tests. Under-girding these tests is that marvelous word: **DISCERNMENT---- judging between good and bad, wholesome and unwholesome, pure and tawdry, genuine and superficial.**

Was Moses opposed to **ALL KINDS** of worship music at Mt. Sinai? Of course not: he only opposed pagan music which violated God's Word and led to sensuality, debauchery, self-centeredness, and self-pleasure. Nor was he opposed to any newly written (contemporary) music composed by a devout Israelite believer----as long as it was music truly honoring God's Word. We have record of two **CONTEMPORARY** songs of Moses----*contemporary to his time: one he himself composed in Ex. 15:1-18, and another composition in Deut. 32: 1-44.* The first song is recorded just a few weeks before the incident at Mt. Sinai and appears in Exodus 15:1-18---a hymn of joy for God's deliverance of the Israelites through the Red Sea and the drowning of the Egyptian army. It is often called **"Victory at Sea"** because it truly was a victory over the Red Sea. The second song is recorded 40 years later at the end of Moses' life and appears in Deuteronomy 32:1-43----a hymn of joy recounting God's historical dealings with Israel, and judgment on disobedient Israelites.

a. Importance of these songs:

FIRST, both songs were sung in the synagogue on the Sabbath evenings as a reminder of God's deliverance from Egyptian bondage, and His care for His people during their 40 year wilderness wanderings. I can imagine some critical Jew complaining, **"We sang that song last Sabbath. Do we have to sing it again? It's boring singing that same song every Sabbath!"** This argument is all too evident today in our churches. But the songs were necessary because of their rich theology about God and His works. This practice of singing the same songs every Sabbath evening teaches us as Christians an important truth: **repeatedly sing hymns rich in doctrine and theology!** Trite, anemic, ditty choruses will not accomplish what these grand hymns produce: Biblical knowledge and spiritual maturity!

SECOND, these two songs of Moses will be sung in heaven by martyred Christians who remained victorious over the beast and his image (Rev. 15:3). They will sing the songs of Moses and the Lamb. Note the time span covered by the songs: the songs of Moses represent Old Testament teaching of God's faithfulness to Israel as a nation in recognition that a large number of Israelites are among these martyred dead, and the song of the Lamb of God reveals New Testament teaching of redemption from sin made possible by the sacrifice of Christ as the Lamb of God, and would include all the saints. What a marvelous blend!

Since we will sing these rich, vibrant, grand, theological hymns in heaven, then we need to practice singing them more in our churches. Watered-down Biblical lyrics wedded to a "pop" catchy, self-centered emotional tune geared to **"make me feel happy"** will not suffice.

Sendry identifies the song in Ex. 15:1-18 as "the first religious national song found in the Bible,"**6** and describes it as "artistically the most relevant, song of the Old Testament," **"Then Moses and the Israelites sang this song to the Lord:"** Verses 2-18 recount the mighty acts of God, His miraculous power in delivering His people. Examine the words and they reveal a total God-centered focus on His majesty, wisdom, sovereignty, and power over all the pagan gods of Egypt and the Egyptian army. There is not the slightest hint in this hymn of any emphasis on Moses' feelings of giddiness, hilarity, or desire to **"feel good,"** by the beat and rhythm of the song.

b. Song of Moses---Ex. 15:1-8

All Hebrew music traces its roots back to the magnificent musical abilities of Moses, and leaders in the Contemporary Christian Music arena today need to learn lessons on quality poetry and music, not from a pop icon Nashville musician with a guitar strapped across his back, but from Moses.

Moses' example of composing the words and music found in Ex. 15:1-18 teach **FOUR** practical lessons: **(1) writing skills are mandatory; (2) musical training is crucial; (3) adaptability is relevant; (4) discernment is monumental.**

(1) First, writing skills are mandatory. Moses did not compose trite, insipid words-----as is too often present in much Contemporary Christian Music, or the "praise and worship" choruses. His words were grand, expressive in poetical brilliance describing the majesty of God's power displayed at the Red Sea-----words requiring deep thought. Slowly read these 18 verses in Exodus 15, pause and reflect at the end of each verse of poetry, and think deeply about their significance. Moses was a great writer because he was a great reader of Egyptian wisdom literature, and possessed a creative gift from God to compose spiritual depth in captivating words.

(2) Second, musical training is crucial. Moses was no novice in musical knowledge; he knew music theory, composition, history, rhythm, and meter. He knew the difference between secular and sacred Egyptian music and the various elements designed to make sound pleasing to the ear and restful to emotions. Great music which has lasted for generations comes from great musicians who disciplined themselves in gaining musical expertise, and we are the benefactors of their long hours of study and creative genius. Yes, on rare, isolated occasions some one with little musical training may compose a tune that is "catchy" but will it last? Only the future will determine it.

(3) Third, adaptability is relevant. We do not have the actual tune or melody Moses created; it is lost in the oral tradition of time. But He did adapt the melody to the existing primitive culture of that time-----singing on a pentatonic scale of five notes and chanted back and forth in antiphonal style. That style would be foreign to our Western ears today because music has developed in epoch ways to include increased range of notes (eight notes with modulating half tones), added harmony, sophisticated rhythm, and orchestral accompaniment. Moses wrote in the time of musical infancy; we exist today in musical maturity. We are confident, however, the musical tune he created at the Red Sea was a tune relevant to his time, and noble in character because of his musical training. The "worship" music around the golden calf was abhorrent---

totally inappropriate for the worship of Jehovah-----but the musical melody at the Red Sea was in a class all together different from the Mt. Sinai music. The burdening task of Christian musical composers today is to write new melodies or adapt existing, excellent tunes to new words. They must make the music relevant to our musical culture-----but only use Red Sea, not Mt. Sinai music.

(4) Fourth, discernment is monumental. Discernment is based on **KNOWLEDGE** and **EXPERIENCE,** and Moses had both----enabling him to know the difference between pagan and Biblical music; between self-centered and God-centered music; between fleshly and non-fleshly music; between **"get happy"** and **"get holy"** music; between hand-clapping and prostrating music; between screaming and hushed music; between giddy and joyful music; between innocuous and thought-provoking music. If Moses was alive today he would be labeled by many people in the pop Contemporary Christian Music movement as ***"intolerant," "legalistic," "judgmental," "Pharisaical," "argumentative," "irrelevant," "old-fashioned," "opinionated," "out-of-touch," and finally an "aesthetic snob."*** He would humbly reply by quoting the words of Paul in I Cor. 2:15: **"The spiritual man (mature man) makes judgment (discernment) about all things, (including music) but he himself is not subject to any man's judgment." DISCERNMENT** remains the Biblically rare, vaunted virtue------despite the epithets of derision thrown against it by many pop Christian pastors, seminary professors, music directors, and worship leaders who pride themselves on their ***"relevancy"*** to modern times, and **"liberation"** from ***"outdated, stuffy , boring, stodgy, traditional hymns."*** Moses would not be welcome in their churches. His two **"contemporary"** hymns are now considered **"traditional"**-------inadequate to meet the needs of modern Christians demanding screeching hot guitars, jazzy rhythms, driving beat, overpowering volume, sentimental tunes, and many repetitiously anemic lyrics labeled **"praise and worship choruses."**

This factual history confirms Moses' training in all phases of music, yet ironically there is no Biblical or historical evidence of musical knowledge in Aaron. Moses could discern between appropriate and inappropriate worship music; Aaron, the appointed worship leader, could not, and 3,000 Israelites were killed from his lack of musical discernment.

This musical composition of Moses here in Ex. 15:1-18 is set to a revised poetical framework by a modern-day poet----Thomas Moore; he entitled it **"SOUND THE TRUPMET."7**

Sound the loud timbrel o'er Egypt's dark sea!
Jehovah has triumphed----his people are free.
Sing---for the pride of the tyrant is broken,
His chariots, his horsemen, all splendid and brave---
How vain was their boast, for the Lord has but spoken,
And chariots and horsemen are sunk in the wave.
Sound the loud timbrel o'er Egypt's dark sea;
Jehovah has triumphed---his people are free.

This song of Moses is a watershed dividing 400 years of Hebrew slavery in Egypt from 40 years of wilderness wanderings, because there is no record in Scripture of the Hebrews singing during their 400 year slavery. All we hear from them during this slavery is **"sighing"**-----

depressed, longing for deliverance. But God's miraculous actions at the Red Sea turned their **"sighing"** into **"singing."**

c. Song of Moses----Deut. 32:1-43

The second contemporary song begins in Deuteronomy 31:30: **"Then Moses recited the words of this song from beginning to end in the hearing of the whole assembly of Israel."** Beginning in Deuteronomy 32:1-44 Moses writes a lengthy song of God's character and prognostication or warning to Israel of their apostasy from God. This song (because of its length) would be classified in musicology today as an **ORATORIO: a long, dramatic musical composition consisting of arias, duets, trios, and choruses sung to orchestral accompaniment.** The song was composed as a **TEACHING INSTRUMENT** for Israel so they would command their children through the rich, deep theology of the song (Deut. 32:44-47). *This song is definitely not trite, infantile, syrupy, nor boringly repetitious-----as are so many modern Christian songs and choruses of today, which in reality "dumb-down" the intelligence level of Christians----retaining them in effect to on-going "babyhood" and spiritual immaturity-----sucking on milk bottles!* **TRITE WORDS PRODUCE INFANTILE CHRISTIANS. SYRUPY TUNES PRODUCE SENTIMENTAL CHRISTIANS!** Where are the poetical lyrics to produce Christians with a strong theological foundation in God's Word? Where are the majestic musical melodies which build spiritual backbone, tear-filled eyes, and a humble, quiet reverence in the presence of God Almighty?

Moses did not compose these words for **"entertainment"** value so the worshipping Israelites would **"feel good"** and experience some nebulous **"holy Ghost feeling;"** no, he composed music **TO TEACH THEOLOGY!** Paul in Colossians 3:16 repeats that same purpose: **"teach and admonish one another with all wisdom, and as you sing psalms, hymns, and spiritual songs."** Much Contemporary Christian Music today is pathetically weak in sound theology, expressing only inane, insipid, superficial truth.

While we do not know the **MUSICAL TUNES** Moses composed and sang, we can be certain the music itself (not just the words) was grand, melodic, and would easily pass the Philippians 4:8 test. After all, remember Moses was trained in **ALL** the realms of Egyptian knowledge-----and this would include training in music. He definitely was a qualified, gifted composer. Absent from this music was any reference or association to uncontrolled emotions, wild celebration, discordant tones, dominating beat, monotonous repetition, or sensual revelry------as was present in the singing of Exodus 32:17-18 around the golden calf.

The Hebrew word for **"sing"** or **"song"** used here in Exodus 15:1 and Deuteronomy 32:1-43 is totally different from the **"singing"** of Exodus 32:18 which occurred just a few weeks after Exodus 15. In Exodus 15:1 and Deuteronomy 32:1 the Hebrew word is **SHIR**, *meaning a song of joy*, but in Exodus 32:18 the Hebrew word for sing is **AW-NAW**, *meaning a chaotic song of depression*. And that is what much of present-day contemporary Christian music does: it claims to worship God, but its poor quality actually depresses true Biblical worship! What a contrast: worship music of joy to God and worship music of depression to God. Both are songs-----but with contrasting results! Discernment is knowing the difference.

Yes, Moses did compose two **"contemporary"** tunes----but separated by 40 long years. The song recorded in Ex. 15:1-18 was at the beginning of the 40 year wilderness wanderings; the song recorded in Deut. 32:1-43 was recorded at the end of the 40 years. There is no record in Scripture (with the exception of the **"chaotic singing"** around the golden calf) of **ANY SINGING** or **INSTRUMENTAL PLAYING** of worship music **DURING THESE 40 YEARS**.

The trumpet (or coronet) was used only as a call to worship during sacrificial services, especially to signal the Day of Atonement (Leviticus 25:9), but there was not singing during the worship. Why? We can only guess, and conjecture is not always accurate. There may be three reasons for the absence of worship music during these 40 years: **(1) NATURE of the Israelites, (2) FEAR of the Israelites, (3) DEVELOPMENT of music.**

(1) NATURE of the Israelites. Singing and instrumental music may be absent because of the grumbling, complaining, carping nature of the Israelites during these 40 years of wanderings in the desert------they were never satisfied with Moses' leadership nor how God supplied their needs. A grumbling attitude normally does not accompany joyful worship music. **(2) FEAR of the Israelites.** They witnessed 3,000 of their fellow Israelites killed by the sword of the Levites as judgment for singing pagan music, and they may have feared any kind of music might be met with duplicating deaths. **(3) DEVELOPMENT of music.** Little is known today of ancient Hebrew music prior to worship in the Temple of Jerusalem, and time may have been needed to develop worship music appropriate for God's enthronement in praise.

They went through the mechanics of sacrifices, but seemingly with lack of joy and rejoicing. They worshipped, but with drudgery! Dead ritualism may describe their worship. Later in the Promised Land when the Temple was built there is an abundance of joy, singing, and instrumental accompaniment-----but not here in the desert. Moses knew how God-honoring music should sound, and the singing of the Israelites around the golden calf was rejected.

We cannot reject **ALL** contemporary music: only what is objectionable. But we must allow and encourage creative, gifted men and women today to compose great Christian music the Church needs for its ongoing worship experiences. Composing great music, however, is not easy: *it is hard work!* It requires giftedness in writing grand, flowing words of rich theology, and majestic, melodic tunes easily sung and remembered. Wedding right words to right music is another monumental task. Such music will meet the eight standard tests of Philippians 4:8 and easily pass through the mesh strainer. The Church needs these men and women. Pray and ask God to raise up these gifted musicians.

d. Contemporary song writers

Excellent music is being written today for worship services as seen in the music and words to **The Power of the Cross**, by Keith Getty and Stuart Townsend, and published by Thankyou Music, copyright 2005. The recent song is not strictly a hymn addressed to God, but would perhaps be classed as a "spiritual song" or known today as a gospel song. In four stanzas it tells the gospel about Christ's ministry on the cross, His suffering, resurrection, the torn veil, and the repeating refrain expressed in "This the power of the cross; we stand forgiven at the cross." The tune flows naturally, is readily singable for congregations, builds to a victorious climax in the refrain, and the words are theologically sound and profound. Thus music and words definitely illustrates the eight standards of Philippians 4:8----an excellent marriage of music and lyrics.

12. Balance traditional with contemporary music.

Traditional music was absent from the worship repertoire of Moses: he only used two contemporary songs he himself composed and sang. No Scriptural record exists revealing the Hebrews in Egypt used any Hebrew hymns; if they and Moses did sing these Jehovah-honoring hymns, we have no knowledge of it. The very term **"tradition"** means reliance on the past and Moses did not use any traditional Hebrew hymns. Today, however, we as Christians have a major advantage Moses did not have: several hundred years of hymns Christians have joyfully used in their worship to God and Christ. These hymns have stood the test of time when measured against the eight bench-mark tests of Philippians 4:8. If Moses was alive today worshipping in our evangelical churches I'm confident he would feel most comfortable singing many of these time-honored hymns.

Moses' two songs are now part of our **"tradition"**------even though no one has ever (to my knowledge) created singable tunes or melodies to his majestic words-----and I longingly wish a gifted musician would create this mighty gift to the Church! This **"traditional"** song would become **"contemporary"**----new and fresh to our generation.

Christian music today is the new **"battleground turf"** of the Church: should we sing traditional hymns or contemporary Christian music? Moses did not face this **"battle"**----we do! And unfortunately an increasing number of Church congregations fight and split over this issue---leaving in the dust fractured families, displaced friends, hurtful feelings, and broken congregations. All Christian music, traditional hymns and contemporary Christian music, can be used in worship-----if both types measure up to the eight tests of Philippians 4:8. That is the standard!

Some new hymns are written today------but many of them are neither singable (meaning melodically tuneful and easily flowing) nor are the words (lyrics) crafted to reflect sound theology: these hymns we must reject------they don't measure up to the strainer of Philippians 4:8. Charles Wesley wrote 6,500 songs, but few remain today in hymnals. Why? Because most of his songs did not endure the test of time----they failed to be true, noble, right, pure, lovely, admirable, excellent, praiseworthy. He was sincere in crafting many songs, but the words and tunes of many songs proved inferior in quality.

Some Contemporary Christian Music (many **"praise and worship"** choruses) written today by a vast number of contemporary musicians must also be judged for the same reasons: lack of sing ability in melody, and triteness (or self-centeredness) in lyrics. The gaveling discernment of Philippians 4:8 comes down hard on these **"ditty"** worship choruses: **REJECTED.** At issue is not traditional hymns or contemporary music, but **EIGHT BIBLICAL STANDARDS OF MUSIC!** Both traditional hymns and contemporary music must be willing to pass through the fine wire mesh strainer of Philippians 4:8.

Traditional hymns and contemporary music can and should be used in worship----but in balance. Singing one hymn and six choruses, or six hymns and one chorus is not balance! There should be a blending appropriate to the worship theme. Moses would feel comfortable singing traditional hymns in our worship services and also some (not all) contemporary praise and worship songs------because they meet the test.

People have their **"comfort zones"** in worship music-----liking a certain kind of music which makes them **"feel good."** We ask the wrong question when we ask ***"What kind of music makes me feel good?"*** Rather we must ask a more fundamental question: ***"What kind of music pleases God?"*** The answer requires more thought, Biblical examination, and exemplifies Paul's own testimony in Galatians 1:10: ***"Am I now trying to win the approval of men, or of God? Or am I trying to please men? If I were still trying to please men, I would not be a servant of Christ."*** Note: when we try to please men with the new "worship style of music" we cease to be a true servant of Christ.

13. Adapt contemporary music to Christian words.

Should all contemporary music be abolished in worship services:? No; of course not. Abolish only contemporary music that does not measure up to the eight standards of Philippians 4:8---music which is neither tuneful or singable, nor geared in rhythm and beat which reflects a worldly, jazzy, syncopated, dominate beat designed to arouse the fleshly nature of man.

Let me give two examples of borrowing great **SECULAR MUSIC** and adapting it for Christian worship. **FIRST**, a popular song composed by Rogers and Hammerstein for the Sound of Music and originally sung by Julie Andrews, **Edelweiss**, is a lovely tune about the Edelweiss flower which grows in the remote Mountains of Austria. The music is certainly tuneful, melodic, harmonious as she sings of the tiny Edelweiss flower. It is a secular, contemporary, song with no hint of irregular beat, nor arousing fleshly lusts.

Someone has written Christian words to this lovely tune as a song of benediction: Here are the words:

May the Lord, Mighty God, bless and keep you forever;
Grant you peace, perfect peace; courage in every endeavor.
Lift up your eyes and see His face, and His grace forever;
May the Lord, Mighty God, bless and keep you forever.

The tune definitely meets the eight standards of Philippians 4:8, and can be used (as in the above words) to a worship service.

Both Martin Luther and Charles Wesley did adapt secular tunes to Christian words----but they did not adapt music reflective of sensuality. They adopted only excellent musical tunes which were excellent in quality. Great music has been written down through the centuries, as well as trashy music. Discernment is knowing the difference, and I believe Christians can adapt these great, secular tunes and incorporate them into meaningful worship by the addition of Christian lyrics.

SECOND, another popular and secular tune composed by Richard Rogers and Oscar Hammerstein II for the Sound of Music and sung by July Andrews is **Climb Every Mountain**==--a song motivating human accomplishment in dreaming great dreams, accomplishing great ambitions. The words are good, but man-centered; I have heard this song sung in worship services, but the song elevates man, not Christ in worship. I have composed new Christian words to this grand, melodic tune and now the popular tune can be truly used in a worship service because the words, wedded to wonderful music, elevate Christ.

Borrowing excellent music cannot be limited to recent years alone, but also include outstanding music from the distant past. Seven examples illustrate this "borrowing" for Christian worship. **FIRST,** is the commonly-used hymn, **Joyful, Joyful, We Adore Thee** in worship services of all denominations. This standard hymn of worship is taken from music composed by Ludwig van Beethoven in 1824, and known originally as **Hymn to Joy.** Almost 100 years later in 1907 Henry van Dyke composed the Christian words of this great hymn to Beethoven's 9th symphony. Henry van Dyke had the spiritual discernment to recognize the stellar music of Beethoven and pen grand Christian words to this majestic hymn of worship. He did not adapt Christian words to cheap, tawdry, sensual, hip-moving, pelvis-thrusting, body-gyrating, volume-penetrating music, but only to a majestic tune which matched noble words.

SECOND, the well-known Christmas carol, **Joy to the World**, illustrates *REVERSE* borrowing----borrowing older words to match a newer tune. Isaac Watts wrote the words in 1719, but the music had not yet been composed. Twenty-two years later Handel composed the tune in 1741, but the words from 1719 were not adapted to the music until Lowell Mason accomplished this "harmonious marriage" in 1848----130 years after the words were first written by Isaac Watts.

THIRD, another example of *REVERSE* borrowing is the Christmas carol, **Hark! The Herald Angels Sing**, words composed by Charles Wesley in 1739, but the tune was not composed until 1840 when Felix Mendelssohn created the familiar music----100 years after Wesley wrote the words. Then in 1856 William H. Cummings became the "spiritual matchmaker" by wedding the words of Wesley from 1739 to the Mendelssohn tune of 1840.

FOURTH, a further example of *REVERSE* borrowing is the worshipful hymn, **Be Still, My Soul** sung in every denomination. The words were composed by a Lutheran Christian, Katharina von Schlegel in Germany in 1768. She was a devout Christian lady who actively promoted congregational hymn singing in the seventeenth century, but the words of **Be Still, My Soul** were not adapted to its present music tune until 100 years later in 1899 by Jane L. Borthwick, a devoted Christian worker in the Free Church of Scotland. She recognized the moving tune of Jean Sibelius in his famous **Finlandia,** composed in 1899, and adapted the words of Katharina von Schlegel to his music. **Finlanda**, another secular tune and the recognized national song of Finland, was a rousing, turbulent piece of music portraying the struggle of the Finish people against Russian influence, but only the penultimate, calming section of the larger musical score was adapted to our present day hymn. Gloria Gaither in 1981 wrote new words to this same musical score, entitling it **I Then Shall Live**, and this new song is now incorporated in many modern hymnals.

A famous painting by Edvard Isto hangs in the National Museum of Finland depicting Finland's struggle for sovereignty from Russia. It visually captures an anonymous maiden personifying Finland defending the book of Finish law from the clutches of the two-headed eagle----emblem of the Russian imperial house.

FIFTH, an additional illustration is the lovely **Theme from Liebestraum Number 3, (A Dream of Love)** written in 1850 by Frantz Liszt, a Hungarian pianist. The absolutely beautiful, flowing song is strictly written for piano performance, but its simple tune is easily sung by a congregation, and I have adapted words of Scripture to accompany this worshipful tune. In a church I served several years ago we often used this simple tune (not the fast cadenza sections) and Scriptural words in our loving worship to Christ. The congregation easily learned the tune, words, and often requested we sing it.

SIXTH, O Sole Mio, a globally known Neapolitan song from Naples, Italy written in 1898 by Eduardo di Capua is a powerfully dramatic song in the tradition of many Italian operatic arias, and has been performed in concerts by famous tenor soloists such as Enrico Caruso, Mario Lanza, Andrea Bocelli, and the Three Tenors: Jose Carreras, Placido Domingo, Luciano Pavarotti. Numerous secular recording artists such as Tony Martin and even Elvis Pressley have adapted secular words to this world-famous tune. Elvis Pressley popularized the song under the title **It's Now or Never**, and it became a world-wide hit, selling more than twenty million copies. This rousing song has since been wedded to theologically majestic lyrics and now appears in some church hymnals under the title, **Down From His Glory**. These Christian lyrics were composed in 1921 by William E. Booth-Clibborn. While the tune is difficult for congregations to sing because of its high and wide range, but it is easily handled by accomplished tenor soloists, and is a rejoicing melody to celebrate the incarnation of Christ who came down from His glory in heaven to become a man and suffer for our sins.

SEVENTH, a popular hymn used in worship services, printed in most hymnals, is **THINE BE THE GLORY,** and often sung at Easter to celebrate the resurrection of Christ. The words were composed by Edmond Louis Budry in 1884, a Swiss clergyman and hymn writer, and adapted to a tune from George Frederick Handle's oratorio, Judas Maccabeus, composed one hundred thirty-eight years earlier in 1746. The political context of the Oratorio is the Jacobite Rising of 1745 in Britain. Handle in 1746 hastily composed the Oratorio for the encouragement of the English. After the success of the British forces at the Battle of Culloden he started a work in honor of the victorious Prince William Augustus, Duke of Cumberland. The chorus became well-known, and the brass bands played this tune at the opening of new railway lines and stations in Britain during the 19th century. The majestic lyrics of the hymn well match the victorious tune of noble triumph. These examples of matching Christ-honoring words to magnificent music meets the standard of Philippians 4:8---music that is true, noble, right, pure, lovely, admirable, excellent, praiseworthy.

14. Define music terms.

Three important words need precise definitions in the area of music: **(1) Psalms, (2) Hymns, (3) Spiritual songs.** These three terms appear in Eph. 5:19 and Col. 3:16 where Paul instructs both the Ephesian and Colossian Christians to sing three categories of songs in the worship services. Sadly these three words are too quickly read and glossed over as unimportant in distinction, but they express different, needed kinds of music for proper balance in our churches.

(1) The first term ("psalms") refers to the Old Testament book of Psalms, for that book was the hymnbook of the early church where Christians actually sang tunes to different passages in the book of Psalms. These Psalms (or other Scriptures) are ***DOWNWARDLY PERSPECTIVE ,*** anchoring worship in the very words of the Bible. Early believers did not have a modern hymn book as we do today in our hymnal racks attached to the back of pews. Rather they used actual Scripture set to music, but the music was totally different from our Western concept of flowing harmony. Instead, the early Church music was more like a chant, something similar to a Gregorian Chant. The **ADVANTAGE** of singing psalms or any Scripture is twofold: ***(1) easy memorization, and (2) foundational doctrine***. Singing Scripture verses is an easy way to memorize the Word of God because a singable tune correlates to the passage. Furthermore, singing Scripture anchors worship on the solid doctrine of the Bible, and avoids triteness so characterized by modern lyrics today. The **DISADVANTAGE** of singing **"only Psalms"** can lead to formalism and deadness in the worship experience.

(2) The second term ("hymns") refers to words of human composition addressed ***VERTICALLY OBJECTIVE*** in praise to God and Christ. A gifted poet and/or musician would read God's Word, capture a doctrinal truth of God or Christ's character, and personally compose words attributing worship to them. That word ***VERTICLE*** is important, because it means the hymn is not addressed to man but to God-----declaring His divine attributes and worth. It focuses all attention upwards to God and Christ, and this type of hymn was the kind of song Moses composed in Exodus 15:1-18 and Deut. 32:1-44. Songs such as **Holy, Holy, Holy, To God be the Glory, Our Great Savior, All Creatures of our God and King, Joyful, Joyful We Adore Thee** are true worship hymns. The **ADVANTAGE** of singing hymns is threefold: ***(1) pure worship of God, (2) theological truth of the lyrics, and (3) avoidance of worshipping our feelings.*** Hymns captures true, unadulterated worship, because they focus on God; teach doctrinal truth of God, Christ, and the Holy Spirit, and like psalms, anchor worship on Scriptural truth. Sailers identifies hymns as "lyrical theology"**8** Furthermore he describes hymns as "theological miniatures" forming the basis of our theology. Strong lyrics leads to strong theology in worshippers; weak lyrics leads to weak theology in worshippers. The **DISADVANTAGE** of singing **"only hymns"** can, like the psalms, lead to formalism, deadness in the worship experience, and stifle testimony from the worshipper.

(3) The third term ("spiritual songs"-----sometimes called **"spiritual odes"** or **"ballads"**) means **"non-fleshly, non-carnal,"** songs **"in harmony with God's character and His Word."** These songs are words of human composition addressed ***HORIZONTALLY SUBJECTIVE*** to man *about God and human experience,* and develop out of the personal experiences of the worshipper----how he/she felt about God, their experience with God, their testimony about God's work in their lives. Historically in the time of the Apostle Paul they are termed **"ballads"** because they express a sentimental song by telling a story with short stanzas, simple words, and repetition of a refrain or chorus. Our modern gospel song and many so-called "praise and worship" choruses would fit into this category. Songs such as **What a Friend**

We Have in Jesus, Love Lifted Me, Down at the Cross, Draw Me Nearer, The Old Rugged Cross, Victory in Jesus, and the short, melodious, effective chorus **God is so God,** are not true hymns----but gospel songs, spiritual songs, or ballads because they are testimony songs-----not true worship hymns. The **ADVANTAGE** of singing these gospel songs or **"praise and worship choruses"** is allowance for personal, subjective experience in the life of the worshipper. The **DISADVANTAGE** of singing **"only gospel songs"** or **"spiritual songs"** is threefold: *(1) Scripture is eliminated, (2) pure vertical worship of God is absent, (3) worship becomes man-centered:* his feelings, emotions, experiences, testimony take center focus-----making the worship experience *SUPERFICIAL---a counterfeit of true worship!*

Balance in music, whether traditional hymns or contemporary Christian music, must include all three categories. A worship service should include songs and tunes using the (1) actual words of Scripture (Psalms or other Scriptures) of **DOWNWARD** teaching, (2) genuine hymns of **VERTICAL** praise to God, and (3) gospel songs or choruses of **HORIZONTAL** testimony about man's experience of God. This diagram visually portrays the need and distinction of these three kinds of worship music; note the **HORIZONTAL** arrow (Spiritual Songs) is often considered worship by sincere Christians, but this category of music is addressed from man to man, rather than man to God.

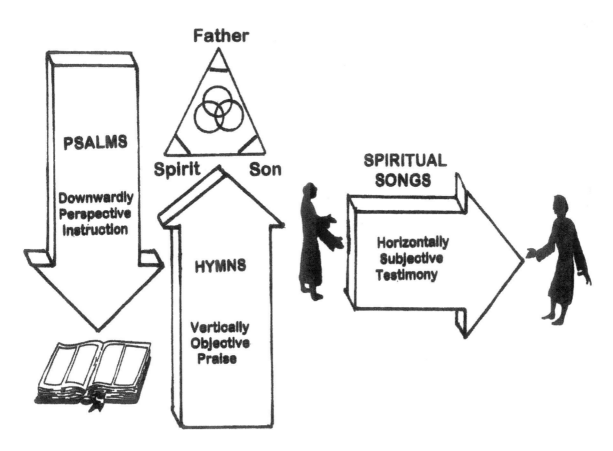

15. Be cautious in hymn "retuning."

"Retuning" is a contemporary attempt of revising existing traditional hymn tunes to a more **"modern"** tempo and rhythm matching the **"contemporary beat of the day,"** but this adaptation is often a return to the golden calf debacle of Exodus 32:17-18: making the music sound more like the world's music. Contemporary music artists will often take an old hymn, rich in music and theology, and add a jazzy, sensuous, syncopated beat, or rock and roll sound so **"the younger generation will like the hymn."** Aaron lives again today in this "new sound."

Hymn tunes are not **"sacrosanct,"** untouchable from contemporary revision------as long as the new tunes or rhythms pass the Philippians 4:8 test. New hymn tunes have been composed to old hymns and some of the music is excellent----a refreshing breeze in worship----excellent because they pass through the fine mesh strainer of Philippians. These new tunes wed well to the old words; but other **"modern, jazzy"** tunes only detract from the doctrinal truth of the hymn. They are a barrier, not an entrance, to worship------an **ILLUSION,** not a **REALISM** of worship.

Often ministers of music think **"let's jazz up this hymn so it sounds more contemporary; let's accent the beat so it becomes more dominant; give it more of a bosa nova sound."** Singing a hymn in such as jazzy, night-club sound detracts from the message of the song. I have heard of some ministers of music actually say, **"Let's sex up this hymn!"** What sacrilege! How crass! How revealing to see the golden calf living again-----with pagan Egyptian music-----in Christian worship!

16. Refrain from entertainment worship.

Entertainment means providing human delight, satisfaction, and amusement to people; it is a self-centered goal. Often pastors and worship leaders will use the right terminology: **"We are here to worship Christ,"** but design the service and select music to amuse the people, entertain them, make them "feel good," give them an emotional "high." These sincere leaders want people to come to church, so they adopt the consumer marketing strategy of *"giving the people what they want: a good variety show of pop music, lighting techniques, hand-clapping involvement, foot-pounding beats."*

Today I viewed a video of a church worship service where the choir and an Elvis Pressley impersonator sang the grand hymn, How Great Thou Art. A man dressed in the white, tapered pants and distinguishing gold cape of Elvis walked on stage wearing sunglasses and hairstyle of the rock'n roll king, Elvis Pressley. He was excellent in his singing style---perfectly matching the breathy, sexy voice of Elvis-----and demonstrated the sexy gyrating hip swaying and pelvis thrusting motions of the rock star. My heart broke as I watched the video: it was not worship, but pure, unabashed, sexy entertainment------in an evangelical church! The golden calf of Mt. Sinai returned to this church.

Will such entertainment draw the crowds? Definitely! Will the offering plates increase in deposited money? Of course! But it is not Biblical worship. It is using worldly methods in worship! After viewing this video an observer sarcastically asked, **"Did you learn more about Jesus in the service?"** Another participant in the worship service replied, **"I don't know. Did he play in the band?"** Sad, so sad!

17. Design worship with freedom and reverence.

The Church Growth Movement and its cousin, Contemporary Christian Music, has reacted against traditional hymns and worship structure as being **"too stuffy, outdated, dead,"** and replaced it with jazzy, pop, sentimental music with its syrupy tunes and trite lyrics repeated hypnotically in monotonous repetition----while standing at attention for 20 straight minutes. Traditional structure is replaced with a new structure of **"follow your feelings"**. The Bible does not give rigid instructions regarding **HOW** in precise detail a worship service should be structured; instead, Scripture gives freedom in designing a worship service------but in Biblical harmony of orderliness, reverence, Christ-centeredness, and conformity to the eight benchmarks of Philippians 4:8. Should the sermon come at the middle or end of the service? Should the Apostle's Creed, Glory Patri, and the Lord's prayer be recited each Sunday? Should the offering plates be passed down the aisles or should worshippers march forward to deposit their offering on the altar? The Bible gives freedom in these areas, but whatever you do, strive for reverence, dignity, joy, and humility before almighty God and His Son. Reject carnality, worldly styles of music, and entertainment focus.

18. Filter out self-centered worship.

a. Count pronouns.

There are three ways to discern self-centered worship in your own personal life and also in a corporate worship service with other Christians: **(1) Count pronouns, (2) compare worshipful content, (3) reflect on personal bodily responses. FIRST,** count the number of pronouns (I, me, my, we, our) used in a song or worship chorus. A true hymn of worship or chorus of worship will have minimal personal pronouns and major on the character and attributes of God and Christ. Two hymns illustrate this important judging tool: **Holy, Holy, Holy**, and **Joyful, Joyful We Adore Thee.** In the first hymn, **Holy, Holy, Holy,** the overwhelming focus is on the holiness of God, the Son, and the Holy Spirit; only one time is a personal pronoun used: **"Early in the morning OUR song shall rise to Thee."** The second hymn, **Joyful, Joyful We Adore Thee,** presents seven pronouns, but again the vast majority of words all point to God, His works, His creation.

In many so-called **"praise and worship choruses"** there exists a subtle shift to self-centered worship by the use of more personal pronouns and personal emphasis on self-fulfillment: my importance, value, dignity, feelings. A contemporary chorus illustrating this self-centered worship is entitled **You Raise Me Up,** containing 33 personal pronouns. Carefully read the words:

When I am down, and oh my soul, so weary

When troubles come and my heart burdened be
Then, I am still and wait here in the silence
Until You come and sit awhile with me.

You raise me up, so I can stand on mountains
You raise me up, to walk on stormy seas
I am strong, when I am on your shoulders
You raise me up---too more than I can be

You raise me up, so I can stand on mountains
You raise me up, to walk on stormy seas
I am strong, when I am on your shoulders
You raise me up---to more than I can be

There is no life—no life without its hunger
Each restless heart beats so imperfectly
But when you come and I am filled with wonder
Sometimes, I think I glimpse eternity

You raise me up, so I can stand on mountains
You raise me up, to walk on stormy seas
I am strong, when I am on your shoulders
You raise me up---to more than I can be

You raise me up, so I can stand on mountains
You raise me up, to walk on stormy seas
I am strong, when I am on your shoulders
You raise me up---to more than I can be

The number of pronouns and emphasis on self-importance, self-enablement, and personal feelings makes this chorus very self-centered-----even though it does make repeated references to an unnamed "You."

Another popular Contemporary chorus is **The Heart of Worship,** by Sonicflood, containing ten pronouns. While the pronouns are minimal, yet the overall thrust of the song is weak, insipid lyrics:

When the music fades
And all is stripped away
And I simply come
A longing just to bring
Something that's of worth
That will bless Your heart
I'll bring you more than a song for a song in itself
Is not what you have required
You search much deeper within

130

Through the ways things appear
You're looking into my heart

     CHORUS
     I'm coming back to the heart of worship
     And its all about You
     All about You, Jesus
     I'm sorry Lord for the thing I've made it
     When it's all about You
     It's all about You

King of endless worth
No one could express how much You deserve
Though I'm weak and poor
All I have is Yours
Every single breath
I'll bring you more than a song
For a song in itself
Is not what you have required
You search much deeper within
Through the ways things appear
You're looking into my heart

Good News Broadcaster magazine, produced by the Back to the Bible organization, published an article on this issue of predominance of personal pronouns: **"If one were to remove all the first and second personal pronouns from much of the contemporary Christian music, they would be humming most of the time."** **9** In the Bible, the greatness of God and His works is extolled; His glory is the central theme, but in much Contemporary Christian Music man's personal interest and benefits take precedence over God's glory.

In both contemporary choruses very little is directly said or even inferred about the grandeur of God, Christ, His death for our sins, His power and holiness. This week I examined closely the lyrics of the top 50 popular songs and choruses listed by a Contemporary Christian Music source. Space prevents me from including here the complete list with all their lyrics, but I formed several categories in my mind of these songs to aid in explaining their content. Other people, I'm sure, would no doubt differently categorize them. I divided them into five categories: (1) songs of pure worship, (2) mixed worship, (3) self-centered worship, (4) testimony, (5) encouragement.

(1) Pure worship is defined as total focus on God, Christ, the Spirit by both exalting them and describing their character traits. (2) Mixed worship adds more self-centeredness and self-absorption to the existing words of pure worship. (3) Self-centered worship includes non-existent or minimal Biblical standards of worship and focuses almost totally on self-achievement and self-worth by using religious terminology. (4) Testimony songs explains personal experience in

overcoming trials or achieving accomplishments through perseverance. (5) Encouragement songs challenge the Christian to endure hardships and trust God.

Two invaluable elements are needed to make any song a memorable masterpiece: the **LYRICS** (words) and a **MELODY (tune)**-----preferably a singable, naturally flowing melody. A song may have excellent words, but joined to a melody which is jerky, jazzy, unbalanced, monotonous, distractingly syncopated, disjointed in melody fragmentation. The opposite is also true: a wonderful, smooth flowing, well balanced tune but improperly connected to mundane, infantile lyrics. Marrying excellent lyrics to excellent melody is a rarity, but when this marriage is achieved the result is a **"great piece of music."**

I located one chorus by Chris Tomlin, entitled **Holy is the Lord,** which in my opinion falls into category #1 on Pure Worship. Read these words from the song:

We stand and lift up our hands
For the joy of the Lord is our strength
We bow down and worship him now
How great, how awesome is he
And together we sing

CHORUS:
Holy is the Lord, God almighty
The earth is filled with His Glory
Holy is the Lord God Almighty
The earth is filled with His Glory
The earth is filled with His Glory.

Note the strong Scriptural references in this chorus, but this strong Biblical backing is either absent or minimized in the other four categories of songs with trite, oblique reference to God. There is a place for songs of encouragement and challenge and personal testimony, but even in these categories and the songs I scrutinized in the list of 50 top popular songs, I believe the lyrics were poorly worded and superficial in their content. I concur fully with Leonard J. Seidel in his book **Face the Music,** (Grand Rapids Publications, Springfield, Virginia, 1998, p113,123) when he states: **"Strong theology encourages strong music........Weak music draws unto itself weak lyrics."**

b. Compare worshipful content.

SECOND, compare these two choruses with the two songs of Moses in Ex. 15:1-18 and Deut. 32:1-44. In Ex. 15:1-18 there are seven pronouns; three expressing Moses' intention to sing to the Lord, praise Him, exalt Him; four pronouns indicate the personal benefit of Moses: the Lord is **MY** strength, **MY** song, **MY** God, **MY** salvation. All these pronouns are expressed in verses 1-2; the remaining sixteen verses describe the different names of God, His power over the Egyptians, His majesty, His breath dividing the Red Sea, His judging hand against the Egyptians, His holiness, His awesome glory, His working wonders, His unfailing love, His strength over other pagan nations, His protection of Israel, His planting them into the land of promise.

Note the conspicuous absence of Moses' feelings, emotions, or concern for himself. There is no indication he is trying to **"get happy, excited, motivated, jazzed up"** into some nebulous spiritual high or holy buzz. Instead he majors on Jehovah and all His power and majesty. ***That is classic worship------free from self-centeredness!!!!!***

Next consider the second song of Moses in Deut. 32:1-44. Only five personal pronouns are used to indicate Moses in the first three verses; the remaining pronouns (**I**) are used by God Himself in describing His works and power, From verse 4-44 the entire lengthy passage describes God's historical record of calling Israel to be His people, His care for them as they wandered for 40 years in the desert, His provision for them, His protection of them, and His predictive judgment on His people for their sin, rebellion, and apostacy from Him.

In both passages of Ex. 15 and Deut. 32 we see clearly what is true worship: ***100% focus on the attributes, character, work, nature of God----lifting and exalting Him.*** Can anyone honestly equate the two illustrated popular "worship choruses" with the lofty worship of God by Moses? In my studied opinion, there is no comparison: no equality. Authors of many popular worship songs may be sincere in their compositions, but exceedingly few match the splendor and grandeur of worship presented by Moses. The content of worship lyrics by many modern day composers is dreadfully trite, insipid, infantile, self-centered, innocuous, and spiritually lethargic, but the content of Moses' worshipful poetry is grand, theological, majestic, humbling, and spiritually building.

Are these two examples of Moses unique or common in Old Testament worship? They are common and represent the many passages in Psalms where David gives worship to God. Every chapter in Psalms is not illustrating worship, but those chapters characterized by worship display a total God-centeredness. Yes, David will use the personal pronoun "I" to state his **INTENTION** of worship then immediately demonstrate his **ACTION** of worship by enumerating and citing the specific character and acts of God.

There are some excellent popular worship songs today, and one of them is **The Majesty and Glory of Your Name,** by Tom Fetke . It is powerful, moving, and God-honoring in its words describing in three stanzas God's creative power in creating the world and the mystery of creating man a little lower than the angels. The refrain or chorus is short but powerful, humbling, melodic in a natural flowing rise and fall in pitch and volume. Shown here are words from only the chorus:

Alleluia! Alleluia!
The majesty and glory of Your Name.
Alleluia! Alleluia!
The majesty and glory of Your Name.
Alleluia! Alleluia!
Alleluia! Alleluia!
Alleluia! Alleluia!

The lyrics are clearly Biblical and perfectly matched to a singable, flowing melody evoking personal worship reaching a crescendo followed by a peaceful resolution of volume. Every time I hear or sing this chorus I want to cry and fall on my face in quiet adoration to God and His Son Jesus Christ. I hesitate to even speak at the conclusion of the song, for I fear any quiet word from me will contaminate the holy presence of God. I merely bask in the quiet, holy presence of Him.

Another vibrant worship song, somewhat dated now, is written by Andre Crouch, **To God be the Glory.** The lyrics and melody are well crafted and support each other in triumphant praise and worship to God and Christ.

c. Reflect on personal bodily responses.

THIRD, discern and filter out self-centered worship by monitoring your own bodily responses and emotions: What effect does the music produce in you? Do you want to stomp your feet, clap your hands, wiggle your hips, thrust your pelvis, scream in hysteria, run down the church aisle, experience a giddy, happiness, or do you feel overwhelmed with the presence of God and desire to fall on your face in humility and tearful reverence before a holy God? ***Fleshly, sensual worship music promotes the former; Biblical worship music guides the later.*** The book of Revelation (5:6-14) records this later experience in heaven of the elders and living creatures in their worship before Christ the Lamb of God. There is no laughter, wild screams, hip-wiggling, pelvis-thrusting, running, hilarity, nor recorded "goose bumps" of emotion------but falling on their faces before the Lamb as they sing **"Worthy is the Lamb, who was slain, to receive power and wealth and strength and honor and glory and praise!"**

You may not know the intricacies of music theory, understand the difference between rhythm and beat, distinguish between a down and upbeat, nor grasp the effect of syncopation, but you can accurately describe what music does to your emotions and body. If listening to so called **"worship music"** makes you feel jittery, uptight, tense, sensually aroused, or giddy with emotion, then you can question the wisdom of this type of music. But if worship music produces in you a calming, reverent spirit, free from sensual urges and aroused emotions of self-satisfied euphoria, then you can affirm it is exalting God----not your human emotions of self.

Rock music and much of its developmental cousin, Contemporary Christian Music, is characterized by three elements: **(1) driving beat, (2) repetition, and (3) loud volume. FIRST,** driving beat is the major, predominate trait of much Contemporary Christian Music; this ongoing, incessant rhythm overwhelms clear thinking and takes commanding control of our bodies. Simon Frith, an English sociologist in his book **Sound Effects, Youth, Leisure, and the Politics of Rock'n' Roll**, New York, Pantheon Books, 1978, p. 14, comments on the effect this driving beat has on our bodies and emotions: **"The sexuality of music is usually referred to in terms of its rhythm---it is the beat that commands a directly physical response."**

SECOND, repetition is saying again and again the same words or same harmonic structure and serves as a controlling measure to create programmed responses in our bodies and emotions. In many Contemporary Christian songs certain phrases are repeatedly sung numerous times in succession. Why? There are two major reasons: **(1) brevity of the text, and (2) mood manipulation. (1) Brevity of the text.** The text (or words) often are short fragments of a phrase, and singing these short phrases occupies about a minute; therefore, the phrase is repeated over and over and over again to add greater length of time in the worship service. **(2) Mood manipulation.** The second reason repetition is used is to manipulate the congregation into **"the mood of worship"** and "**deeply imprint the phrase in their minds**. This technique is popularly labeled as **"7-11 music----seven words repeated eleven times."** The result of this repetition is boredom and monotony.

Is all repetition wrong and unwise? No! Even in great music such as Handle's **Hallelujah Chorus** sung at Christmas and Easter, there is repetition: "**King of Kings and Lord of Lords......Hallelujah! Hallelujah! Hallelujah!**" Why is this world famous, triumphant music not boring and monotonous? Because the repetition of words occurs at different chords, at different times, and in antiphonal manner (meaning the tenors sing back to the altos, and the sopranos answer back to the bass). The repetition is present, but it is written in a variety of ways. **CONCLUSION**: Repetition is a useful technique when used with variety of differing chord structures, differing intervals, and differing styles.

THIRD, loud volume of the drums, electric guitars, electric keyboards, brass instruments is used further to capture and control the thinking, emotions, and bodily responses of the worshipper. All three traits of rock music and Contemporary Christian Music is identical to the pagan Egyptian worship music used by the Israelites as they danced, skipped, whirled, and cavorted around the golden calf. At Mt. Sinai the music was not called rock 'n' roll-------it was euphemistically called **"worship music"**. And today pastors and worship leaders are reviving in our services this same Egyptian "worship music." The Hebrews had limited musical instruments at Mt. Sinai, but through **VOLUME** of sound, and **PERCUSSION** on the drums and tambourines the worshippers could be controlled by the sheer overpowering of the music. Today in churches this same technique is used: the volume in the public address system is increased and matched with the thudding of the drums felt each time in your chest.

Steven Halpern is an expert on nutrition, proper eating habits, and other factors impinging on good physical and mental health. He comments on music and its impact on mental health in this statement: *__"The loud volume, drums, and repetition of music of the contemporary rock genre bears a not-coincidental resemblance to trance music found in other parts of the world."__*10

Note the word **"trance"** in Halpern's observation. What is a trance? The dictionary defines it as a state resembling sleep; a form of hypnosis; a stunned condition; daze; stupor. The driving beat, repetition, and loud volume all combine to create a trance-like state in the worshipper, and the sad commentary is worship leaders call this experience "worship." I have personally witnessed this physical response in sincere Christians from the music. They will sway horizontally from side to side, bow and bend repeatedly in a downward fashion, roll their head in a circular manner, wave their hands and arms from side to side or in a forward position, sometimes gyrating with their legs and feet-----all the while keeping their eyes closed. They appear in a trance-like stupor. What caused this physical response? The driving beat, repetition of words or harmonic structure, and over powering volume of music. Mt. Sinai and Egyptian worship music is reincarnated each Sunday morning in many evangelical churches!

Pagan Egyptian worship music of 3,000 years ago is now baptized and given the born again, sacro sanct term of Contemporary Christian Music! Do we find Moses in Ex. 15 or Deut. 32 manifesting this trance-like stupor and loss of bodily control? Definitely not! What about David in the Psalms: is there any indication he looses bodily or mental control and falls into this worshipful daze and stupor? No! Yes, the scriptures teach we may lift up holy hands to God in worship, but this singular act is not a trance, but a symbol of surrender and praise to God, and is not associated with any other bodily movement.

19. Define precise worship.

Worshipping God is important, and this study has looked both at **INCORRECT** worship in Ex. 32:15-17 with the golden calf, and **CORRECT** worship with the two songs of Moses in Ex. 15:1-18 and Deut. 32:1-44, but I have not precisely defined worship. Before defining the term, observe and listen to ordinary, sincere Christians on Sunday morning as they worship God. Usually you will hear them say repeatedly either in prayer or in song: *"Lord, I worship You; I worship You; I worship You; I worship You; I praise You; I praise You; I praise You; I exalt You; I exalt You; I exalt You; I magnify You; I magnify You; I magnify You; I magnify You."*

What do you obviously notice? That's right-------repetition, repetition, and more repetition of the same words. Is this worship? Well, yes-------partly! These three word simple phrases state the **_INTENTION_**, but not the **_ACTION_** of worship. Properly defined, the word "worship" **means ascribing, declaring, or reciting the worth and character of God-----telling** God what He already knows about Himself: He is holy, just, merciful, gracious, kind, gentle, judging righteous judgment, Creator of all things, Lord of Hosts, the Great Physician, omnipotent, omniscient, omnipresent, eternal, unchangeable, provider, guardian. Worship recites these attributes to God in verbal prayer or in song; worship is far more than repeating fifteen times **"Lord, I worship You."** This sincere statement is only the beginning of worship, and must be followed by reciting back to God and Christ their divine qualities listed above.

Moses' two songs illustrate this verbal recitation. In both Ex. 15 and Deut. 32 Moses goes into great detail describing who Jehovah is: His names, His works as Creator and Judge, His provision and care for His people the Israelites, His powerful defeat of the Egyptian army and Pharoah, His guiding and guarding of His people from harm, and this recitation is the heart and soul, the "meat and potatoes" of Biblical worship.

Is much effort required to repeat fifteen times **"Lord, I worship You?"** Definitely not! But more effort, energy, and knowledge is needed to worship God the way Moses did by reciting back to God his divine character traits. You need to know what they are before reciting them. But this knowledge is necessary for Biblically mature worship.

Since music is a major component of worship, it must include lyrics (words) reflecting this Biblical and theological knowledge of God. But sadly many, many contemporary praise and worship songs fail to use Biblical words and theological ideas describing God and Christ; instead they use trite, anemic, watered-down clichés reducing God to a **"powerful pal, a good buddy, my friend"** who will help me be successful in my business relationships and career. Traditional hymns of worship are more precise in using strong words of theology and doctrine in worship.

I compare a steak dinner with apple pie topped with luscious whipped cream. Which is more nutritious, the steak dinner, or the mounds of whipped cream on the apple pie? The answer is obvious, but many people want more and more whipped cream. Yes it is attractive and tasty----but definitely not wholesome: we can't develop strong muscles and a healthy immune system from whipped cream.

Hymns teaching strong doctrine and theology is the steak dinner; many contemporary pop songs and choruses represent the whipped cream. When you pray, don't merely repeat fifteen times "I worship You," but go beyond this **INTENTION** and pray with **ACTION:** **"Father, I worship You because you created this world out of nothing; You formed the seas and dry land; You designed the entire solar system with all its planets and moons; You created Adam and formed Eve from one of his ribs, then breathed the breath of life into man."** This is true worship: it clearly expresses Biblical truth in a knowledgeable, mature manner.

Expect and demand the hymns you sing in your worship service also express this same degree of Biblical knowledge which exalts Christ, rather than many of the pop, jazzy, syncopated, rock and roll style of music with its anemic, watered-down words often expressing self-centered feelings of self-benefit. Don't repeat the painful lesson from the Israelites who borrowed pagan music around the golden calf to use in worship of Jehovah: they were misguided then, and sincere Christians today are also misguided by using pagan music patterns in worship to God.

20. Reject Pagan Methods.

The previous nineteen points of application have centered on pagan music styles seeping into our evangelical churches of worship, but now I want to address pagan methods as illustrated by the **"strange fire"** of Nadab and Abihu in Leviticus 10:1-8 and their instant death from God's judgment. The issue there is not strictly music styles, but borrowing pagan coals of fire from pagan altars-----mixing pagan fire with God's fire on the Brazen Altar, and thus diluting God's holiness and allowing the demonic influence from false gods. What precisely does "pagan" mean? It is defined in many different ways with no consensus of agreement; for the purpose of this book I define it as any atheistic, agnostic, polytheistic, or humanistic belief or practice opposed to Biblical revelation of God and Christ.

The Egyptian music at the golden calf in Exodus 32:17-18 was pagan music because it originated in the polytheistic beliefs and practices of Egyptian worship. The Israelites merely borrowed this musical style to their own destruction. But the "strange fire" of Nadab and Abihu was not confined to music, but pagan methods or practices of the polytheistic Midianites. Today we do not face polytheism of the Midianites, but a more subtle deception of humanistic (man-centered) beliefs and methods advocating human betterment, personal success, personal self-esteem, financial wealth, material freedom, and popular acclaim. A godless culture abounds in promoting these goals through a variety of sophisticated methods.

I have articulated some of these questionable methods in previous chapters and their allurement to the church today. Recently I heard of an evangelical church offering a raffle at a cost of $10.00 each with the chance to win a Harley Davidson Motorcycle----one for a man and one for a woman-----as an inducement to attend the worship service on a selected day. Big crowds attended on this Sunday and the two popular motorcycles were awarded to the two raffle tickets drawn. Did this method work? Certainly! But was it a Biblical method? I don't think so!

Pastors and other Christian leaders face a constant temptation to use some pagan, humanistic method to increase attendance and evangelistic opportunity. The church is looking for better methods; God is looking for better men! What can the evangelical church do in the face of these tempting pagan methods? Ephesians 6:10-18 describe this pull from unseen demonic sources, and lists the spiritual weapons we have, but one of the least popular weapons is in verse 14: "Stand firm." Resist the temptation------and stand firm against it. Other pagan methods and techniques have yet to be developed by a worldly system, but they must be resisted. Allowing and using pagan methods is reliving the experience of Nadab and Abihu----it is corrupting the holiness of God and allowing demon influence to get a foothold in the church.

21. Expunge self-worship.

Self-worship centers on our personal emotions------seeking gratification and stirring of our emotions of love, contentment, mystical experience with God, feelings of happiness and exultation. These emotions are normal and commonly experienced at various times by all of us, but they are not the **motivation** for worship. Do you attend worship service expecting to experience these emotions? If so, then you are guilty of self-worship: we are commanded to worship and love God, not ourselves. Worship is giving honor and praise to God for His person and character: it is not praising and experiencing the subjective worth of our emotions. Self-worship violates the second commandment: **"You shall not make for yourself an idol or any graven (carved) image of Me." (Exodus 20:4)**

The worshippers around the golden calf violated the second commandment with an actual idol, and pagan music which stirred their emotions of giddiness, hilarity, sensual feelings, and resulting orgiastic practices. They did not anticipate in advance these emotional feelings, but when the music played they realized the music made them "feel good," it stimulated their self-absorbed, narcissistic feelings. They learned through experience what kind of music promotes subjective feelings. They worshipped the true God-----in the wrong way!

An idol involves a **MATERIAL** and **MENTAL** image. We commonly know a physical, material, visible idol is prohibited, but we fail to realize a mental, non-material, unseen idol is also prohibited by this commandment when we form in our minds before worship an anticipated stirring of our emotions. In effect we are worshipping our emotions! We mentally carve in our minds an image of our satisfied emotions, and judge worship by whether or not these emotions were stirred and exalted. ***We are worshipping worship: adoring,*** *honoring, satisfying the subjective experience of worship, instead of giving praise to God in worship.*

Much CCM in its philosophy and music practice gears toward using songs that stimulate the sensual, ecstatic emotions of man---giving the worshipper what he wants, meeting his anticipated needs. Pastors and worship leaders will never say "We are here to worship our feelings," but design the music to accomplish that unstated objective. The worshipper today, like the Israelites around the golden calf, learn the style of music which will meet their subjective emotions, and approach worship with this **MENTALLY CARVED IMAGE** of musical anticipation.

All of us are emotional creatures----though we may express them in different ways. Sometimes I am moved to tears by the meaningful words of a hymn; other times I sing the same hymn with no outward emotional display. Sometimes in a worship service I sense in my spirit the overwhelming majesty of God and bow my head in reverence; other times my emotions seem absent. Why the difference? Because my emotions, and yours as well, are quite changeable----- and unreliable. We all have good days, bad days, and in-between days. God knows our emotional constitution and He in His sovereignty knows when and how to meet these emotional needs. We approach a worship service, however, to give honor to Him----not to ourselves. You may tell God you love Him-----yet feel no gushing upsurge of emotional excitement. Are you being hypocritical with no emotional attachment? Of course not! Your words of love are sincere, genuine, despite the numbness of your emotions.

These same changeable emotions are everyday manifested in marriage. As I sit before this computer writing this book I sense no romantic passion generated toward my wife. Does the absence of passion mean I don't love her? Definitely not! My love for her is a settled issue---- after more than forty-six years of marriage. But there are times I do sense deep, romantic passion for her, and in those times my words of love to her take on profound emotions.

Expunge self-worship; eliminate it; crush it. Don't enter worship with the mental idol of **"What can I get out of it,"** but **"How can I adore God?"** Don't desire music to make you "feel good," but music and words expressing the grandeur and holiness of God. Don't judge a worship service by how your emotions were stimulated, but by how God was honored. Don't violate the second commandment by erecting a mentally carved idol of anticipated, self-generated emotional narcissism.

22. Seek the spirit, not the letter, of commands.

In the absence of a specific, precise command from God prohibiting pagan coals of fire, Nadab and Abihu misused their freedom and acquired coals of fire from the pagan altars of the Midianites. They also failed to grasp the positive example of God providing the burning coals of fire on the Brazen Altar. Their approach was strictly legalistic: wanting a specific, prohibiting command.

What pagan methods will be introduced into the church in the next ten or twenty years? We don't know, and the Bible does not offer a specific, written prohibition addressing each of them in detail. Are we free, therefore, to adopt and adapt these pagan methods to increase the success of the church? If your approach is legalistic, like Nadab and Abihu, you will not feel guilty in going outside Biblical teaching to endorse and embrace them. But the major issue is discovering the spirit of God's commands----the intent, the over-arching aims of God's holiness. A rule of hermeneutics clarifies this procedure, and is expressed in this manner: ***Include all passages on a given subject to correctly state Biblical teaching.*** Each passage must be considered, correctly interpreted, and jointly focused on the stated, or inferred, teaching.

Suppose there are twenty passages of Scripture on a given subject----stewardship, for example---- but you only read and interpret ten. What is the problem? You are ignoring ten other passages which may give additional insight to the subject: your conclusion will be inadequate, short-sighted, skewed. All twenty passages must be correctly interpreted in order to properly judge the overall import and divine principle undergirding them. This rule also applies to the subject of methods of ministry: isolate all passages on the subject of methods, correctly interpret them, and discern the divine principle or principles uniting these passages. Allegiance to this rule will permit the spirit of the commands to capture your mind, give clarity to your thinking, and reject certain pagan methods because they conflict with these Biblical principles. Furthermore this hermeneutical process is both **OBJECTIVE** and **SUBJECTIVE:** *objective in interpretation of these passages, and subjective in discernment of sensing their direction.* Through objective interpretation of these passages you will subjectively sense the direction, the aim where these passages are focused. Yes, subjectivity (discernment) is involved, but based on objectivity.

23. Evaluate methods based on holiness---not pragmatism.

Why did God instantly kill Nadab and Abihu in the Tabernacle? They violated His holiness, as recorded in God's message to Moses in Leviticus 10:3: ***"Among those who approach me I will show myself holy; in the sight of all the people I will be honored."*** We can show the holiness of God through our righteous conduct, or suffer judgment through our unrighteous conduct: Nadab and Abihu suffered the later. God's judgment demonstrated to all the people that day His essential quality of holiness: **"in the sight of all the people I will be honored."** The Israelites observed this fire from God kill the two priests, and these worshippers instantly perceived the unmatchable holiness of God. Note God did not say **"I prefer to be honored,"** or **"I would like to be honored,"** but **"I will be honored."** As Sovereign God, He demands in our worship music, personal conduct, or methods of outreach we exalt and extol His holiness. Nor did God say He will be honored through His goodness, power, omniscience, omnipotence----but holiness----the essential attribute undergirding all other qualities of His Godhead. These additional attributes are merely the rays of light in God's spectrum----all streaming from His holiness.

Nor did He say **"I will be honored through pragmatism----whatever works."** Nadab and Abihu operated on the basis of pragmatism---any source of fire will be sufficient; any fire will "work;" any fire can be brought into the Tabernacle. But they were wrong! And God killed them! Pragmatism, as discussed previously, means whatever works, gets results; it does not consider morals or values in methods, only what **"gets the job done."** Note the implied time difference in Nadab and Abihu securing coals of fire from the pagan altars of the Midianites. This pagan altar may have been located near the Tabernacle, one quarter mile, one half mile, or removed even one mile. There they secured the coals of fire, placed incense over the hot embers, and walked toward the Tabernacle. God's judgment did not fall, but when they came into the Tabernacle and offered **"unauthorized fire"** before, or in the presence of the Lord, then the fire of God fell on them and instantly killed them. During their seeming **"walk to the Tabernacle"** their pragmatism seemed to "work." The coals continued burning; the sweet-smelling incense continued rising and filling the atmosphere with its pleasant aroma. Their pragmatic method worked------for a period of time!

The church today is enamored with pragmatism----casting about for any method to attract crowds, build large congregations, and fill the offering plates. One church uses a shot glass (small glass of liquor) to invite people to its worship services. Empty shot glasses were ordered with the name of the church printed on the glass along with bold printed message on the glass: **"Give our church a shot!"** Church members walked the streets, entered saloons, dance halls, and offered free shot glasses to strangers. Did this "shot glass" method work? Certainly! New visitors came to the church as a result of this pragmatic marketing technique. But at what cost to holiness?

Pragmatic music in worship does not exalt the holiness of God, but targets the emotional needs of the worshipper. Yes, a church may sing the hymn Holy, Holy, Holy but the song and message is contaminated by other pragmatic "praise and worship" choruses sung to a driving beat, jazzy sound, sensual feelings and thunderous volume of musical instruments all seeking to give the worshipper "a holy buzz," and self-centered feeling of self-esteem. As a pastor or music director, select music and methods where God's holiness is exalted. Does this mean the hymn Holy, Holy, Holy must be sung each Sunday? Of course not! But all songs must be sung in reverence and respect to God------apart from the pagan sounds and sinful associations of secular tunes.

God's judgment on Nadab and Abihu did not occur immediately upon their securing coals of fire from the Midianites, but seemingly afterwards----perhaps ten minutes, one half hour, or maybe even an hour later. His judgment may have been postponed! And God's judgment on the pragmatic church today may also be postponed-----by a year, five years---or deferred at the judgment seat of Christ when pastors and church leaders must give an account to Christ for their adoption of pagan methods and pagan music used in worship. But immediate judgment occurs to the church in superficial worship, "lite" sermons with minimal Bible teaching, immaturity in believers, and demon-contamination of sinful practices in Christians. Some people may be "converted" through pagan, pragmatic methods and music, but does their "conversion" eventuate into rocky (superficial) or thorny (temporary) soil? The goal of evangelism is good soil that produces growth and reproduction of holy living, but pragmatism and paganism is powerless to achieve this supernatural aim.

24. Refute "preference" in music selection.

Many sincere Christians believe **"taste"** or **"preference"** is the undergirding issue in music, and this false belief is being taught in seminaries, Bible Colleges, and universities. This false thinking is typically expressed in the following statement: **"I have my own taste and preference in worship music; you have yours, and my preference is just as good as yours."** Is worship music, or any other kind of music, merely a matter of "taste" or "preference?" If you have read the previous chapters, the answer should be obvious: all musical "taste" is a cultivated fondness because it meets our needs. We listen to certain kinds of music because we enjoy it, receive pleasure from it. But the major question is: Does the Bible give guidance on music selection? Does the Bible direct us in the kinds of music we hear? Does the Word of God give standards for judging Christian and secular music? The answer is definitely yes!

How would Moses respond to Aaron at the golden calf had Aaron said, "This Egyptian worship music is my preference; my personal taste? I like its sound; it meets my personal desires, and gets response from people."? How would Paul answer the Colossian Christians in Colossians 3:1-2 if they said, "We prefer to set our affection on earthly things; we have a taste for music which meets our self-centered needs-----------music that is popular in the MTV style."? How would Paul reply to the Philippian Christians in Philippians 4:8 if they said, "We prefer to listen to music that is false, superficial, morally low, lacking in reverence, evil, impure, offensive, depraved, mediocre, dishonorable, substandard, lacking in commendation from knowledgeable, mature Christians"? What would God say to Nadab and Abihu in Leviticus 10 if they stated: "Our preference is to acquire coals of fire from pagan temples as a legitimate method of worshipping the true God?" Many Christians interpret I Thessalonians 5:21 not as it is stated: "Test everything," but "Test everything----except music: in this area let your personal taste and preference be your guide."

Taste and preference in worship music must be cultivated by Biblical standards-----not by our selfish desires for pleasure, enjoyment, or **"relevant sound."** Yes, each Christian has certain "tastes and preferences" in worship, but are they tastes and preferences God commands, endorses, and instructs in His Word? We learn to like, taste, and prefer music to which we are ***repeatedly exposed,*** whether it is rock, soft rock, jazz, classical, blue grass, country western, hip hop, heavy metal. The command of Paul in Philippians 4:8 is to think on eight standards of measurement in order to gain an acquired skill of discernment, and develop Biblical taste and preference for music that is true, noble, right, pure, lovely, admirable, excellent, praiseworthy. Does your "taste and preference" in music meet these eight standards?

CHAPTER 8

Conclusion

"In a multitude of words transgression is not lacking, but he who restrains his lips is prudent." (Proverbs 10:19---Amplified Old Testament). A shorter way of repeating this wise proverb is: "Use words sparingly." That is sound advice! Solomon in this verse is talking about personal speech----not about books. Some topics can be summarily discussed in a few pages of a book, but other subjects require more detail and explanation. This book does not address every facet of controversy on worship music, but I hope what is written in these pages stimulates you to read further and become more discerning in judging between poor, good, better, and best in worship music----between appropriate and inappropriate. I have attempted to give a Biblical exposition of several key passages and their application to worship music in our churches. Many technical aspects of music structure, harmony, rhythm, and beat are not included here, but are important to consider in judging the worth of music as determined by the eight tests of Philippians 4:8. Books providing this information are listed here:

1. **Music in the Balance**, by Frank Garlock and Kurt Woetzel, published by Majesty Music, 1992. (Presents a Biblical plan of music that good men considerable reasonable. Trained musicians will appreciate the scholarship of their studies, and novices will understand and gain valuable insight.)

2. **Measuring the Music**, by John Makujina, published by Old Paths Publications, 2002. (This book is very thorough in documenting the false reasoning and philosophy of Contemporary Christian Music. Presents arguments made by advocates of CCM, and Biblically refutes them.)

3. **Face the Music**, by Leonard J. Seidel, published by Grand Rapids Publishing Co., 1998. (The author is a lecturer and seminar director on the subject of Church music. Warren W. Wiersbe says: "You may not agree with him, but you cannot safely ignore what he writes.")

4. **Music and Morals**, by Kimberly Smith, published by Winepress Publishing, 2005. (A mini-reference guide to different musical styles and their origins. Examines the effects of music on the listener, putting to rest the myth that music is amoral. A CD of music examples accompanies the book.)

5. **Let Those Who Have Ears to Hear**, by Kimberly Smith, published by Winepress, 2001. (Smith presents ways the reader may begin to discern music. She also exposes fifty "excuses" used to defend CCM.)

Included here is a chart by Kimberly Smith and taken from her book, Let Those Who Have Ears to Hear.**1** The chart visually summarizes the contrast of Contemporary Christian Music and Godly Christian Music.

Christian Music Comparison Chart	
Contemporary Christian (offbeat or jazz rhythms, etc.)	**Godly Christian** (straight-forward rhythms)
1. Disorderly. (I Cor. 14:33)	1. Orderly. (I Cor. 14:40)
2. Rhythms originated from pagan culture. (Jer. 10:2a; Rom. 8:7)	2. Religious music of Western civilization originated in New Testament church. (Eph.5:19; Col. 3:16)
3. Appeals to the flesh. (Rom. 8:5a, 8:7)	3. Appeals to the spirit. (John 4:123-24; Rom. 8:6b)
4. Pictures conflict of our spirit with our flesh. (Rom. 7:14-25; Gal. 5:17)	4. Pure; pictures denial of flesh and self control. (Rom. 8:12-14; Gal. 5:22-23; Titus 2:11-12)
5. Tickles the ears to draw people to the church. (II Tim. 4:3)	5. Acknowledges that it is God who draws people to Christ through the Holy Spirit. (John 6:44)
6. Imitation of the world. (I John 2:!5; Luke 16:15b)	6. Separateness from the world. (Rom. 12:2; II Cor. 6:14-17)
7. Use of sensual techniques. (I John 2:16)	7. No such techniques used. Morally righteous. (Rom. 13:14; I Pet. 1:15-16)
8. Contributes to emotionalism in worship. (John 4:23-24; I Cor. 14:33)	8. Encourages true, spirit-filled worship. (John 4:23-24; Phil. 3:3)

NOTES

Chapter 1

1. John I. Durham, *Word Biblical Commentary, Vol. 3, Exodus,* (Waco: Word Books Publisher, 1987), page 430.
2. Nehama Leibowitz, *Studies in Shemot Exodus*, (Jerusalem: The World Zionist Organization, 1981), page 599.
3. S. R. Driver, *Exodus*, (Cambridge: University Press, 1985). page 354.
4. John I. Durham, *Word Biblical Commentary, Vol. 3, Exodus,* (Waco: Word Books Publisher, 1987), page 400.
5. Alfred Syndrey, *Music in Ancient Israel*, (London: Vision Press Limited, 1969), page 323.
6. Ibid., page 167.
7. James I. Mursell, *The Psychology of Music*, (Westport, Connecticut: Greenwood Press Publishers, 1964), page 216.
8. Arthur W. Pink, *Gleanings in Exodus*, (Chicago: Moody Press, 1972), page 105.
9. Alfred Syndrey, *Music in Ancient Israel,* (London: Vision Press Limited, 1969), page 40.
10. Hans Hickkmann, *Die alesten Musikernamen, Musica* (March 1951), Vol. 3, page 90.
11. Justin Martyr, *Apologia Prima pro Christianmis*, 44, PGL, VI, page 395.

Chapter 2

1. Alfred Syndrey, *Music in Ancient Israel*, (London: Vision Press Limited, 1969), page 163.
2. Ibid., page 163.
3. Ibid., page 480.
4. Ibid., page 481.

Chapter 3

1. Alfred Syndrey, *Music in Ancient Israel*, (London: Vision Press Limited, 1969), page 176.

Chapter 4

1. Richard S. Hess, *Bulletin for Biblical Research, "Leviticus 10:1: Strange Fire and an Odd Name,"* 12:2, page 187-188.
2. Bryan D. Bibb, *Ritual Words and Narrative Worlds in the Book of Leviticus*, (New York: T & T Clark, 2009), page 120.
3. Hess, *Bulletin for Biblical Research, "Levitics 10:1: Strange Fire and an Odd Name,"* 12:2, 2002, page 187-188.
4. Philipp J. Budd, *Leviticus, NCB*, (London: Pickering Grand Rapids: Eerdmans Publishing Company, 1996), page 151.
5. Frank M. Cross, *The Biblical Archaeologist Reader*, ed G. Ernest Wright and David Noel Freedman, (New York: Anchor Books, 1961), page 217.
6. Ibid., 217.

Chapter 5

1. *New Dictionary of Thoughts*, (New York: Standard, 1955), page 477.
2. A. J. Hoover, *Don't You Believe It*, (Chicago: Moody Press, 1982), page 7.
3. Ibid., page 79.
4. Norman L. Geisler and Ronald M. Brooks, *Let Us Reason*, (Grand Rapids: Baker Book House, 1990), page 95.
5. Ibid., page 95.
6. S. Morris Engle, *With Good Reason, An Introduction to Informal Fallacies*, (New York: St. Martin's Press, 1976), page 8-9.
7. Normal L. Geisler and Ronald M. Brooks, *Let Us Reason*, (Grand Rapids: Baker Book House, 1990), page 134.
8. Ibid., page 134.
9. Ibid., page 134.
10. Ibid., page 137-138.
11. Stephen Naylor Thomas, *Argument Evaluation*, (Tampa: Worthington Publishing Company, 1991), page 140.

Chapter 6

1. F. F. Bruce, *An Expanded Paraphrase of the Epistles of Paul*, (Palm Springs: 1965), page 121.
2. Gerhard Kittel, *Theological Dictionary of the New Testament*, Vol. 4, (Grand Rapids: William B. Eerdmans Publishing Company, 1964), page 284.
3. Kimberly Smith, *Let Those who Have Ears to Hear*, (Enumclaw, Washington: Winepress Publishing, 2001), page 42.
4. John Diamond, *Your Body Doesn't Lie*, (New York: Warner Books, 1980), page 164.
5. Ibid., page 161.
6. Frank Garlock and Kurt Woetzel, *Music in Balance*, (Greenville: Majesty Music, 1992), page 46.
7. Ibid., page 46.
8. John Diamond, *Your Body Doesn't Lie*, (New York: Warner Books, 1980), page 164.
9. Ibid., page 166.
10. V. P. Furnish, *Theology: The Place and Purpose of Philippians III, NTS*, 10, (Nashville: Theology and Ethics in Paul, 1963), page 89.
11. Gordon Fee, *Paul's Letter to the Philippians*, (Grand Rapids: William B. Eerdmans Publishing Company, 1995), page 375.
12. Carol Merle Fishman and Shelley Katch, *The Music Within You*, (New York: Simon & Shuster, 1995), page 189.

Chapter 7

1. Neill Postman, *Amusing Ourselves to Death*, (New York: Penguin Group, 1985), page 85.
2. John Makujina, *Measuring the Music*, (Willowstreet, Pennsylvania: Old Paths Publications, 2002), page 219-265.

3. Robin A. Leaver, *Luther's Liturgical Music: Principles and implications,* (Grand Rapids: William B. Eerdmans Publishing Company, 2007), page 13.

4. Flavius Josephus, *Antiqiuities,* Writings of Josephus, 184-10, 18:23; 20:12.

5. S. Lewis Johnson, *BibSac, "Beware of Philosophy,"* Oct. 1962, page 119.

6. Alfred Syndrey, *Music in Ancient Israel,* (London: Vision Press Limited, 1969), page 163.

7. Robert Atwan and Laurance Wieder, *Chapters into Verse: Poetry in English Inspired by the Bible,* Vol. 2, (New York: Oxford University Press, 1963), page 129.

8. Don E. Sailers, *Music and Theology,* (Nashville: Abington Press, 2007), page 135.

9. Harold E. Richards, *Good News Broadcaster, "Has Contemporary Christian Music Had It?"* Nov. 1982, page 38.

10. Steven Halpern, *Tuning the Human Instrument,* (Belmont, California: Spectrum Research Institute, 1978), page 240.

Chapter 8

1. Kimberly Smith, *Let Those Who Have Ears to Hear,* (Enumclaw, Washington: Winepress Publishing), page 183-184

BIBLIOGRAPHY

Atwan, Robert and Laurance Weider, editors, <u>Chapters into Verse: Poetry in English Inspired by the Bible,</u> New York: Oxford University Press, 1993.

Bibb, Bryan D., <u>Ritual Words and Narrative Worlds in the Book of Leviticus,</u> New York: T & T Clark, 2009

Bruce, F. F., <u>An Expanded Paraphrase of the Epistles of Paul,</u> Grand Rapids: Eerdmans Publishing Co., 1965.

Budd, Phillip J., <u>Leviticus, NCB,</u> London: Pickering, 1996.

Burroughs, Jeremiah, <u>Gospel Worship or The Right Manner of Sanctifying the Name of God in General,</u> Orlando: Soli Deo Gloria Publications, 1648.

Cross, Frank M., <u>The Biblical Archaeologist Reader,</u> New York: Anchor Books, 1996.

Diamond, John, <u>Your Body Doesn't Lie,</u> New York: Warner Books, 1980.

Driver, S. R., <u>Exodus,</u> Cambridge: University Press, 1985.

Durham, John I., <u>Word Biblical Commentary, Exodus,</u> Vol. 3, Waco: Word Books Publisher, 1987.

Engle, S. Morris, <u>With Good Reason, An Introduction to Informal Fallacies,</u> New York: St. Martin's Press, 1976.

Fee, Gordon, <u>Paul's Letter to the Philippians,</u> Grand Rapids: William B. Eerdmans Publishing, 1995.

Fishman, Carol Merle, and Shelley Katsh, <u>The Music Within You,</u> New York: Simon & Schuster, 1985.

Frame, John M., <u>Contemporary Worship Music,</u> Phillipsburg, New Jersey: P & R Publishers, 1997.

Frith, Simon, <u>Sound Effects, Youth, Leisure, and the Politics of Rock 'n' Roll,</u> New York: Pantheon Books, 1978.

Furnish, V. P., <u>Theology: The Place and Purpose of Philippians III, NTS,</u> 10, Nashville: Theology and Ethics in Paul, 1963.

Garlock, Frank and Kurt Woetzel, <u>Music in the Balance,</u> Greenville: Majesty Music, 1992.

Geisler, Norman and Ronald Brooks, <u>Let Us Reason,</u> Grand Rapids: Baker Book House, 1990.

Halpern, Stephen, <u>Tuning The Human Instrument,</u> Belmont: Spectrum Research Institute, 1978.

Hess, Richard S., <u>Bulletin for Biblical Research,</u> "Leviticus 10:1: Strange Fire and an Odd Name," 12:2, 2002.

Hickkmann, Hans, <u>Musica,</u> Die altesten Musikernamen, March 1951.

Hoover, A. J., <u>Don't You Believe It,</u> Chicago: Moody Press, 1982.

Johnson, S. Lewis, <u>BibSac,</u> "Beware of Philosophy," Oct. 1962.

Josephus, Flavius, <u>Antiquities,</u> Grand Rapids: Zondervan Publishing, 1982.

Kittel Gerhard, editor, <u>Theological Dictionary of the New Testament,</u> Vol. 6, Grand Rapids: William B. Eerdmans Publishing Co., 1964.

Leaver, Robin A., <u>Luther's Liturgical Music: Principles and Implications,</u> Grand Rapids: William B. Eerdmans Publishing C., 2007.

Leibowitz, Nehama, <u>Studies in Shemot Exodus,</u> Jerusalem: The World Zionist Organization, 1981.

Makujina, John, <u>Measuring the Music,</u> Willow Street, Pennsylvania: Old Paths Publications Publishing Co., 2002.

Miller, Steve, <u>The Contemporary Christian Music Debate,</u> Waynesboro, Georgia: OM Literature, 1993.

Mursell, James, L., <u>The Psychology of Music,</u> Westport, Connecticut: Greenwood Press, Publishers, 1964.

<u>New Dictionary of Thought,</u> New York: Standard, 1955.

Peck, Richard, <u>Rock: Making Musical Choices,</u> Greenville: Bob Jones University Press, 1985.

Pink, Arthur W., <u>Gleanings in Exodus,</u> Chicago: Moody Press, 1972..

Postman, Neil, <u>Amusing Ourselves to Death,</u> New York: Penguin Group, 1985.

Richards, Harold E., <u>Good News Broadcaster,</u> "Has Contemporary Christian Music Had It?", November 1982.

Saliers, Don E., <u>Music and Theology,</u> Nashville: Abingdon Press, 2007.

Seidel, Leonard J., <u>Face the Music,</u> Grand Rapids: Grand Rapids Publishing Co., 1998.

Smith, Kimberly, <u>Music and Morals: Dispelling the Myth that Music is Amoral,</u> Enumclaw, Washington: Winepress Publishing, 2005.

Smith, Kimberly, <u>Let Those Who Have Ears to Hear,</u> Enumclaw, Washington: Winepress Publishing, 2001.

Syndrey, Alfred, <u>Music in Ancient Israel,</u> London: Vision Press Limited, 1969.

Thomas, Stephen Naylor, <u>Argument Evaluation,</u> Tampa: Worthington Publishing Co., 1991.

Watson, Thomas, <u>The Ten Commandments,</u> Carlisle, Pennsylvania: The Banner of Truth Trust, 1692.

Wright, G. Ernest and David Noel Freedman, <u>The Biblical Archaeologist Reader,</u> New York: Anchor Books, 1961.